*ADVENTURES IN TWO WORLDS*

# BOOKS BY A. J. CRONIN

A. J. CRONIN

# Adventures in Two Worlds

McGRAW-HILL BOOK COMPANY, INC.

NEW YORK   LONDON   TORONTO

ADVENTURES IN TWO WORLDS

Library of Congress Catalog Card Number: 51–13125

Published by the McGraw-Hill Book Company, Inc.

Printed in the United States of America

# PART ONE

# Chapter One

WHEN I AWAKENED, that April morning, in my attic bedroom, my head still cloudy from late hours of study, I felt constrained, reluctantly, to review my financial position. Thanks to the gratuity which I had received on my demobilization from the Navy three months before, the fees for my medical classes were paid up until the end of the year. The gold watch and chain I had inherited from my father, once again judiciously pawned, had provided me with the requisite instruments and secondhand textbooks. I had even managed to discharge in advance my annual dues to the Students' Union. In an academic sense I was strictly solvent.

But, alas, the other side of the ledger was less satisfactory. In my anxiety to ensure that nothing should interrupt this resumption of my studies, I had given slight heed to the minor consideration of keeping body and soul together. For the past month I had been subsisting on an occasional tearoom snack, supplemented by bizarre bargains from the local market brought into my lodging of an evening in a paper bag. I was, moreover, two weeks behind with my room rent, while my total assets—I counted the few coins again—were precisely three shillings and fivepence. Viewed from the rosiest aspect, it seemed scarcely an adequate sum on which to feed and clothe myself for the next eight months. Something must be done . . . and quickly.

Suddenly I burst out laughing, wildly, hilariously, rolling about on the lumpy flock mattress like a colt in a meadow. What did it matter? I was young, healthy, filled with that irrepressible spirit only to be found in a ruddy, towheaded Scot whose veins were infused with a dash of Irish red blood corpuscles. I would work, work, work. I would live on air, sleep in the park, sing in the streets, do anything and everything, to enable me to take my doctor's degree. I would win through at all costs. Was I not free again, and alive, miraculously, after those weary and dangerous years when, in the destroyer *Melampus,* we had patrolled the leaden, perpetually agitated waters of the North Sea, darting across, a solitary decoy, to Torchelling, Zeebrugge, and Jutland, through uncharted mine fields and submarine-infested shallows, half frozen by icy spray, sleeping in sea boots and a lifesaving jacket, riven by seasickness and the firm belief that any moment we might find ourselves blown to smithereens? Yes, the war, thank God, was over—there would never be another! And spring was here, glorious spring, touching even this smoky old city of Glasgow with its tender tints and sudden shafts of radiance. And—this above all—was I not immeasurably, hopelessly, and utterly unsuitably in love? She was a slender, brown-eyed young woman of eighteen, with soft russet hair and sun-warmed complexion, of a sweetness and innocence that melted the heart, also studying medicine at the University of Glasgow, and bent upon becoming a doctor attached to one of the Uganda foreign missions. Upon a foggy February day, some weeks before, in the pathology department I had come upon her, dissecting an endocarditic heart with grave application. On looking up from her work she had noticed me, and at the blinding moment the seeds of an unreasoning affection were sown. My first remark was breath-taking in its fatuity. I said, "Isn't it foggy today?" But I learned that her name was Mary.

We began to go out together. This dreary city which we inhabited had two redeeming features—the excellence of its tearooms, where for a modest twopence one could sit long over a refreshing cup, and the superb beauty of its surrounding countryside. Already we had expended more twopences than I could afford—an excuse to be together and to talk. Then on Saturdays we escaped to the nearby woods and hills, travelling through the suburbs by tramcar, then walking many miles across the moors, wind-burned and carefree.

In our serious moments we realized how impossible was our

4

relationship. Not only were we temperamentally opposed, for every practical purpose we were the last two people in the world to consider, even remotely, the business of matrimony. She was quiet, modest, and reserved, brought up in a strict Nonconformist circle and still, presumably, treasuring ardent hopes of converting the natives of the Congo. I was both happy-go-lucky and fiercely ambitious, while the religion into which I had been born, though it exercised me little, was not likely to commend me to Mary's family.

Our various friends had been kind enough to point out our mutual unsuitability, and from time to time we had met in agonized confabulation, whereat, over more tea and buns, we palely pledged ourselves to common sense, then parted, heroically, forever. But no sooner had we done so than, next morning, we came together by a force stronger than Newton's law of gravity and called Heaven to witness that we would never give each other up.

I jumped up, threw open the window, and began those backbreaking exercises with which I tortured my lanky body in a vain effort to become a second Sandow. Then, in the rickety bathroom, two flights down, I set my teeth and plunged into an icy tub. I dressed quickly, regretting the necessity which made me wear my old naval uniform. Not from choice was I attending classes like a juvenile admiral of the fleet—on my return from service I had found the moths in possession of my sole civilian suit. Still, why not carry through with it in style? I set my peaked cap at an angle, picked up my textbooks, and ran downstairs.

Unluckily, my landlady lay in wait for me, guarding the front door with broom and bucket, a little cadaverous woman with adenoids and broken whalebone stays, whose execrable performances upon the parlour harmonium every Sunday afternoon were torture to the dogs of the neighbourhood.

"Good morning, Mrs. Grant."

She did not respond to my greeting, but continued to regard me with her lacklustre yet accusing eye.

"Did you cook a herring in your room last night?"

"Well . . . , as a matter of . . ."

5

"The smell went all through the house. My Indian gentleman was fair upset. Forby, you were wasting my gas."

"I didn't use much gas, Mrs. Grant. In fact"—I forced a jovial laugh—"I ate the thing half raw."

She was not amused, but shook her head in melancholy disapproval.

"I've nothing against you, lad, you back from the war and all. But you're away behind with your rent. If you cannot pay . . . , you'll have to go."

Silence. I clenched my fist and banged it down hard on the well-worn covers of Osler's *Practice of Medicine*.

"Mrs. Grant," I assured her, "I swear by Hippocrates, I'll pay you. Something is going to turn up for me. And soon!"

Outside, the breeze was soft and fresh. As I strode through Kelvingrove Gardens a mavis was singing in the flowering red-currant bushes, and crocuses dappled the new grass surrounding the art gallery, where hung my favourite portrait, Rembrandt's "Man in Armour," before which, lost in admiration, I had often sighed, "Ah, to possess a painting such as that, one day!" Upon the hill beyond, the low outline of the University lay clear against the morning sky, chill despite the warmth of the day, and with a massive, brooding air, as though burdened by the weight of its five hundred years. How many Scottish country boys, poor yet ardent, had come to these grey cloisters, bringing with them, in the early days, from the farm, a sack of meal to make the porridge that would sustain them through months of study—in commemoration of which there was instituted a special students' holiday, "Meal Monday." How many of these ambitious lads, or perhaps how few, had won through in the end, and how many, ah, how many more, despite their desperate striving, had been coldly rejected, returned to their native villages, spent and defeated, stigmatized as failures!

The thought galvanised me: I could not, must not fail; at all costs I must succeed. That, indeed was my dominant passion, the leitmotif of my life, the very reason of my being, implanted in my breast by those ten years of unbelievable hardship which had followed upon the death of my father—an event which had transformed my easy,

6

affluent, and pampered existence to a struggle for bare survival. Nothing can exceed the longing of a poor youth, beaten down by circumstances, to rise above misfortune and justify himself, not only in his own eyes but in the eyes of others. Upon the heart of such a one is blazoned the motto: "Conquer or die." With every pulse beat I seemed to hear, throbbing in my ears, the words "get on, get on, get on . . . , to riches, high position, fame."

On the south side of the University, upon a slightly lower level, stood the Western Infirmary, and as the town clock struck nine, I passed through the students' entrance. This morning, in the main surgical clinic, the excision of a cerebral tumour was to be performed —a special treat which I had no wish to miss—but beyond that, my hopes were centred upon a plan which I meant to put into execution as soon as the operation was over.

Despite my apparent bravado, I was only too well aware that the opportunities for a student to support himself at this small northern university were practically nonexistent. Indeed, the only chance lay in securing an appointment as "dresser" or "houseman" to one of the Infirmary surgeons, a position which, though unpaid, entitled the fortunate incumbent to free board and lodging at the hospital. Now, I had been privately advised that the dresser to my surgery professor, Sir William MacEwen, was presently to be promoted to the position of registrar. I felt that I stood well with MacEwen; before going into the Navy I had received evidence of his consideration, and in each of the three monthly examinations conducted since my return, I had gained the first place. In brief, I had decided to ask him for the position.

Already, in the operating theatre, most of the class were assembled, filling the circular tiers of benches that rose to the white-glassed roof, but my friend Chisholm had reserved a seat for me in the front row. As I squeezed in beside him a low, expectant buzz filled the air, intensified as the patient, a middle-aged woman, already under the anaesthetic, was wheeled in.

I was no stranger to suffering, yet as I saw her lying inert, upon her face, breathing hoarsely, her head, completely shaven and swabbed with iodine, resembling a huge billiard ball, there was in

7

her appearance something inhuman and grotesque which moved me strangely, and with a dramatic instinct altogether out of place in one dedicated to science, I began to reconstruct her history.

At the outset, as she went about her household tasks—getting the children off to school, preparing her husband's midday dinner—she had heard a faint ringing in her ears, like a peal of distant bells or wind whistling in the chimney, a sensation so odd it actually made her smile. As the noises recurred at intervals during the next few weeks, she dropped a little warm oil in her ears. There was not much improvement. And then her eyes began to trouble her, the newsprint of the daily paper seemed blurred and indistinct. Ah, that was it, of course! Why hadn't she realised that her glasses needed changing? She went to the optician straightaway.

But no, the stronger spectacles did not help her, and now, indeed, she felt singularly out of sorts. Her head ached, her appetite was gone, and at times the roaring in her ears assumed the intensity of a train thundering through a railway tunnel. What on earth was the matter with her? Worried and alarmed, she paid a visit to her family physician.

The doctor listened sympathetically to her story, put the stethoscope to her chest, and nodded wisely. She was a trifle run-down, he told her, too bound up in her children, too unsparing of herself. She must take things easier, eat more green vegetables, spend an occasional weekend at the seaside. He gave her a tonic which would put her right in no time. He also syringed her ears.

Reassured, clutching hopefully this marvellous medicine, she returned home. Next morning, when she rose, she felt giddy, reeled, lost her balance, and fell sideways to the floor. Thereafter, inexorably yet quite unrecognised, the frightful malady progressed. Accompanied by her husband, she visited a new doctor and then another, receiving always a different diagnosis which blamed in turn the liver, the nerves, the stomach, and always a fresh treatment that failed miserably to alleviate her sufferings.

At last, in despair, she had recourse to the Infirmary and here came under the care of one who was neither an ignoramus nor a charlatan. She was examined thoroughly, scientifically—all manner

8

of tests were carried out. Then the fatal words were uttered: "A tumour of the brain. . . . The only hope, and that a faint one, immediate operation." With what anguish, what nightmare terror had she contemplated this prospect? And then finally, this very morning, she had surrendered herself to the unknown, to that void wherein sharp steel would bite into her head, break apart the skull, and pierce to the very seat of life. . . .

Suddenly, a silence in the theatre recalled me—the professor had entered, unheralded and unaccompanied, but with a calm dignity, a look of interior purpose which made him at once the central figure in the drama about to be enacted before us. At this time Sir William MacEwen was past seventy, yet his tall spare figure, erect as a lance, his regular, clean-cut features and handsome profile, his tanned skin taut over high cheekbones, even the sweep of silvery hair that framed his striking head, conveyed a sense of youthful indomitable vigour. Simply to look at MacEwen was to recognise instantly a great man whose powers remained undiminished. Indeed, for more than three decades, he had been acclaimed as the finest brain surgeon in Europe. We students—a thoroughly hardened and disrespectful lot—loved and revered him, knew him among ourselves as "Billee," repeated with affection the legends that had grown around his name.

He was already gowned for the operation, and after quietly studying a few X-ray photographs, he turned toward the class. His voice was soft yet incisive, his manner courteous, a model of politeness.

"Gentlemen, we have today an interesting case which we believe"—in addressing us he always used the royal plural—"which we believe exhibits unmistakably the symptoms of intracranial glioma."

He paused, and his eye, roving the benches, came to rest—no doubt because I sat at the end of the front row—upon me.

"What are these symptoms?"

"Intense headache, vomiting without apparent cause, unrelated to the taking of food, and extreme vertigo."

"Continue."

"There is usually marked optic neuritis with choked disk. The relative degree of neuritis is a reliable guide to the side on which the tumour is situated."

"And if this tumour were situated in the cerebellum?"

"The speech would be slow and jerky, the head retracted. The patient would tend to fall toward the side opposite the tumour. Unilateral paralysis would occur."

"The prognosis?"

"The outlook is grave. Tumours of the base of the brain, though usually circumscribed, are difficult to reach. Death may occur from sudden haemorrhage, asphyxia, or pressure on the vital centres."

"Admirable. I congratulate you."

With an effort, I maintained my air of studious detachment. Above all, at this moment, I had wished to impress Billee with my earnestness and efficiency. I felt that in offering me this opportunity fortune could not have been kinder to me.

Now the patient's stertorous breathing had lapsed to a low sibilation, the theatre sister had clipped the last sterile cloth around her neck, and with a glance at his anaesthetist, MacEwen approached the operating table.

Like an artist defining the outline of a great picture, he took a lancet and made the first incision. Swiftly he reflected the scalp, exposed the shining table of the skull. Then the whir of the trephine filled the room as he began to cut away a circle of bone as large as a good-sized saucer. The work was hard, for he did not use an electric drill. If MacEwen had a foible, it was to disdain modern appliances and to employ only the simplest equipment, relying entirely upon his own superb skill. Once, when called as an expert witness in a high court of law, he was asked by the presiding judge if he boiled his instruments. "My Lord," Billee replied, holding out his hands, small and delicate as a woman's, "how could I boil these?"

Now he had laid aside the trephine and with a retractor lifted out the disk of bone. Beneath, the pink membranes of the brain were revealed, frail and delicately veined as a butterfly's wing. Skilfully he turned them back. But apparently the aperture did not satisfy him, and boldly, calmly, he proceeded to enlarge it. I held my breath as the metal forceps crunched through the skull bone, wrenching at the very roots of the cervical vertebrae. When it was done, and the meninges parted, a low murmur, almost a sigh, broke from the class.

10

There, dark and angry red in the white substance of the brain, was the tumour. Under the bright beam of the professor's frontal mirror, ringed by forceps, within that frightening, pulsing cavity, it blossomed like a malignant jungle flower, or like some strange marine organism, swaying in a subaqueous light, a sea anemone, whose scarlet fronds brought death by their embrace.

And now MacEwen, slowly and deliberately, began to dissect out the growth from the complex tracts and convolutions with which it was entwined and which, if severed, would cause the patient's instant dissolution. What miracles of skill and knowledge, what judgement and intuition, what imperturbable courage were displayed in this technique! Watching, fascinated, as he touched and made to tremble the chords of life, I longed with all my heart to achieve something of the mastery which had brought him to such pre-eminence. Ah yes, that was the battle cry . . . get on, get on, get on.

At last, it was done—the gliomatous growth, oozing red, large as a pomegranate, enucleated in its entirety, and whisked away by a nurse in a tissue of gauze. And swiftly, with unbelievable dexterity, the professor cauterized the vessels, removed the clamps, and replaced the aponeurosis. The scalp was stitched up and, although there seemed little sign of shock, a saline administered. Then MacEwen tied the final suture.

"Thank you, gentlemen. That is all for this morning. In three days' time it may be necessary to drain accumulated fluid. Otherwise we look for an uneventful recovery."

The patient, her head swathed in a great turban of bandages, was wheeled out by the house surgeon and two nurses. The class began to leave the theatre, not with the usual shuffling of boots and babble of tongues, but silently, as though overwhelmed. Later there would be talk in plenty. And in the afternoon when MacEwen appeared in the lecture room they would give him an ovation. Now, however, this stillness held a greater tribute.

I let the others get away, remaining seated, in the pretence of making notes, in reality gathering my forces for the effort I meant to make. The anaesthetist had risen, stretched himself, and, taking a cigarette from his case, quitted the theatre. MacEwen, attended only

11

by the sister, showing no signs of fatigue or strain, was quietly washing up, as though the superb exhibition he had given were nothing more than ordinary routine. Presently the sister left him—he was alone.

I took a deep quick breath and went forward.

"Excuse me, sir. May I speak to you a moment."

He turned, wiping his hands on the stiffly laundered towel.

"Certainly. . . . We are always prepared to listen to the young."

His tone, the indulgence in his gaze, gave me confidence. After all, I had done brilliantly in the examinations. In the wards my answers to his questions had seemed to interest him, and more than once my more daring flights of fancy had made him smile. All that I sought was the lowest position on his staff. Taking courage, I asked him for it.

For a moment he observed me.

"Why do you wish to be my dresser?"

In all sincerity I answered:

" I want to specialise in surgery."

Again there was a silence, a long silence. Then, gently, yet firmly, he shook his head.

"No. I have already made the appointment."

His sharp eye remained bent upon me kindly, yet with that unerring judgement that never failed him.

"In medicine, or some other field, I believe that you may make your mark. But of one thing I am sure. You will never be a surgeon."

# Chapter Two

LOCHLEA ASYLUM: WANTED: a clinical clerk. Full board and lodging provided at the institution. Honorarium 100 guineas. The candidate appointed will be permitted to attend classes at the University.

Two anxious and depressing weeks had passed since my rejection by MacEwen when this notice, pinned on the board in the Students' Union among dozens of dog-eared intimations of surgery lectures, midwifery courses, post-mortem demonstrations, and final-year dances, caught and held my desperate eye. It seemed so miraculously the chance of my salvation I scarcely dared to hope, and lest any of my needy friends should forestall me, I turned quickly, tore down Gilmore Hill, and boarded a green tramcar—one of the sedate and splendid vehicles which, in those days, bore the citizens of Glasgow immense distances for a single penny.

The asylum, situated in nicely wooded country, four miles west of the city, was dismayingly imposing—a great castellated mansion, set in well-tended gardens, surrounded by meadows and orchards, the whole domain encircled by a high stone wall. At the gate lodge, when I had stated my business, I was admitted and conducted up the long beech avenue by an attendant who brought me, finally, through an arched doorway and a vestibule, adorned by marble statuary, to the office of the superintendent.

Dr. Gavinton, acknowledged as one of the leading alienists of his time, was a tall, spare, iron-grey man, gaunt and sallow-featured, with a quiet, rather baffling aloofness in his manner. As he gazed at

13

me in silence from behind his desk, his penetrating, strangely hypnotic yellow eyes increased my nervousness. Conscious of my deficiencies, sadly shaken in my self-esteem, I steeled myself for a searching and painful interrogation. To my surprise, he repeated my name, mildly, then remarked:

"Are you related to the youngster who captained the eleven in the Scottish Shield three years ago?"

"Well, sir," I stammered, "as a matter of fact I . . ."

He nodded, his severity broken by a human and friendly smile.

"I saw the game. You played well. If the ground had been less muddy you might easily have won. Sit down. You'll find that chair reasonably comfortable."

I took a long breath, scarcely daring to believe in my good fortune —that this should be my reward for that grim and gruelling match, lost in a rainstorm by a single penalty goal, a defeat which had reduced me, in the dressing room, to bitter tears. Yet it was so. Frank Gavinton was a football enthusiast, an old International, who had played regularly for Queen's Park, the premier Scottish amateur club, and twice represented his country at Hampden Park. For half an hour we discussed football, with the intimacy of those who know and love the game. Then, abruptly, he stood up, held out his hand.

"Report here tomorrow at nine o'clock. I know that you'll be punctual. Oh, by the way." He called me back. "We pay in advance here. You'd better have this . . . , your first quarter's stipend."

He took his pen, wrote for a moment, and not looking at me, handed me a cheque for twenty-five guineas. My heart was too full for speech. I hoped he had not guessed how hard up I was—yet I rather suspected he had. But at least I could now settle my indebtedness to Mrs. Grant, get my watch out of pawn, and retrieve my impounded valise. I was saved.

Nothing could have been more supremely opportune than this appointment, which was, of course, far superior to anything I could have obtained at the Infirmary. I was free, in the forenoon, to continue my medical education; I had my splendid honorarium. My new quarters, a comfortable sitting room, with easy chairs and a fireplace, communicating with a snug, red-carpeted bedroom and a

14

well-fitted bathroom, were, by contrast with the wretched "digs" I had quitted, palatial. My diet, no longer limited by the state of my purse, was equally improved, for at Lochlea everything was done in admirable style. Breakfast now consisted of cereal and cream— thick and fresh from the home farm—an inexhaustible platter of crisp bacon and eggs, fragrant coffee, fresh rolls, and fruit. For lunch, which was served to the staff with some formality, we had soup, a joint of meat or roast chicken with several vegetables, an excellent dessert, and cheese. Tea, brought to my sitting room at four o'clock, displayed always the housekeeper's skill in baking, since the tray bore, every day, a tempting plate of milk-and-soda scones and those delicious iced pastries which, for some reason, are known in Scotland as "French" cakes. Supper, a movable feast, usually brought several cold dishes to the sideboard, with kedgeree, macaroni, or curry kept hot for us on an electric plate. Add to this the privilege of dropping in at any hour to the great basement kitchen for a snack, and it becomes possible to imagine the change in circumstances and outlook for a famished youth who for weeks had been keeping body and soul together on an odd stale bun and an occasional mug of tea.

In addition to the superintendent, two other physicians made up the medical staff of the asylum: Dr. Peters, a rotund elderly little man with a jolly face and a passion for grand opera which caused him to hum Verdi and Offenbach on his rounds; and Dr. Jane Carmichael, a charming and brilliant woman who, scarred and disfigured in her youth by a laboratory accident, had refused to let her life become a tragedy but thereafter had devoted her career magnificently to the care of the insane. Nor must I forget to mention the matron, Miss Montgomery, a frail, slender, silver-haired lady, demurely quiet in speech, patrician in manner, in whose delicate hands rested much of the complex management of the establishment and who, by one soothing word, a single tranquil glance, could calm the most refractory patient. All these good people displayed toward me a kindness and indulgence which I tried to repay by pulling my weight in my new team, in short, by a conscientious attention to my work.

Certainly, the duties of the "clinic" at Lochlea lacked neither interest nor variety. All the dispensing was under my charge, the

15

preparation of the huge Winchesters of stock solutions of potassium, sodium, and ammonium bromide, of chloral hydrate, paraldehyde, and many other drugs which were widely used as sedatives. I undertook the bacteriological work and microscopical examinations of pathological specimens. I also had the rather odd duty of feeding those patients who refused to eat, an operation which demanded the passing of a stomach tube, a recondite art in which I soon became extremely proficient. In addition, I kept the case records, made the evening round of the galleries when one or other of the doctors had the day off, and in general made myself useful and agreeable to my betters. Most of all, at Dr. Gavinton's request, since he set a high therapeutic value on this line of treatment, I was expected to mingle with our patients in a social way, to organise their games, play tennis, cricket, and handball with them, take part in the concerts and dances that were regularly held for their benefit and entertainment.

Much has been written of the inmates of mental institutions that is not only in extremely bad taste but also arrant nonsense. It is customary, for example, to portray such afflicted persons as highly amusing individuals who frequently believe themselves to be important historical characters, such as Napoleon, Julius Caesar, or Lady Godiva, and whose consequent aberrations in these roles are made a subject for exquisite mirth. Nothing could be further from the fact. Not once in my stay at Lochlea did I come across a patient with such obligingly diverting tendencies. The sober truth is that mental disorders are always pitiful. Yet they are fascinating to those who study them, who essay the stupendous task of probing the mysteries of the human mind.

Lochlea was an advanced institution, one of the best in Scotland, and although it supported the usual quota of incurables, it received many "breakdown" cases, people thrown out of gear by the stress and strain of life—a businessman brought to attempted suicide by bankruptcy, a poor young mother pathetically deranged through the loss of her first baby, a wife broken by family trouble and an unfaithful husband. . . .

To heal and rehabilitate these patients, to see them go forth, clear-eyed again, from this walled citadel, fit to resume their daily avoca-

16

tions and take their part in the battle of life, this was the main objective and the real reward of Gavinton and his co-workers at Lochlea. It was in many ways a thrilling work. But there was danger in it too.

Of all the inmates of Lochlea, the one to whom I had become most attached was George Blair. Known to everyone as Geordie, this young man had a history which, made more moving by his open and engaging disposition, particularly aroused my sympathy. Five years before, he had killed his cousin—had, indeed, strangled him to death. Yet the circumstances of the crime seemed, to a certain extent, to exonerate the culprit. When we talked the matter over together— this process of self-revelation was always encouraged—Geordie confessed to me that the murdered youth had insulted his sister; had, indeed—to put the matter in its least offensive form—tried physically to force his attentions upon her. It was this outrage that had temporarily unbalanced Blair: a fact which, with such an upright young fellow, was quite understandable. Certainly the verdict of the court had been "Guilty, while of unsound mind." Thus Geordie, sentenced to detention "during His Majesty's pleasure," found himself removed, mainly through family influence, to Lochlea, where he must spend the rest of his days.

This burden of lifelong punishment, heavy and unjust though it seemed to me, had been accepted manfully by Blair, a fact which prejudiced me more strongly in his favour. No one in the place was more cheerful or energetic. He sang at the concerts, in a fine baritone voice, led the church choir every Sunday. At the monthly assemblies he appeared in a dress kilt, was up for every dance, led the grand chain, was tremendous in the eightsome reels. Although somewhat short and thickset in his figure, he was endowed with a remarkable physique and took enthusiastic part in all the games organised at Lochlea. It was this, in the first place, which brought us together. I have always loved all kinds of sport and at this period made a fetish of physical culture, rising every morning at six for an ice-cold bath, which was followed by half an hour of Müller calisthenics, by a sprint round the grounds or a game of some sort, before I set out for the University to attend my classes. Thus Geordie and I had many

17

rattling exchanges at tennis and squash racquets. Often on Saturday forenoon when I was free we took out a ball and punted it to each other in the recreation ground. He was such a likable fellow, so gay and virile—so obliging, too, going out of his way, without being asked, to perform many thoughtful personal services for me—that I became extremely fond of him. Indeed, I went so far as to bring his case before the superintendent.

After the day's work, Gavinton was fond of a game of billiards, and since Dr. Peters didn't play, he often asked me to his house, where he had an excellent table and would give me twenty in a hundred up. One evening when we were so engaged, I said to him:

"It's very hard, sir, that Blair should be condemned to spend the rest of his life at Lochlea."

"Indeed." He chalked his cue. "Do you think so badly, then, of our little place here?"

"Oh, no, sir. It's . . . it's extremely pleasant in many ways. But after all . . . , it's shut off from the world by a high stone wall."

"That wall serves a fairly useful purpose."

"Of course, sir. But surely not for Blair. He's such a decent chap. And he's had a rotten deal. Don't you think some sort of appeal could be made to the authorities . . . or a petition got up?"

There was a silence during which Dr. Gavinton, stroking his upper lip with a characteristic gesture, gave me an odd look. Then, he smiled faintly and, bending to take his shot, remarked:

"My dear clinic, I think our friend Blair will do very well at Lochlea."

Of course, that closed the discussion. But I was not satisfied. I went out of my way to make things as pleasant as possible for my friend Geordie.

One evening, a few weeks after this conversation, I was on duty in Dr. Peter's absence—he had gone, in high glee, to a performance of *La Bohème* by the visiting Carl Rosa Company—and I went to make the round of the men's galleries. I had been studying in my room, and it was later than usual, almost eleven o'clock, when I entered the ward kitchen where old Currie, the night attendant, was

18

busy making a brew of hot Ovaltine, which, according to custom, he took to a number of the less robust patients. Currie was over seventy, a steady-going, grey-bearded Highlander, bowed by age but still hearty, who for nearly fifty years had kept night watch in the galleries of Lochlea, who used to tell me, with a chuckle, in his soft Inverness accent, that for half a century he had rarely seen the sun. I had enjoyed many chats with Currie over a measure of his nourishing beverage, but tonight as he poured and handed me a cup he glanced at me sideways.

"Geordie had a nasty turn this evening. They've put him in Number 7."

I gazed at the attendant in amazement.

"Blair . . . in Number 7?"

"Ay." Currie nodded. "He was real bad."

I could not understand. *Number 7, in this gallery, was the padded cell.* I thought for an instant that the old man was joking, but the expression on his face dismissed that thought. Puzzled and distressed, I started out of the kitchen, still holding the cup of Ovaltine. If Blair were really ill, he might be glad to have it. As I went down the gallery I heard Currie call after me, but I paid no heed, and using my key, without which one could not pass anywhere in Lochlea, I let myself into Number 7.

At that instant, before I had adjusted myself to the interior gloom, I received a smashing blow on the chest which jerked the hot Ovaltine into my eyes and threw me violently against the door, which instantly slammed shut. Almost blinded—the high, grilled roof light gave only the feeblest gleam—I nevertheless saw enough to recognise my danger and to realise what a fool I had been to incur it. There was raging mania in Blair's expression and an indescribable menace in his posture as he rushed at me again, tore the empty cup out of my hand, and smashed it down on my head.

"Geordie . . . , for God's sake . . . , don't you know who I am . . . ? Your friend. . . ."

He did not answer but drove at me again. Then, with a shudder, I became aware that I was locked up with a homicidal lunatic in the

19

place most dangerous, most dreaded in the whole asylum, a cell so isolated, so insulated and impervious to sound, that my cries for help would never reach the gallery.

A cold wave of fear and horror swept over me. I could feel the blood from my lacerated scalp trickling down my neck. But at all costs I must try to defend myself. As Blair advanced I hit him with all my strength. Although the blow staggered him, I might as well have tried to halt a rushing bull.

I can lay no claim to be a fighter. Caution has always been the key-note of my character, and I shall have to disclose, later on, instances of lack of courage which still cause me to wince. Yet I had studied the art of self-defence and, during my service in the Navy, had been fortunate enough to spar many rounds with Seaman Hall, lightweight champion of Britain, who was then my shipmate in the destroyer *Melampus*.

Everything I had learned from Hall I brought out now with the intensity of desperation. Keeping away from Blair as best I could, I hit him repeatedly with a straight left and crossed my right to the jaw. He was an easy target, making no effort to guard himself, yet all that I could do failed to stop him. Normally he had far greater strength than I, and in his present state of dementia—a state which, while rendering the nervous system impervious to pain, excites the muscles to their highest pitch of action—he completely outmatched me. Again and again he charged in with flailing arms, and although many of his wild swings missed, the weight of these attacks was overwhelming. Terrifying, too, was his congested face, the look of indescribable malice in his eyes, the hoarse panting of his breath as he pressed against me. Utterly spent, I felt my head turn giddy as, with a final rush, he hurled himself upon me and flung me to the floor. Sick and dizzy, I was conscious of his fingers on my throat, compressing my windpipe, despite my struggles, choking the breath from my body. Sparks shot before my eyes, I recollected dimly how he had throttled his cousin.

At that second, while my senses swam, I vaguely heard the door burst open and, as in a dream, saw Currie, followed by two young male attendants from the adjoining gallery, dash into the cell. Even

20

as they threw themselves on Blair and the agonising pressure on my throat relaxed, I realised that old Currie, by going first for adequate help rather than coming to the cell himself, had saved my life. And then I fainted.

Later that night Dr. Gavinton put ten stitches in my head—I still have the scar—and for days afterward my throat was so painful I could scarcely swallow.

One morning in the following month, as I walked down the avenue to attend Professor Stockman's lecture at the Western Infirmary, a gay and cheerful greeting made me turn my head. It was Geordie—brisk, smiling, affectionate as ever. As I stood there he ran up to me and warmly, glowingly, shook my hand.

"How are you, my dear fellow? Wonderful to see you again . . . , simply wonderful. You know, I hated to have to knock you out. But really, it was very wrong of you to make such horrible proposals to my sister."

I stared at him aghast, but had wit enough to mutter:

"I'm terribly sorry, Geordie. . . . I was carried away. . . . I'll never do it again."

Often, after that, Geordie begged me to play tennis and racquets with him or stood disconsolately with the football hoping for the resumption of our Saturday games. But during the remainder of my sojourn at Lochlea I was wise enough to keep my distance.

Shall I say that I had learned never to trust a man who believes he has a sister, when he happens to be an only child.

# Chapter Three

As WE LEFT the cross-channel steamer at Dun Laoghaire and hailed a jaunting car to drive us to the city, my heart expanded in the soft evening mist, filled with the intimations of spring, with the exquisite fragrance of peat smoke and that indefinable sense of growing green things which somehow is the mark and charm of Ireland. All my Irish blood effervesced as the lights of Dublin came into sight and we spanked over the Liffey Bridge down O'Connell Street toward the Rotunda.

My fellow traveller was a classmate, Hugh Devers, and before sitting the final professional examination in June we had come to take a three months' midwifery course at the Rotunda Hospital, which was then, under the mastership of Dr. Fitzgibbon, the finest obstetrical school in Europe. Fresh from Lochlea, with forty guineas of my honorarium still remaining in my pocket, I was ready to make the most of the experience. Devers was an American who had been sent to Glasgow University because his father, a doctor in Texas, had worked at one time with Professor Ralph Stockman and wished his son to study in the wards of his old friend. In Hugh's nature, however, there was nothing of the respectful acolyte. Tall and rangy, with a wide smile that revealed strong white teeth, he had an independent, happy-go-lucky disposition which made him the best companion in the world.

In the days which followed we stole some hours, mostly at Hugh's prompting, from our lectures and the heavy schedule of practical work. We found time to visit the Abbey Theatre, at Leopardstown we lost a few shillings on the races, and by borrowing some clubs, we played a round of golf on the famous Portmarnock Links. We even drove out to the River Boyne one afternoon and tried, without success, to poach a salmon.

But it was in the slums, in the pulsing and sorrowful heart of Dublin, that most of our days and not a few of our nights were spent. This was the district served by students from the Rotunda. The work was incredibly hard. Often when we had come in, tired out from a long vigil at a protracted confinement, and were on the point of getting to bed, word would come in that we were wanted for another case, and with a burst of profanity, off we would trudge, with our black bag, along the ill-lit streets, climbing the dark stone stairs of a high tenement to a poor single room where, again, we would officiate wearily, perhaps clumsily, yet with willing care, at the great mystery of birth.

In addition, we had, thereafter, to visit our patients twice daily for a period of two weeks, to wash and change the newborn babe, to learn all that pertained to the postnatal care of mother and child. Such close contact in this dreadful environment with the dolorous realism of motherhood could not but have its effect on us. Gradually we lost our earlier exuberance, became attuned to a more sober mood. Indeed, it was here, in the slums of Dublin, that I became aware, for the first time, of the patience and endurance, the sublime fortitude of the very poor. Many moving instances of courage and self-sacrifice came to our notice, and one in particular, so tender and so tragic, made a lasting impression upon me.

We first saw her on Loughran Street, fetching water from the public faucet with the baby in her arms, a heavy infant of nine months, bound to her skimpy person by a tattered shawl. Her name was Rose Donegan and she was about fourteen, red-haired, with deep blue eyes which somehow seemed enormous in her serious little face. Three other children, their ages between five and nine, hung about her skirt, a certain similarity of feature and the uniform redness of their hair proclaiming them to be Donegans also.

The contrast between the squalor of her background and the intrepid brightness of her gaze aroused our curiosity. We began by

23

wishing her good morning, and after a few days, this greeting drew from her a grave and bashful answering smile. Gradually—for her reserve was not easy to overcome—we progressed to terms of friendship.

We learned then that Rose, the three younger children, and baby Michael had lost their mother eight months before. They lived with their father, Danny Donegan, in a basement in the teeming warren of Loughran Street. Danny, who worked occasionally at the docks, was a weak, utterly good-natured character. Soft-spoken and full of the best intentions, he spent most of his time and money at the adjacent Shamrock Bar. Thus it fell upon Rose to sustain the burden of the household, to keep the two rooms clean and tidy, to manage her errant father, to salvage the remnants of his earnings as best she could, to cook and attend to the children.

Although there was affection for all of them in Rose's heart, beyond everyone she adored baby Michael. As she carried him on sunny afternoons to the outskirts of Phoenix Park she staggered under his weight, but that did not daunt her. Nothing daunted her. As we saw her go resolutely along the crowded, unsavoury pavement, bent on some errand, to bargain with the butcher for an end of ham or coax the baker to extend her credit for an extra loaf, we marvelled at the temper of her spirit. She was not blind to the sights around her. She had the slum child's elemental knowledge—an absolute unblushing understanding of the hard mysteries of life, mingled with an innocence that was sublime. Those wide, reflective eyes, set in that small grimy face, held the wisdom of the ages. But more than that—they held a fathomless fount of love.

Our first interest in this child turned gradually to deep concern. We felt we must do something for her, and having discovered by chance that her birthday was imminent, we had a parcel delivered to her from an outfitter's in O'Connell Street. It was good to think of her in a warm tweed dress, with sound shoes and stockings, everything to match.

We kept out of the way for a few days, but we chuckled as we pictured her in her finery, marching proudly to Mass on Sunday, her shoes squeaking magnificently down the aisle. Yet when we saw her the following Monday, to our dismay, she was still wearing her ragged clothing, still bound by her tattered shawl to the infant.

"Where are your new clothes?" Devers exclaimed.

She coloured to the roots of her hair, then said:

"It was you." After a long pause, not looking at us, she added simply, "They're pawned. There was nothing in the house. Michael had to have his milk."

We stared at her in silence. Would she always sacrifice herself, yield everything that was hers to this baby brother? Not if I could prevent it. Next day I went to Father Walsh, who had charge of the Loughran Street parish.

His face lit up when I spoke of Rose, and after I had made my plea he considered for a few moments, then slowly nodded assent.

"We might get her to the country for a bit. I have friends . . . the Carrolls . . . good people . . . in Galway. But you'll have a job to persuade her." He smiled wryly as he accompanied me to the door. "She's a perfect little mother. That's the force that fills her life."

A week later, after an exchange of letters, I went determinedly to Loughran Street. The children sat around the table while Rose, with a worried frown, was slicing the remnants of a loaf.

"Rose," I said, "you are going away."

She gazed up at me without comprehension, pushing back the strand of hair that fell across her puckered brow.

"To Galway," I went on, "for a fortnight. To a farm, where you'll have nothing to do but feed the chickens and run wild in the fields and drink gallons of milk."

Momentarily, expectation flooded her face, but it swiftly faded. She shook her head.

"No, I have to see to the children . . . and Dad."

"That's all arranged. The Sisters will take care of them. You must do it, Rose, or you'll have a breakdown."

"I can't," she said. "I couldn't leave the baby."

"Confound you, then. You can take him with you."

Her eyes sparkled. They shone even brighter when, on the follow-

25

ing day, we packed her and her charge into the train. As the engine pulled out she was dandling the baby on her bony knees and whispering in his ear:

"Cows, Michael. . . ."

It was good to have news of them from the Carrolls. Rose was putting on weight, helping in the farmyard. Her own misspelled postcards breathed a happiness she had never known before—and ended invariably with a glowing account of how well the country suited Michael.

The two weeks slipped away. Then, near its end, came the bombshell. The Carrolls wanted to adopt Michael. They were a middle-aged couple, childless and prosperous. They had grown fond of the child and could offer him advantages far beyond anything he would have at home.

Danny, of course, thought the opportunity "stupendous." But there was Rose to consider, and the decision was left to her. None of us knew what that decision was, or how much it cost her to make it, until she came back—alone.

She was glad to see the other children and her father, but all the way from the station she sat silent and withdrawn.

"It's for his benefit," she sighed at last. "I wouldn't stand in his way."

At Loughran Street she pulled herself together and gradually took up her old position. She was, indeed, more conscientious than before. Under her promptings Danny actually signed the pledge. There was no guarantee of permanence in his regeneration; still, while he kept sober and in steady employment, Rose was able to redeem the pledged household goods, so that the basement rooms really took on an air of home. Some Saturdays she managed even to tuck away a few shillings in the tea canister on the mantelpiece.

Good news came of the baby's progress. Michael's foster parents spared no effort to make him happy; already they spoke of him as their own. Then one morning a different letter arrived. Michael was down with pneumonia. With pale cheeks and compressed lips Rose sat staring at the letter. Then she moved rigidly to the canister on the mantel, counted out the money for her railroad fare.

"I'm going to him."

She brushed aside all opposition. Didn't they know that she could do anything with the child—make him take nourishment when he was feverish and his medicine when he was fretful? Why, by stroking his forehead, she could even send him to sleep. With a fixed expression she made herself ready for the journey, arranged with a neighbour to care for the children, then set out by tram for the station.

That same evening at the Carroll farm, taking no denial, she established herself as Michael's nurse. From Father Walsh we learned afterward what took place.

It was a serious attack. The coughing was the worst. With her arm round Michael's neck, heedless of the danger to herself, she supported him until the spasm was over. She spent herself upon him, day and night.

At last the crisis passed; she was told that Michael would recover. She rose dizzily from beside the bed, pressing both hands against her brow.

"Now I can rest." She smiled. "I have such an awful headache. . . ."

She had caught the germ from Michael. But it did not attack her lungs. What happened was worse. She developed pneumococcal meningitis and never recovered consciousness. As I have indicated, she was just fourteen years of age.

Many years later I made a pilgrimage to Rose's grave. In the lonely moorland churchyard, a soft west wind was blowing from Galway Bay, carrying from nearby whitewashed cottages the tang of turf smoke—the breath, the very soul of Ireland. There were no wreaths upon the narrow mound of green, but, half hidden in the grass, I saw a tiny shoot of brier, bearing upon the thorny stem a single white wild rose. And suddenly, from behind grey clouds, the sun came forth and shone with all its radiance upon the white flower, upon the small white tablet that bore her name.

# Chapter Four

"Look, my dear! Did you ever in your life see such an absurdly comic creature!"

A smartly dressed woman, first-class passenger on the *Rawalpindar*, about to sail from Liverpool on the long voyage to Calcutta, made this remark, in a high, "well-bred" voice, to her companion, a young man with a military yet foppish air, as they stood before me on the liner's upper deck. Following their amused gaze, my eyes came to rest upon a squat, very ugly native seaman, with short legs and a large disproportionate head, scarred by a cicatrice which ran from ear to temple, whom I recognised as the Indian serang, or quartermaster of the ship. He was quietly superintending the crew of lascars now completing the loading of baggage into the hold from the Mersey lighter alongside.

"Looks hardly human," agreed the man of Mars, twisting his embryo moustache, with a superior smile. "Inclines a chap to believe, don't you know, that dear old Darwin was not altogether wrong . . . what?"

I turned away silently and went below to my cabin. Three weeks before, to my inexpressible joy, I had taken my medical degree. Never shall I forget that breathless moment when, in a fever of anxiety and suspense, scanning the list pinned upon the University notice board, knowing that my small store of money was finally exhausted, that I had neither the funds nor the energy to repeat that culminating effort—sitting up night after night over my text-

28

books with a wet towel round my forehead till the crack of dawn—I discovered, not only that I had passed, but that the examining board had given me honours as well. Nor am I ashamed to confess to the moisture that rushed into my eyes, almost blinding me, although "Doggy" Chisholm, who stood beside me and who had also passed, commented ironically as he gripped my hand:

"Slight lachrymal-gland activity this morning, Doctor. May I prescribe a hundredth of atropine? Or a good glass of beer?"

He could afford to be lighthearted. His father, provost of Winton, owned the Laughlan steelworks.

And then, as if this were not enough, I had been fortunate enough, through the good offices of my old chief Professor Stockman, to be appointed temporary ship's doctor on the S.S. *Rawalpindar*. While he was putting me through my medical "oral," Stockman had decided that I was extremely run down, that the trip to India and back would set me up again.

The voyage began favourably in calm, clear weather. We crossed the Bay of Biscay without suffering unduly from the turbulent waters of that shallow sea and soon were through the Strait of Gibraltar, traversing the tranquil Mediterranean under azure skies. The *Rawalpindar* was a stout old tub, manned by white officers, with an entirely native Indian crew. She had done fine work in the war, but since her coal-burning engines had not been lately reconditioned, she was exceedingly slow—capable, indeed, of a bare ten knots. This, however, was no defect to the young physician, for whom every day of balmy breezes, of brilliant sunshine and entrancing novelty—swift visions of foam-girt islands, the mysterious African coastline, distant white-walled villages, porpoises gambolling in the creamy wake—was an added source of sheer delight.

The ship was crowded, packed with passengers from stem to stern. Transportation had been impossible for the four years of hostilities, and with the restoration of peace everyone wanted to travel, not only the usual tourists and pleasure seekers, but businessmen tied up at home for many months by DORA regulations, cotton and jute merchants bound for Calcutta and Bombay, Ceylon tea planters and Cawnpore mill owners, together with a large number of Anglo-

Indian army officers, many of whom were accompanied by their wives and families.

From the first night out there was tremendous gaiety on board. This was the beginning of that postwar era when, after the murderous holocaust of the trenches, the years of slaughter, mud, and misery, of anxiety, frustration, and fear, the world suddenly went mad and, like a revivified corpse, embarked on a wild and frantic spree. Lunch and cocktail parties, sweepstakes on the ship's run, "horse racing" and deck sports of every kind, impromptu concerts and fancy-dress galas—these were but a few of the diversions afforded by these halcyon days and feverish nights. For such junkets the ship's doctor is always in demand, and although my inclination lay to more meditative ways, I was usually drawn into the festivities.

Chief among the social promoters—those people who on shipboard excel at "getting things up"—was Miss Jope-Smith, the woman whom I had overheard on the boat deck the morning of our departure and who, with her brothers, Ronald, a cavalry subaltern posted to Bengal, sat, unfortunately, at my table in the dining saloon. Madge Jope-Smith was a thrusting person, handsome in a hard sort of way, obviously over thirty, though got up in a dashing style to look younger. She was not only a snob but a bore, an assertive bore, who talked incessantly of her "place" in Cheltenham, her titled friends, her "personal maid," her horses, dogs, and exploits in the field of fox-hunting—though I suspected that her quarry in the chase, whom, to her infinite chagrin, she had not so far brought to bay, was a man. Never at any meal did she fail to inform us of how welcome she would be in the best society of Peshawar and Darjeeling. Arising from the prospect of her sojourn in India, the leitmotif of her conversation, reduced to its elemental note, was the superiority of the English upper classes and the need for impressing this upon the subject native races. She constantly abused the table steward, a nice Parsee boy who was well-meaning but slow, and having scolded him into complete confusion, she would cast her bold glance around the table.

"These people have to be kept down, you know. Don't you agree, Ronnie?"

"By Jove, yes." Her brother, quite innocuous, was a dependable echo. "You're absolutely right."

"If you let them get away with it, there's no knowing what ideas they'd get in their heads."

"Yes, by Jove. I mean, well, after all . . . , remember how we had to shoot them down in the Mutiny."

"Exactly. Now I'm a liberal-minded woman. But they're such a poor lot at best. Not an ounce of stamina. No loyalty. And treacherous, too. . . . Why, I remember Colonel Bentley once told me. . . ."

We reached Port Said. Everyone went ashore, excitedly, came back loaded with purchases from Simon Artz, with silks, shawls, cigarettes, scent, and jewellery. That night, as the anchor was weighed and we glided past the De Lesseps statue into the snaky waters of the Suez Canal, the orchestra played louder than ever, the dance waxed faster and more furious. The desert reached away on either hand, camels and Bedouin encampments were silhouetted against the purple sunset. Then we were through the Red Sea, past the barren rocks of Aden, and out upon the wide Arabian Sea.

On the following morning, as I held my consultations in the surgery adjoining my cabin, the serang, Hasan, appeared, bringing with him two of his lascar deck hands. Waiting in the doorway until I bade him enter, he inclined his head in a respectful salaam and addressed me. His voice, as if broken long ago in its conflict with the roar of wind and water, was hoarse, yet it had a steady undertone.

"Doctor Sahib, I fear these men are sick."

The seamen certainly did not look well; they complained of general malaise, of intense headache and racking bone pains. They looked frightened, too, as though suspecting something serious to be amiss, rolling the whites of their eyes as I asked them to strip and began my examination. Both were fevered, with thickly furred tongues and that dry skin, burning to the touch, which is nature's gravest warning. As yet there was no sign of lung involvement. No inflammation of the throat. Nothing abnormal in the abdomen. Instinctively I thought of malaria. And then, to my horror, as I once again took the pulse, my palpating fingers became aware of

31

a scattering of hard little nodules, exactly like lead shot, under the wrist skin of each man. It was an unmistakable symptom, and immediately, inspecting more closely the areas behind the knees and beneath the armpits, I found in each case a definite papular eruption.

Young and inexperienced in my profession, I had not learned to control my feelings, nor had I yet acquired that dissimulation which masks the sentence of death with a comforting smile. My expression must have altered visibly, for although the serang said nothing, his lined and battered face assumed a look of deeper gravity. For a moment I looked into his eyes, and even then, while realising that he knew as well as I the nature of the malady before us, I could not but experience, as a kind of shock, the resolution, the intrepid calmness of his gaze. Still he said nothing. When I told him in a low voice to wait in the surgery with the men, he again simply inclined his head.

Hurriedly, with beating heart, I made my way to the bridge. Captain Hamble was not there, but in the chartroom below. He looked up sharply as I burst in.

"Sir"—my voice broke—"I have to report smallpox on board. Two of the deck hands."

I saw his lips draw tightly together. He was a thickset man of fifty-five, with close cropped hair and sandy, bushy eyebrows, known as a strict disciplinarian, something of a martinet, but also as a just and fair-minded officer. Now his brick-dust complexion assumed a deeper tinge.

"Smallpox." He repeated the word under his breath. "You're sure?"

"Quite, sir." And I added, "We have no lymph in our medical supplies."

"Would we carry enough for fifteen hundred passengers? Don't be a fool!"

He bit his lip angrily and, frowning deeply, began to pace up and down the narrow chartroom.

"Doctor," he said, drawing up at last and coming close to me, his words unmistakably grim, "forget that remark of mine. . . . I

32

was upset and didn't mean it. Now, listen, you are in charge of the health of the ship. It's entirely up to you. I can't give you any of my officers; I'm overloaded and understaffed. But I am going to give you the serang. He understands these fellows. And believe me, he's the finest man I have. Between you, you've got to keep this thing from spreading. And what's more, don't let a whisper of it get out, or with this fancy lot we have on board we'll have a bloody panic, as sure as God's my Maker."

I left the chartroom, realizing, with a weakness in my stomach, the desperate responsibility of my position. Gone now was the care-free ease I had enjoyed, reclining in a deck chair reading Pierre Loti and dreaming romantically into the sunset of my own secret desire to write, treating nothing more serious than a cut finger or a case of mild seasickness. Here we were, in the middle of the Arabian Ocean, fifteen hundred passengers aboard, no means whatever of vaccinating them, and smallpox . . . The most deadly contagion in the whole dictionary of disease.

Back in the surgery one of the lascars was in the grip of a violent rigor. I turned from the shivering man to the serang, whose incalculable eyes remained fixed upon me.

"You know?" I asked him.

"Yes, Sahib. I have seen this before."

"We've got to isolate these men . . . , check on the contacts. . . ." As I spoke, trying to assume a cheerfulness and confidence I did not feel, Hasan quietly acquiesced.

"Yes, Sahib. . . . I shall do what I can to help you."

There was no sick bay on board, not an inch of available cabin space. One look at the crowded forecastle showed the impossibility of segregating the infected men anywhere in the crew's quarters. Baffled, I looked at the serang who, undismayed, again turned upon me the full force of his eyes.

"We will make a shelter on the afterdeck, Doctor Sahib. Very cool there. With plenty of fresh air."

In the stern of the ship, admirably protected from view by a battery of derricks and donkey engines, he set to work, moving about, squat and noiseless, his powerful head and long pliant arms

33

conveying the same impression of strength and composure that was reflected upon his flattened and misshapen face. Within an hour, he had erected, with silent efficiency, a large canvas shelter, tautly secured, and roped off from the surrounding deck. Mattresses and sheets were then brought up and the two patients comfortably installed.

Our next step was to muster the crew for a thorough medical inspection. One of the stokers, who complained of fever and headache, showed the prodromal nodules with the beginnings of the typical rash. He was isolated with the other cases.

"And now . . . who is going to help me attend to these men?"

Hasan glanced at me in surprise.

"Why, naturally it is I."

"You must be careful. This disease is most contagious."

The serang, had he known me better, might perhaps have smiled. As it was, the austerity of his expression did not relax.

"I am not afraid, Doctor Sahib."

Together, Hasan and I sponged the patients with permanganate solution, administered to each man a strong antipyretic, hung sheets soaked in disinfectant round the shelter, and set up within this little secret area of quarantine a cooking stove where liquids could be heated and simple meals prepared. Finally, while the passengers were at lunch, we cleared the night watch from the forecastle and, with some sulphur candles which Hasan disinterred from the ship's stores, thoroughly fumigated the crew's quarters. With this accomplished, I felt somewhat easier in my mind.

Next morning, however, brought fresh cause for concern. At the muster which I held at daybreak, I found three fresh cases among the deck hands. The men already segregated were much worse, covered from head to toe by that foul purulent eruption which is the most horrible symptom of the disease. And that same afternoon, four more of the crew sickened. We now had ten cases in our makeshift lazaretto. It was a situation to test the strongest nerves. But the serang, calm and unperturbed, his eyes steadfast beneath the misshapen frontal bones of his dark, cicatrised face, gave me fresh heart. Merely to be beside him made it difficult to despair.

34

In tending the patients he was indefatigable, giving them water, relieving their intolerable skin irritation with the lotion I had made up, cooking for them on the makeshift galley, always on hand when I needed him to help me lift and sponge a semiconscious man—and all this carried out with complete and contemptuous disregard for his own safety.

"Be careful of yourself," I had to beg him. "Do not go quite so close."

Now, indeed, he showed his strong teeth, stained pink with betel nut, in a sudden, fleeting smile . . . yet a smile so faint, so transitory and, above all, tinged with such native sadness that it broke only for an instant his deep and natural tranquillity.

"Are you careful of yourself, Doctor Sahib?"

"Indeed I am. Besides, this is my work."

"Do not worry, Doctor Sahib. I am strong. And it is my work too."

By this time, except for emergency calls, I had placed myself more or less in quarantine. At the captain's suggestion, to allay suspicion, it was given out that I had caught a chill and was indisposed. I ceased to go to the dining saloon, and all my meals were brought on a tray to my cabin. In the evening, as I sat at my solitary dinner, hearing the music of the string band and the sway and shuffle of the dancers on the deck above, it was difficult to restrain a mood of bitterness. In that frenetic whirl, how little they guessed their danger! There came to my mind Barbey d'Aurevilly's tale of the *bal masqué* held by the French king at Avignon, whither the court had retired to escape the pestilence prevailing in Paris, and where, at the height of the gaiety, when all unmasked themselves, a gaunt stranger stood revealed in their midst, bearing on his hectic features the fatal stigmata of the Black Death. With equal morbidness I watched my own person for the first sign of the disease, not from fear—oddly, I was so weighed down by responsibility that I had slight concern for myself—but with a queer detachment and the conviction that I would contract the malady; fatally, no doubt, since I had not been vaccinated since I was a child. And in this state of heightening tension I cursed the slowness of the ship, that

35

lack of speed which had previously given me cause for satisfaction. Although we were moving full steam ahead, Colombo, the nearest port of call, was still eight days away.

Twice a day I reported to the captain. His anxiety, without doubt, far exceeded mine, but his years and the habit of command helped him to control it. When he heard what I had to tell him he nodded once or twice, considering me with harassed, irascible eyes, seeming almost to look beyond me to his board of company directors in distant Liverpool. Then, dismissing me, he forced out a word of encouragement:

"Good. You're doing all right. See you keep it up."

But could we keep it up? In the course of the next forty-eight hours first one, then three more of the stokers, who had been suspect overnight, went to join the others on the afterdeck. A total of fourteen now. And one of the earlier victims had lapsed into coma, seemed likely to die at any hour. Under this added load, I could not sleep, and though I spent most of the daylight hours in the lazaretto, even at night I could not keep away from the stern of the ship. And there, where I knew I should find him, watchful and mute under the stars, was the serang.

How shall I describe the solace which flowed toward me from him as he stood there, in meditation, brooding rather, silhouetted against the taffrail, with his long arms folded on his bared chest, motionless as a statue? A silver whistle, symbol of his office, hung by a lanyard from his muscular neck. The tropic moon, rolling in the velvet sky, brought out the deep lines on his face which, despite its latent energy, had the immobility of carved ebony. When a sick man groaned faintly with the pain of his tormented universe, he would step forward, without sound, to succour him. And then, returning, he would fold his arms, while the ship, an atom detached from earth and lost upon the ocean, surged slowly forward.

He had no fondness for speech. But despite the silences of our long night vigils I gathered, gradually, some fragments of his history. He was from the Punjab, whence his parents, sturdy and nomadic Pathans, had wandered to southern India. There, like so many in that coastal area, he had, as a boy, taken to a seafaring life. For

36

nearly forty years he had given himself to the oceans of the world, and fifteen of these years had been spent on the *Rawalpindar*. Small wonder he regarded the old ship as his home. Indeed, he had no other, no place on shore, neither family nor friends in the great land mass of India. He had never married. The tackle block which, falling from the masthead, had so frightfully broken and disfigured his features had turned his thoughts from women.

By religion he was a Jain, yet there was in him something far beyond the teaching of the sects, a faith inculcated by the purifying eternal wind, the beauty and the desolation of great waters, by waves pounding on grey rocks, on palm-fringed beaches, by blue-white snow upon distant mountain peaks, lush jungles steaming in the tropic sunset, by the united mysteries of a thousand landfalls and departures.

In all his life he had acquired nothing, neither property nor money—his few possessions, contained in his ship chest, might be worth a few rupees. The thought hurt me, and in an access of mistaken sympathy, I exclaimed:

"Hasan, you are doing so much in this emergency, the company must give you extra pay."

His forehead creased perplexedly. He was silent for a long moment, a disconcerting silence broken only by the slow thud of the propeller shaft and the wheezing rattle of the sick. Then he answered:

"What use is money, Doctor Sahib, to one who has all he needs? I am well enough the way I am."

He was unmistakably sincere, completely detached from the usual hope of reward, austerely contemptuous of all personal advantage. Money had no interest for him, he had always despised it. He knew none of those feverish desires with which it is inseparably linked. Instead he had courage, self-control, and faith. The men he worked among lived poor and died poor. It had become the habit of his mind to disregard tomorrow.

Standing with him, in the liquid moonlight, I was stung by a strange pang. Besides his clear simplicity the world's values suddenly seemed dross. A great party had started in the saloon, brilliantly illuminated by coloured electric globes. The raised voices and bursts of laughter, the popping of champagne corks, the incessant backward drift of jazz intensified in me the feeling that mankind had sacrificed the spirit for the flesh, had become sapped of virtue, dreading any prospect not insulated by ease, by the smug protection that can be bought with gold.

Indeed, as I viewed my own outlook toward the future, my passionate desire for success and wealth, I was conscious of a secret shame. I turned my back upon the tumult and from the milky white sea beyond, from the sighing emptiness of the night, there came to me the echo of those immortal words: "O ye of little faith! Take no thought, saying, What shall we eat? or, What shall we drink? or, Where withal shall we be clothed?"

On the following day we lost two of our patients. It was Hasan himself who sewed their shrouds, who in his hoarse and hollow voice read aloud a short passage from the Koran before their bodies, wrapped in sailcloth, with a weight at their feet, were cast overboard at midnight.

No fresh cases developed. And a week later, in the sulphurous light of early dawn, we anchored off Colombo, the Cingalese port doctor and officials came aboard, all formalities were completed. Before the first of the passengers was awake, the yellow flag had been lowered and the sick men taken off to hospital. Several of the patients showed signs of having passed the crisis, but three, helpless and delirious, a mass of running sores, were carried to the lighter, like children, in the arms of Hasan. As we stood together, watching the flat launch bobbing toward the shore, I saw that the serang's dark cheeks were wet with tears.

Our passage through the Bay of Bengal was brief and uneventful. I had barely time to recover myself, or to realise that the epidemic had been confined, before we had navigated the mud flats of the Hoogly and were anchored alongside the quay at Calcutta. A general celebration marked our arrival—sirens blowing, favours floating in the breeze, final rounds of drinks, the decks crowded with people waving and shouting greetings to friends meeting them on the dock. Suddenly, at my elbow, I heard the familiar shrilling of Miss Jope-Smith.

"Oh, look, look, Ronnie. There's that absurd creature again."

Once more I followed their united gaze. And there, again, down in the afterhold, knocking out the hatch battens to unload the baggage, his squat figure foreshortened from above, with long arms swinging, more ungainly than ever, was the object of their mirth —Hasan.

The huntress from Cheltenham swung round, bent her wit, her fascinations upon me.

"Where did you keep him all the voyage, Doctor dear? In a special cage?"

Silence—a vision of the serang's nobility rising before me.

"Yes . . . , in a way . . . it was a cage. . . . But isn't it queer, Miss Jope-Smith—the animals were all outside."

Though I kept my voice even, I thought that I should suffocate. Abruptly I turned away, went below to my cabin, and beat my clenched fists hard against the wooden bulkhead.

# *Chapter Five*

---

SCOTLAND AGAIN, and real Scots weather—sad contrast to the sunny skies and spicy breezes of the tropics. On the deserted little platform of Dundonald Junction I stood in the blinding wind and rain, wondering if I should take a cab. Economy denied the cab, dignity demanded it—not my own dignity, but that of my new position.

At length I beckoned to the red-faced cabby in the long green coat, who, from beside the one flyblown four-wheeler that graced the station exit, had been considering me for the last three minutes with a stealthy, speculative eye.

"How much to Tannochbrae village? Dr. Cameron's house."

Auld Geordie cautiously came over. None of your southern alacrity, none of that "Cab, sir!" nonsense about Geordie. He knew his worth, did old Geordie Dewar, and never sold himself for less.

"How much luggage have ye got?" he parried, though the luggage was plainly seen—one portmanteau upon the pavement, and a small black Gladstone bag, a very new bag, which I gripped in my right hand. Then he added:

"You'll be Cameron's new assistant, I'm thinkin'?"

"Just so!"

"Two shillings to you, then—Doctor."

He threw a cunning emphasis upon the title, but for all that I kept my head and said sternly:

"I mean the short cut." I who had never been in Tannochbrae before! "Not the long way you proposed to wander round with me!"

40

"As Goad's my Maker. . . ." protested Geordie.

A lively argument ensued, at the end of which a compromise—one shilling and "the price of a pint"—was effected with expressions of good will on both sides.

The portmanteau was slung upon the roof, old Geordie climbed rheumily upon the box, and I was rattled off along the stony moorland road.

At the end of the voyage home, Captain Hamble had pressed me to remain with him on the *Rawalpindar* but at the same time had honestly advised me against lapsing into a routine which, to his knowledge, had turned many an eager and ambitious young man into a lazy and lackadaisical ship's surgeon. The captain had been extremely kind to me and in Calcutta had taken me ashore many times to lunch at the Grand Hotel and to see the sights—the great temples and gilded palaces, the teeming bazaars where sacred cattle roamed and ravaged the stalls at will, the gorgeous botanical gardens filled with exotic birds and blossoms, the grisly burning ghats that lined the waters of the Hoogly. All this had fascinated me, had stirred within me a longing to record my impressions of so exciting a scene. Yet I was fully aware of the sound sense in Hamble's warning, and hearing from a classmate at the University that there was an assistantship vacant in Tannochbrae—"Not much, mind you. . . . Regular country practice . . . , and he's a hard nut, old Cameron, though a rare good sort at heart"—I had, not without reluctance, quitted my berth in the ship.

So here I was, hunched in this mouldy four-wheeler, clattering down the cobbled street of a small West Highland village. Halfway down we swung to the right, into the drive of Arden House, a soundly built white stone dwelling with a coach house at the side and a semicircular spread of lawn in front.

The rain dripped miserably as I sprang up the front steps and rang the bell. After a minute, the door opened and the housekeeper, a thin, elderly woman, dressed entirely in black, confronted me. Her hair was tightly drawn, her person spotless, and in her bleak face was stamped authority mingled with a certain grudging humanity; she had the look, indeed, of one tempted terribly to smile, who guards perpetually against a single sign of levity, lest it ruin her self-esteem.

For a few seconds she inspected me, my bag, my hat, even my boots; then, with a slight elevation of her brows, my luxurious background of horse and cab.

"Ye've a cab!" she observed severely, as though I had arrived in the state coach drawn by four cream horses. A pause. "Well! I suppose you'd better come in. Don't forget to wipe your feet."

I dutifully wiped my feet and "came in," feeling that I had made a bad beginning.

"The doctor's out," she announced. "He's fair run off his legs, poor man, since the last assistant left. Aah! He was no good, that one—no good ataaal!" And with a faint shake of her head, as though, in her considered judgement, I would not prove much better, she left me marooned on the hearthrug.

Somehow I had to smile. Then I glanced round the big, comfortable room—the dining room, it was—with warm red curtains and Turkey-red carpet, a blazing coal fire, and furniture of sound mahogany. No aspidistra, thank God! A big bowl of apples on the dresser, a full glass barrel of biscuits, and whisky in the square-cut decanter. No pictures, no photographs, but, of all things, three yellow violins hanging on the walls. A good—oh, a decent room to live in. I was warming myself pleasantly at the blaze when the door was flung open and Cameron came stamping in.

"That's right," said Cameron, without a handshake or a word of preamble, "warm your backside at the fire while I work myself to death outside. Dammit to hell! I thought Stirrock said ye would be here this mornin'. Janet! Janet!"—at the pitch of his lungs— "For God's sake bring in our tea."

He was a medium-sized, oldish man with a face beaten bright crimson by Scots weather and Scots whisky, and a pugnacious little grey imperial, now dewed with raindrops. He stooped slightly, so that his head had a forward, belligerent thrust. He wore gaiters, cord breeches, and a big, baggy tweed jacket of a nondescript, vaguely greenish colour, the side pockets stuffed to the bursting

42

point with everything from an apple to a gum-elastic catheter. About him there hung invariably the odour of drugs, carbolic, and strong tobacco.

Obtaining a good three-quarters of the fire, he inspected me sideways and asked abruptly:

"Are ye strong? Sound in wind and limb?"

"I hope so!"

"Married?"

"Not yet."

"Thank God! Can ye play the fiddle?"

"No!"

"Neither can I—but I can make them bonny. Do ye smoke a pipe?"

"I do!"

"Humph! Do ye drink whisky?"

My dander had been rising under this interrogation. I don't like you, I thought, as I looked at the odd, unprofessional figure beside me, and I never will. I answered surlily:

"I drink what I like, and when I like!"

The spark of a smile gleamed in Cameron's sardonic eye.

"It might be worse," he murmured, and then: "Sit in and have your tea."

Janet had swiftly and silently set the table—cake, buns, toast, preserve, brown bread, home-baked scones, cheese, and bannocks— and now, with the big brown teapot, she brought in a huge dish of cold ham and poached eggs.

"There's no falderals in this house," Cameron explained briefly as he poured the tea—he had beautiful hands, I noticed, hard-skinned, yet supple. "Breakfast, middle-day dinner, high tea, and supper—plain food and plenty. We work our assistant here, but —by your leave—we don't starve him."

We were well through the meal when Janet came in with more hot water. Only then did she say impassively:

"There's a man been waiting this last half hour—young Lachlan Mackenzie, him that has the steading up Inverbeg way. His bairn's badly, he makes out."

43

Cameron arrested a piece of oatcake halfway to his mouth to let out his favourite oath:

"Dammit to hell!" he cried, "and me up at Inverberg this mornin' and passed his very door. Th'infernal eediot! I'll wager the child's been sick for days. Do they all think I'm made of steel?" He checked himself. Then, with a sigh which seemed to let off all his boiling steam, he added in quite a different voice, "All right, Janet. All right. Let him come in here the now."

In a moment Mackenzie stood in the doorway, cap in hand—a poor, shiftless-looking crofter, very much abashed by his surroundings, and terribly nervous under the doctor's interrogating eye.

"It's the boy, Doctor," he muttered, twisting his cap. "The wife thinks it's the croup."

"How long has he been poorly, Lachlan?"

This friendly use of his name gave the young fellow confidence.

"Two days, Doctor—but we didna' think it was the croup. . . ."

"Ay, ay, Lachlan. The croup! Just so, just so." A pause. "How did ye get in?"

"I just walkit in, Doctor—it's no that far."

Not far! It was seven miles from Inverbeg to Tannochbrae.

Cameron rubbed his cheek slowly.

"All right, Lachlan man! Don't you worry. Away with Janet now and have your tea while the gig's bein' got round."

Silence in the dining room when he had gone. Cameron reflectively stirred his tea. Almost apologetically he said:

"I can't be hard on a poor devil like that. It's a weakness I never seem to get over. He owes me for his wife's last confinement—he'll never pay it. But I'll get out the gig, drive seven miles, see the child, drive seven miles back. And what do you think I'll mark against him in the book? One and six—if I don't forget. And what does it matter if I do forget? He'll never pay me a red bawbee in any case. Oh, dammit to hell! What a life for a man who loves fiddles!"

Silence again; then I ventured:

"Shall I do the call?"

44

Cameron took a long pull at his tea. The bright satire was back in his eye as he said:

"That's a braw wee black bag ye've got—ay, I see it on the sofa —brand-new and shiny, with your stethoscope and all the new contrivances inside, bonny and complete. No wonder ye're fair itchin' to use it." He looked me straight in the face. "All right! Ye can go. But let me warn you, my lad, in a practice like mine it's not the bag that matters—it's the man!" He got up. "Do the call then, and I'll do the surgery. Take some antitoxin with you to be safe. It's on the right-hand shelf as you go in the back room. Here! I'll show ye. I'm not wantin' you to drive seven miles to find out that croup is liable to mean diphtheria."

The gig was waiting outside the front porch, with Lachlan already in the back, and Jamie, the groom, standing ready with the waterproof sheet. We set off through the wet, blustery night.

In the village the rain fell heavily enough, but when we crossed the bridge and breasted the hill it broke upon us in torrents. The wind drove full into our teeth like a hurricane.

Fifteen minutes, and I was half drenched; my hat saturated, trickles of water oozing down my neck, and my precious bag, which I held upon my knees, streaming like a wet seal. I wanted to curse the weather, the practice, and Cameron; but I shut my teeth and said nothing.

It was bad, bad going. The road was dark, too, the gig lamps so blurred by a film of mud that Jamie had difficulty in keeping the horse upon the road. Away to the right, behind massed firs, were the lights of Darroch, vague, unfriendly; and to the left, lying like a great dark beast, the amorphous bulk of the Ardfillan Hills.

We went on through the pitch blackness and the rain in silence. Then from ahead came the quick lapping of water against some hidden shore.

"The loch!" said Jamie, by way of explanation. They were the only words spoken during the journey.

The unseen road wound now by this angry, unseen water. Then, three miles on, we bore sharply to the left and stopped finally at a small steading where a single illuminated window seemed some-how swamped and hopeless in the great void of sodden blackness.

As we climbed out of the gig, Lachlan's wife opened the door. She looked no more than a girl despite her clumsy sacking apron and uncouth brogues. A coil of hair fell carelessly down her neck, and her big eyes were dark and youthful against the anxious pallor of her face. She helped me out of my wet coat in silence; then, though she still said not a word, her worried eye indicated the kitchen bed. I walked over to it, my boots squelching on the stone-flagged floor.

A little boy of three lay tossing under a single blanket, his brow damp with sweat, his face completely livid as he gasped for breath. I asked for a spoon, but did not use it; instead, with my finger I depressed the child's tongue. Yes! The whole of the fauces covered with thick, greenish-white membrane. Laryngeal diphtheria!

"I've made him some gruel, Doctor," the mother murmured, "but he doesna' . . . doesna' seem to fancy it."

"He can't swallow," I said.

Because I was nervous my voice sounded unsympathetic, even harsh.

"Is he bad, then, Doctor?" she whispered, with a hand at her breast.

Bad! I thought, with my fingers on the pulse. She doesn't dream how bad he is! Bending down, I made a complete and careful examination. There was no doubt at all—the child was dying. What a horrible position, I thought again, that this should be my first case.

I went to my bag, opened it, filled my big syringe with 8,000 units of antidiphtheritic serum. The child barely moaned as the needle sank into his thigh and the serum slowly filtered in. To gain time I went back to the fire. Jamie and Lachlan were in the room now, too, for it was the only warm place in the house. They stood together by the door. I could feel their eyes on me, watchful, expectant, together with the terrified eyes of the mother. I was the centre of that humble room. They looked to me to do something for the child.

What was I to do? I knew very well what I should do. But I

46

was afraid. I returned to the bed. If anything, the boy was worse. In half an hour, before the serum could act, he would be dead from obstruction of the windpipe. Another wave of fear came over me. I had to make up my mind. Now—at once—or it would be too late.

Automatically I faced round. I felt myself so young, so utterly inept and inexperienced in the face of the great elemental forces which surged within the room. I said in a manner wholly unimpressive:

"The boy has diphtheria. The membrane is blocking the larynx. There's only one thing to do. Operate. Open the windpipe below the obstruction."

The mother wrung her hands, and screamed:

"Oh, no, Doctor, no!"

I turned to Jamie.

"Lift the boy onto the table."

There was a second's hesitation; then slowly Jamie went over and lifted the almost senseless child on to the scrubbed pine table. But at that Lachlan broke down.

"I canna' stand it! I canna' stand it!" He cried weakly, and looked around desperately for an excuse. "I'll away and put the horse in the stable."

Blubbering, he rushed out.

Now the mother had recovered herself. Pale as a ghost, her hands clenched fiercely, she looked at me.

"Tell me what to do, and I'll do it."

"Stand there and hold his head back tight!"

I swabbed the skin of the child's throat with iodine. I took a clean towel and laid it across those glazing eyes. The case was far beyond an anaesthetic; madness to think of using it. Jamie was holding the oil lamp near. Setting my teeth, I picked up the lancet. I made the incision with a steady hand, but I felt my legs trembling beneath me. A deep incision, but not deep enough. I must go deeper, deeper—go boldly in, yet watch all the time for the jugular vein. If I cut that vein . . . ! I widened the incision, using the blunt end of the scalpel, searching desperately for the white cartilage

47

of the trachea. The child, roused by pain, struggled like a fish in
a strangling net. God! would I never find it? I was muddling hopelessly, messing about—I knew it—the child would die; they would
say that I had killed him. I cursed myself in spirit. Beads of sweat
broke out on my brow, as I remembered, suddenly, MacEwen's
fatal words: *You will never be a surgeon.*"

The child's breathing was terrible now, thin, infrequent; the
whole of his tiny thorax sucked and sobbed over each frightful, useless breath. The neck veins were engorged, the throat livid, the
face blackening. Not a minute longer, I thought! He's finished, and
so am I. For one sickening instant I had a quick vision of all the
operations I had known—of the cold, immaculate precision of the
Infirmary theatre, and then, by frightful contrast, this struggling,
desperate thing dying under my knife upon a kitchen table by the
flare of an oil lamp, while the wind howled and stormed outside.
Oh, God, I prayed, help me, help me now.

I felt my eyes misting. A great emptiness possessed my whole
being. And then under my searching knife the thin white tube
sprang into view. Swiftly I incised it, and in the instant the child's
gasping ceased. Instead, a long clear breath of air went in through
the opening. Another—another. The cyanosis vanished, the pulse
strengthened. Swept by a terrific reaction, I felt that I was going
to collapse. Afraid to move, I kept my head down to hide the smarting tears that sprang into my eyes. I've done it, I thought; oh,
God, I've done it after all!

Later I slipped the tiny silver tracheotomy tube into the opening.
I washed the blood from my hands, lifted the boy back to bed. The
temperature had fallen a point and a half. As I sat by the bedside,
watching, cleaning the tube of mucus, I felt a queer, benign interest
in the child—I studied his little face, no longer strange to me.

From time to time the mother replenished the fire so silently she
was like a shadow in the room. Jamie and Lachlan were asleep
upstairs. At five in the morning I gave another 4,000 units of serum.
At six the child was sleeping, far less restive than before. At seven
I rose and stretched myself. Smiling, I said:

"He'll do now, I expect!" And I explained to the mother the

method of cleaning out the tube. "In ten days it'll all be healed up good as new."

Now there was no terror in her eyes, but a gratitude—moving and inarticulate—like the gratitude of some dumb creature to a god.

The horse was harnessed, the gig brought round. We all drank a cup of tea standing. The rain had stopped long since. And at half past seven Jamie and I were off, striking through the pale glory of the morning. Strangely, Jamie was no longer taciturn; he had a word for this and that—a word of comradeship which fell graciously upon my ears.

It was close on nine when, tired, unshaven, and clutching the mud-splashed bag, I stumbled into the dining room of Arden House. Cameron was there, fresh as a new pin, whistling a little tune softly, between his teeth—he had an exasperating habit of whistling in the morning!—as he inspected a dish of bacon and eggs.

He looked me up and down; then with a dry twinkle in his eye, before I could speak, he declared:

"There's one guid thing has happened anyway! Ye've taken the newness off your bag."

# Chapter Six

THE VILLAGE, as the spring came, lost all its bleakness. Wrapped in soft airs, the blue sky feathered by fleecy clouds, the cottage gardens filled with the scent of honeysuckle and the hum of bees, the hillsides alive with the bleating of lambs, Tannochbrae became a sweet and pleasant place. Trout were leaping in the mountain burns, and whenever I had a spare hour I sought them with all the throbbing eagerness of an insatiable fisherman. I was happy in my work, becoming attached to my crusty old colleague, free, on my occasional day off, to travel to Glasgow to visit the girl I could not forget, who still was attending medical classes at the University. I even felt myself winning some faint signs of favour from our primly disapproving housekeeper when, unfortunately, I was involved in a serious and most worrying dispute.

An outbreak of scarlet fever had occurred in the district, starting in the month of May, a severe form of the disease, affecting chiefly the children of the village, and it showed no signs of abating in the ordinary way. As the days passed, and one case followed another despite all our efforts at treatment and isolation, I lost patience and told myself I must get to the root of the matter. Some specific factor was definitely disseminating the disease, and I pledged myself to find it.

At the outset I realised that I could expect little help from the public health authorities. At this time the post of medical officer of health to the county was vested in the person of Dr. Snoddie, a rather self-important practitioner who lived in the neighbouring town of Knoxhill. This worthy doctor was not a Highlander—he came from the Borders—but he had married a Knoxhill woman, a rich widow slightly older than himself. Since his marriage he had set out to cultivate the best "county" families. He wore a cutaway coat and kept a brougham. He had come to regard his public office as a sinecure and was content to draw his honorarium of fifty guineas a year without in the least exerting himself to earn it.

There was one point common to all the cases I had met, and that was the milk supply, which came in every instance from the farm adjacent to Tannochbrae known as Shawhead. The more I thought about it, the more I was convinced that the Shawhead milk was the origin of the epidemic. I had no proof, of course, merely a suspicion, but it was enough to make me resolve to act. On the forenoon of the following Tuesday, as I was passing Shawhead, I drew up the gig and called in at the farm.

It was a pretty place, as snug and sonsy as any man could wish, with whitewashed farm buildings, against which rambler roses were already beginning to bloom. Everything, as far as the eye could see, was sweet and clean, the yard orderly, the outbuildings sound, the surrounding fields well cared for and in good heart.

Small wonder it was that Rob Hendry should be so proud to own this fine dairy and the pedigree Ayrshire herd which often won him prizes at the local show. Known colloquially as Shawhead— taking the name from the land that was his patrimony—Rob was something of a character, a big, craggy man of about fifty, with iron-grey hair. Shawhead's whole life was bound up in two interests: his farm, that had come down to him in the family line, and his young wife Jean, whom he had recently married and whom, for all his dourness, he plainly adored.

Much sly gossip went the rounds of Tannochbrae over Shawhead's fondness for his young wife, who was of humble birth and had been his dairymaid before Rob put the ring upon her finger, and the saying, "Nae fool like an auld fool," was freely bandied among the cronies. But Shawhead was quite content and could afford to snap his fingers—a customary gesture!—in the face of local gossip.

When I knocked at the bright green-painted door of the farm, it was Jean herself who answered, and at my question she smiled and shook her head.

"No," she answered, "the good man's out. He's gone to Ardfillan market with some calves. He'll not be back till this afternoon."

She was a bonny lass, the new mistress of Shawhead, plump and brisk, with pink cheeks and fine coppery hair braided trimly behind her ears. Not more than twenty-three, she had an air that was both innocent and buxom. Her skirt, kilted in the true kailyard fashion, revealed a petticoat of striped cloth, beneath which her ankle, for all its coarse hand-knitted stocking, was well turned and firm. Her sleeves, rolled up above her elbows, exposed clean, competent arms. As I surveyed her against the background of the well-kept steading, the suspicions I had formed began to waver.

"So Shawhead's out," I temporised.

"Ay," she answered, "but he'll be home the back of four. Will you look in then, or is there any message I could give him?"

I hesitated.

"As a matter of fact, Mrs. Hendry, it's rather an awkward business I've come about. This outbreak of scarlet fever. . . . It's spreading, you know, and I find that in all my cases . . . , well, not to put too fine a point on it—the milk has come from Shawhead. I want to be quite open with you. I wondered if I might look into things, and see if, by any chance, the cause of the trouble might be here."

At my words, though they were spoken gently, her frank expression altered. Her face clouded, she tossed her head.

"The fever!" she cried indignantly. "To mention it even . . . in the same breath as our good milk! To be sure, Doctor, if it's that you've come about, you'd better see the master."

And without further parley she closed the door sharply in my face.

Discouraged by this setback and, for some obscure reason, inclined to be annoyed myself, I got back to the gig and continued my morning round. I had half a mind to let the matter drop, but at the next house when I found that the Prentice boy, one of my fever cases, had taken a turn for the worse, and that his brother showed signs of sickening with the complaint, I felt I could not abandon my original purpose. In fact, at midday, when he got home, I mentioned my intention to Dr. Cameron. Cameron listened; then the corners of his mouth drew down dubiously.

"It looks like the milk," he said slowly, "when you reason it that way. And yet I can't think it either. Shawhead has a model place out there." He paused. "Go and see him, by all means, but be careful how you set about it. He's a touchy deevil, and his temper's like tinder."

That afternoon I returned to Shawhead farm and knocked once again on the bright green door. There was no immediate answer, and imagining that Shawhead might be in the dairy, I wandered across the yard, past the barn, and into the dairy, which, however, contrary to my expectations, was empty. I then turned into the byre.

As I entered the byre, the cows were at that moment brought in by the byreman in preparation for the evening milking.

Leaning against the doorway, I observed the fine, sleek animals as, breathing softly, they took up their places quietly in the stalls. I then watched the byreman, David Orr, known familiarly as Davit, take the three-legged stool and, sitting close to the first animal, press his cheek against its dappled side and begin the milking.

My eyes dwelt in a kind of fascination upon Davit, for Davit had a pale and sickly look, and round Davit's throat was wrapped a twist of red flannel.

Advancing cautiously, I greeted Davit, who looked up with a kind of rustic simplicity.

"It's you, Doctor!" said Davit. "I'd no idea you were here. Are you after a glass of milk?"

Unsmiling, I shook my head.

"I'll have no milk today, Davit." And then, indicating the red flannel casually, "What's like the matter with your neck?"

Davit paused in his milking and gave a conscious laugh.

"Oh, it's nothing—nothing at all, ye ken. I had a sore throat some weeks past, and it's left me kind of poorly, but it's nothing at all—nothing at all."

My gaze became more intent.

"A sore throat!" I echoed; then slowly, "Did you have any rash, Davit, with the sore throat that ye had?"

"Rash?" echoed Davit stupidly. "And what in the name of wonder might that be?"

I made to explain, to press my inquiries; then all at once I caught sight of Davit's hands and stopped short. Now there was no need to seek further. The answer came from Davit's hands, so busily employed in milking the cow, for from each of those hands fine particles of skin were peeling.

The evidence was conclusive—the fine powdery desquamation, like a dust of bran, which invariably follows scarlet fever, and which, coupled with the fact of the sore throat, convinced me beyond all shadow of doubt that Davit had had the disease in ambulant form—a mild yet most dangerous type—and that he had not only contaminated the milk, but had almost certainly infected the udders of the cows.

Suddenly a loud voice broke the stillness of the byre.

"So you're here, are you? Spying around and shoving yourself into other people's business?"

Shawhead himself had appeared, dark with anger. Behind him stood his wife, gazing resentfully at me. It was a painful moment, yet now I could not possibly avoid the issue.

"I'm sorry, Shawhead. I'm not here from choice. It's plain necessity." I pointed to the staring byreman. "Davit here has had scarlet fever, probably a slight attack, but enough to do a lot of damage." I tempered my words as best I could. "It looks as if you might have to shut up your dairy for a week or two."

"What!" Shawhead exclaimed, between amazement and indignation. "Shut up my dairy! God in heaven, ye're not blate!"

"Be reasonable," I pleaded. "You're not to blame. But the fact remains, it's here the infection has come from."

"The infection! How dare you, man. We're all clean folks in this farm."

"Yes, but Davit . . ."

"Davit's as clean as the rest of us," cried Shawhead. "He's had a bit sore throat and no more. He's better now. Better, d'ye hear! It's rank lunacy to make out we maun shut up because o't."

"I tell you," I persisted, with as much patience as I could muster, "that he has had scarlet fever. He's scaling all over his body. That's what is contaminating your milk."

Here the veins on Shawhead's forehead stood out. He could not contain himself.

"That's enough! I'll hear no more from ye. The very idea! My fine milk contaminated! It's pure sweet milk, and always has been. Don't ye know we drink it ourselves?"

And in an access of indignation he took the dipper and plunged it in the milk. Raising the brimming measure in a gesture of defiance, he drank half himself, then gave the rest to Jean.

"There!" He flung down the dipper. "That'll show you. And if you speak another word you'll bitterly regret it."

There was a pause. I understood the farmer's wounded pride. But I had my duty. I turned away in silence.

That afternoon I went to the house of Dr. Snoddie in Knoxhill and put the matter before him, asking that he take steps immediately, in his official capacity to meet the situation.

The health officer, seated at his desk, pressing his finger tips together, inspected me over his gold-rimmed pince-nez. He had little love for Dr. Cameron and was obviously pleased that I had come to seek a favour of him in his official capacity.

"I'll look into it, of course," he remarked in a patronising tone. "But, frankly, I cannot see that you have any real grounds for your request. There's no positive evidence—no rash, no fever, nothing but a mere supposition on your part. You must remember that it is an extremely serious matter to shut down a man's business on what may be merely unfounded conjecture."

I flushed hotly.

"Conjecture be hanged! That farm is the focus of the trouble. I'll swear to it."

"Indeed!" said Dr. Snoddie, with an astringent smile. "Well, we shall see." A suave gesture of dismissal. "You'll hear from me in the course of a day or so."

Fretting under this manifestation of officialdom, I had, nevertheless, to make the best of it. For twenty-four hours nothing happened; then, on the day following, as we sat at lunch, the expected note was delivered by hand.

I read it, then passed the paper to Dr. Cameron, who studied it, gazed at me covertly, and sighed:

"It's what you might expect of friend Snoddie. But what can we do? If he won't close we must sit tight and hope for the best."

"And find ourselves with a dozen more cases? No, thanks!" I spoke with sudden violence. "If we can't get official action, we'll do it the other way."

"Now, be careful," remonstrated Cameron. "He's a dangerous man, is Shawhead."

"No more dangerous than his milk." And before Cameron could reply I walked out of the room.

All the stubbornness in my character was aroused. In the course of my visits during that day and the next I asked my patients, guardedly yet emphatically, to refrain from using the Shawhead milk supply. Despite my vexation, and a burning sense of being ill-used and misunderstood, I spoke with discretion. Like a young fool, I had forgotten what my older and wiser colleague would undoubtedly have foreseen. Far from being treated as a confidence, in no time at all the news went round, the place rang with my words.

The resultant storm thoroughly dismayed me. All the excitement which local controversy arouses in a small community was in active operation. People took sides, tongues wagged, the dispute became the chief topic of interest in the district.

Sustained but little by the consciousness that I was in the right, I could do no more than stick grimly to my guns. But on the Friday of the same week a document arrived which shook me even more severely. It was no less than a writ issued by the farmer through Logan and Logan, Knoxhill solicitors, for slander. In the local parlance, Shawhead was "having the law on me."

Without delay I took the ominous blue parchment to Dr. Cameron, who studied it in silence.

"I can justify myself," I muttered. "You know I acted for the best."

56

"Well," said Cameron slowly, "that's what you must tell the court."

Slight encouragement, perhaps, for Cameron said no more. Yet I knew, for all his reticence, that the old doctor was behind me. Nevertheless, as the days went on and I became more fully aware of my position, realising that I must go into open court to face the charges laid against me, with my reputation hanging upon the decision that was to be given, I was far from confident.

Had I been correct in my diagnosis? Had I been justified? Did my motives spring from devotion to my profession, or merely from an obstinate desire for self-justification? No, I told myself fiercely, a thousand times no. But the very emphasis of my answer did not save me from sleepless nights and days which were a misery of uncertainty and suspense.

I found people looking at me oddly, even in the streets of Knoxhill. Dr. Snoddie, driving past in his brougham, avoided my gaze with an obviousness which told me I should receive no support from him.

Another day passed, and the silence which existed between Cameron and myself at mealtimes was more than I could bear.

And then, late the next afternoon, as I sat moodily in the surgery, worrying over all that had passed and all that must so shortly take place, my colleague came in with a strange expression upon his face.

"Have you heard?" He spoke in a low, restrained tone. "She's down with it. Acute scarlet fever. Shawhead's wife, Jean Hendry herself."

One astounded instant. Then a terrific wave of vindication swept over me. In a flash I remembered Shawhead's defiant gesture as he passed the dipper of milk.

"They'll never go on with the case now," Cameron meditated. "They tell me Shawhead's near off his head with anxiety. It's a judgement."

I was silent, fighting with all my strength the depth, the intensity of my relief.

The village gasped at the turn of events, and allowing due sympathy for Shawhead, opinion swung round like a weathercock in a change of wind. I became at one stroke protector of the people and of the public health of Tannochbrae. But I would have none of the congratulations which folks tried to offer me as I went about my work, for now it was known that Jean Hendry was desperately ill. The attack was of the fulminating type, her temperature was reported to be mounting rapidly, and she was delirious.

Shawhead had forbidden her removal to the hospital at Knoxhill, and now, in truth, was the dairy closed, the whole farm isolated, and the cows out in the pasture by day and by night. Dr. Snoddie, with a sour and worried face, was in close attendance, and a specialist had been summoned from the Ruchill Hospital in Glasgow.

In spite of all this, Jean Hendry grew worse. On the Sunday it was reported that she was sinking, and a kind of silence, greater far than the ordinary Sabbath stillness, settled over Tannochbrae. Not a word passed between Cameron and myself. Then, toward the evening of that quiet day, as the sun was setting in a pool of light behind the Winton Hills, Janet, the housekeeper, entered the living room. Her face was drawn in noncommittal lines, her hands were folded tightly over her bosom, and her voice was sombre as she said:

"It's all done with now. Jamie just brought in the word. She's gone."

Still not a word was spoken. I turned my head away. Outside, a bell began to toll.

Six weeks later, I met Shawhead for the first time since our encounter in the byre. The farmer, aged and broken by his loss, was returning from the churchyard, which lay on the hillside, beyond the village kirk. Awkwardly, I stopped in the middle of the pathway, and almost mechanically Shawhead stopped too. Our eyes met, and each read in the face of the other the knowledge of what might have been, the terrible knowledge that his wife might now have been quick and alive beside him, not cold in her narrow grave.

A kind of groan broke from Shawhead's pale lips, slowly he reached out his hand, which met mine in a long and tortured grasp.

# Chapter Seven

ONE EVENING, when consultations in the surgery were so few that I sat glancing idly through the *West Highland Advertiser,* a long, thin man, with bad teeth and sandy hair streaked over his bald head, called to see me. I recognised him as Dougal Todd, the village painter and carpenter.

"I hope I'm not disturbing ye, Doctor," he began, in a melancholy, sanctimonious style, and with accent and idiom so broad that I am forced, in some measure, to translate it. "The truth is, I've just dropped in to have a word with you about my poor old mother." He shook his head and lowered his eyes. "Ye see," he explained, "my mother's a frail little body, and pretty old—believe me or not, she's eighty if she's a day. It's but right she should see the doctor once in a while. I wouldna' have it otherwise, I'm so fond of her. Forby, I've got her life insured in a society or two, which makes it more or less obleegatory.

"Now, Doctor, I was wonderin' "—his voice became ingratiating, confidential—"seein' that my mother is just a poor old woman and me so ill off myself, I was wonderin', seein' that you're just the assistant here, I was wonderin', I say, if ye wouldna' see her for half the ordinary fee."

I stared at my dismal-faced visitor, quite baffled by his astounding proposition.

"I'll think it over," I said at length, resolving to put the matter before Cameron later in the evening.

"Ay, ay," agreed Todd. "Think it over, Doctor, do. As a kindness to a poor old done woman, ye understand."

He hung about for a minute with a hesitating, meanly propitiating air; then, remarking that it was a chilly evening, he bared his bad teeth in a smile and scraped himself out.

That night at supper Cameron answered my query with emphasis: "Don't! Not on any account! If the old woman comes in of her own accord about her rheumatics or a touch of bronchitis, it's quite different. Don't charge her a penny piece. Consultation and as much physic as she needs for nothing. Mind you, she'll want to pay you with the few pennies in her purse—she's the decentest, honestest old body ye'd meet in a day's march. But if Dougal has you in to her for his demned insurance societies or the like, make the fee double. He's the nearest, whingiest miser in the whole of Tannochbrae."

The Todds lived in the main street, beside the general store. Todd was too mean to have a shop himself; he had "premises," as he put it—a big corrugated shed littered with shavings and scaffolding—in the yard behind.

Perhaps Todd's avarice was catching, for his wife, Jessie, a big, stout woman with a shrewd eye, had the name for hardness, while Jessica, their only child, had never been known to give a sweet away. When observed chewing in the school playground and asked by a schoolmate for a share of her candy, the invariable reply of the red-cheeked little Jessica was: "Oh, dear! Oh, dear! I've just put the last bit in my mouth."

From which a saying arose in Tannochbrae: "Never ask the Todds for anything—they've aye just put it in their mouths."

Not that they weren't decent folks, the Todds; oh, yes, they were self-respecting, hard-working, God-fearing folks! Six days of the week, without thought of half-holiday, Dougal could be seen in his dirty white coat attached to a paintbrush and a ladder, while on the seventh, in his sober blacks, he escorted his wife and daughter to the kirk.

In this household lived old Mrs. Todd, a quiet, timid little woman, with a wrinkled, cheerful face and an almost sparrowlike chirpiness of manner. How this modest, kindly body had ever propagated a son like Dougal remained a mystery to Tannochbrae. All her life she had worked hard and done her best for Dougal. But now she was old, with, as Dougal sadly remarked, little enough but himself to show for it.

She had a very small room right at the top of the house where she kept her treasures—a small bottle of cough syrup to ease her bronchitis, a few strong peppermints in a round, tin box. Her meals, by gracious permission, were taken downstairs with the family, except when the Todds had company, but most of her time was spent in the broken armchair in her attic by the minute spark of fire—which she displayed a genius in nursing. On rare occasions, when the weather was warm, she made a brave sortie and went out. Dougal discouraged these small excursions.

"Now, now, Mother, remember your age. Ye ought to be thinkin' about your last end instead of jauntin' down the town."

A kindly protest, of course! To the old woman, Dougal never seemed anything but kindly. True, he would watch her with a harassed eye if she took a second scone at teatime. "Mother! Ye oughtna' to eat so much at your time of life."

And he would wince to see her labouring upstairs with the tiny scuttle of coal from which she fed her fire; not because she laboured, but because, alas, she used his coal.

Despite his parsimony, Dougal was not rich—in business his meanness cut both ways—but he was rich in hope. He had insured his mother for "a heap of silver." When she was dead, this money would be Dougal's. The only trouble was that quite steadfastly the old woman refused to die.

Despite the most sympathetic encouragement—"Mother, ye're lookin' verra poorly today," or "Mother, would ye not like to take to your bed and let me fetch the minister?"—old Mrs. Todd went on meekly consuming food, tea, and coal, as though she meant to live to be a hundred.

Late at night Dougal and his wife would sit up, thinking of the food, the tea, the coal—of the heavy insurance payments mounting

61

up from week to week—not saying a word, but both of them brooding over the loveliest diseases, from pneumonia to apoplexy, which
might have taken the old woman off, and didn't.

A few weeks after Dougal had called on me, old Mrs. Todd visited
the surgery herself. It was one of her treats—which she enjoyed so
much and experienced so seldom—a jaunt "doun the street." She
had bought herself some tape she needed at Jenny McKechnie's—
fancy goods and millinery—and enjoyed the long gossip with Jenny
into the bargain. At the store she had got herself two pennyworth of
black striped balls—less delicate in the flavour than the peppermints, but infinitely more lasting. And now, tired but triumphant,
she dropped in on me at Arden House on her way back to her garret.

"I've heard tell of ye so much, Doctor, I just had to come and see
ye. Would ye give me a drop cough mixture for my hoast? I've a
tickly in my tubes at nights."

She beamed at me with her dark, sparrowy eye—a cheerful, taking little body—withered, perhaps, like an apple that has been kept,
but sound to the core for all that.

I loved her instantly.

"Certainly you'll have some cough mixture. And strong at that.
I'll make it up for you myself."

"Something to warm my chest, Doctor," she suggested, coming out
of her shell.

"Ay, ay!" I agreed heartily. I gave her the best, a good stiff
chlorodyne concoction, fit, as I assured her, for the Queen herself.

"And the dose—it's two teaspoonfuls at night," I announced, lick-
ing on the label.

"What's that ye say, Doctor?" she inquired, and then, with a comi-
cal simplicity, "Ye ken, I've turned that deaf since I broke my
spectacles."

I had to laugh. It was so infectious that in a minute old Mrs. Todd
joined in.

"Ye've a joke in ye, Doctor," she complimented me archly, as I
showed her to the door. "Fine! I aye liked a doctor with a joke in
him."

Next morning, which was Saturday, the Todds sat down to breakfast in the kitchen. Porridge was supped in silence by Dougal, his wife, and Jessica. Old Mrs. Todd had not appeared. Next, tea was poured, and Dougal's egg, shelled and in a cup, produced from the oven. And then, with a sour look at the wag-at-the-wall clock, Jessie remarked to her husband:

"Can that mother of yours not get up in time for her breakfast? I've put up with plenty from the same old faggot—and for long enough and all. Things are coming to a bonny pass. She'll like to have me runnin' up with trays to her, no doubt."

"I don't think she's even out of her bed yet," said Jessica, taking her cue from her mother and tossing her head. "Auld lazybones!"

Dougal steered a spoonful of egg past his lugubriously drooping moustache.

"It's a waste of guid gas"—he masticated glumly with an eye on the meter—"to keep things warm for her."

"Here, dearie!" cried Jessie to her pet, in an access of spite, "run upstairs and shake her out of bed this very minute."

Jessica slid agreeably from her chair and, clutching her buttered scone, went bouncing upstairs.

Silence—silence above and below. Then a sudden wail, a wild scampering, and Jessica flung back into the kitchen.

"Aw, maw!" she blubbered. "Granny's dead!"

Dougal exploded a mouthful of tea back into his saucer; Jessie drew bolt upright in her chair.

"Dead, hinny," she whispered gently. "Did you say . . ."

"Ay," Jessica whined, with a wisdom beyond her years. "That's what I did say. She's streiket out stiff as a poker."

A long exhalation that might have been a sigh came slowly from Jessie's bosom. At the same moment Dougal thrust back his chair.

"Come on."

He made a masterful gesture to his wife. They hurried up to the top floor. They burst into the attic. Then, suddenly, they paused.

The old woman lay on her back with her mouth fallen open and her cheeks fallen in. Her eyes were gummed, her nostrils pinched.

"Mother!" exclaimed Dougal, lifting her hand. But it slipped out of his grasp and fell stiffly on the bed.

There was a pregnant pause while Dougal and his wife stared at the rigid figure on the bed. Then from over his shoulder Jessie whispered reverently:

"It's all over, Dougal! Ay, ay, she's by with it all now."

And taking the end of the sheet she solemnly covered old Mrs. Todd's pallid face.

Dougal looked at his wife, sniffed, and whined:

"Oh, dear, oh, dear! My poor mother's deid."

"She's with her Maker, Dougal," said Jessie, turning up the whites of her eyes. "We mustna' question His holy will." And taking him by the arm she led him gently downstairs. But in the kitchen Dougal sank into a chair.

"Pity me!" he groaned. "My poor mother's deid at last."

"Ye canna' reproach yourself, Dougal," said Jessie firmly. "Ye were aye a good son to her. And aye I did my best for her myself. A decent old body she was. She had to go sooner or later. And what a peaceful end. Will ye have a drop spirits to steady you up?"

Dougal groaned again, and shook his head. But it was no time for economy. Jessica fetched the bottle from the parlour dresser, and with a show of repugnance Dougal took off a good four fingers.

"That's better," said Jessie. "Ye maun draw yourself together, man. There's plenty for ye to do. There's the doctor's certificate to get, and the undertaker to see, and the insurance . . ."

Dougal lifted his head.

"Ay—there's the insurance." He sighed deeply. "Ah, weel, I'll better get on with it—though it's bitter, bitter work to do."

He got up, took his cap, and went.

He went first to Arden House, where Janet answered the door.

"Janet! I want the doctor," Dougal blubbered, for the whisky had intensified his grief. "My dear old mother—she's passed away in her sleep."

"Poor body," Janet exclaimed involuntarily. Then, inspecting him sternly, "Ye canna' have the doctor the now. They're both of the two of them out. I'll send up the assistant when he comes in from Marklea." And she slammed the door in his face.

No sympathy, thought Dougal; oh, dear, oh, dear—no sympathy

64

in the woman at all. My poor old mother! I'm crying like a bairn. On the way to the undertaker's, in neighbouring Knoxhill, he stopped folks in the street to tell them, weeping, of his loss.

At Gibson's, the undertaker's, he ordered the coffin—a nice coffin, a beautiful coffin, fine value for the money, and not too dear. Sam Gibson was a good lad with a kind word, and a fair promise of 5 per cent discount for cash. He promised to send round to lay out the old woman that evening.

It was dinnertime when Dougal got home. Jessie had been busy; she had made a beautiful steak-and-kidney pie. That and a baked custard stood on the table. The whisky was there, too. Jessie exclaimed sensibly:

"At a time like this we've got to have our food. What with the shock and one thing and another. . . ."

They sat in.

"I don't feel like it," Dougal protested, as he accepted his plate. Then, as he put a large tender piece of steak below his moustache, "But I suppose we must keep up our strength."

Jessie said:

"Come to think on it—what was the insurance, up to date?"

"Near enough five hundred pound," Dougal answered solemnly, and forked a promising potato.

"Dear, oh, dear. It's a heap of money."

"Ay, it's a heap of money. Wheesht! There's the doorbell. It'll be the doctor."

On my return from Marklea, Janet had given me the message, and I had come on directly, worried and rather upset that the old woman should have died so soon after consulting me. Jessie met me in the lobby.

"Ye don't mind if I don't come with ye, Doctor. The shock of it has fair upset us all. The very idea of entering the poor old body's room's enough to make me grue. It's the left-hand door on the top landing."

I went up and into the room alone. I drew up the blind. Then, on the table by the window, the first thing I saw was my chlorodyne mixture. I stared at the bottle. One third of it was gone.

65

Quickly I went over to the bed, lifted the old woman's eyelids. Pin-point pupils. I took her wrist, held it. Then a faint smile came to my face. From my bag I took a vial of strong spirits of ammonia and held it under her nose. For a moment nothing happened. Then, with great enthusiasm, the dead woman sneezed.

Drowsily she opened her eyes, stared at me, and yawned while I shook her.

"Doctor, Doctor—what are ye doin' here in all the world? But, oh, I've had the most wonderful sleep."

Bending over her, I bawled in her ear:

"How much of that medicine did ye take?"

"Eh, what? Two tablespoonfuls—like ye telled me."

"No wonder ye slept," I shouted. "But now I'm thinkin' it's high time ye were up."

I corked the chlorodyne, thrust it in my pocket, and went downstairs.

"Will ye have a drop whisky, Doctor?" Dougal asked me mournfully in the kitchen.

"I think I will," I said, heartily, "though it's the first time I've heard you offering anyone a drink, Dougal."

The bereaved son shook his head pathetically.

"It's the occasion, Doctor. My poor old mother! I'm heartbroken she should be taken from us!"

"We're all heartbroken," Jessie echoed piously.

"Well! Here's health, Dougal," I said.

"Your good health, Doctor," said Dougal sadly. "We'll want four certificates. I had her in four insurance societies, the poor old body!"

There was a loud noise upstairs, followed by the banging of a door.

"Goodsakes!" cried Jessie, turning pale. "What's that?"

"Grand whisky, Dougal." This, with great heartiness, from me.

There was the sound of someone coming downstairs.

"Do ye hear it?" cried Jessie again. "There's something coming down the stairs."

The door opened, and old Mrs. Todd walked into the room. Jessie shrieked.

66

"God Almighty!" said Dougal, and he spilled the good whisky all over his dickey.

Paralysed, they watched the old woman draw in her chair to the table and help herself to pie. First she yawned, then she tittered— then, with a look at the pie, the custard, and the whisky, she exclaimed:

"It's a grand dinner the day. And I'm fair famished with hunger!"

She began to eat with a rare good appetite. And at that I left her to it.

# Chapter Eight

As SPRING WORE toward summer, Tannochbrae was ablaze with flowers. Strange though it may seem in such northern latitudes, the Scottish people love their gardens and cultivate them with surprising skill. My patron was no exception to the rule, and in his gardener, Alexander Deans, he possessed a horticultural treasure who came every day, regular as the clock, from the neighbouring township of Knoxhill, to keep the grounds of Arden House blooming, trim, and tidy.

One day, Deans was planting in the front bed of lawn when Dr. Cameron came down the gravel drive.

"Day, Alex," he called out across his shoulder; then, drawing up short, "Good God, man! What do you think you're doing?"

Alex was planting calceolarias in the big round bed—masses of beady, yellow calceolarias.

"Don't ye know I cannot endure that yellow trash?" Cameron exclaimed. "Where's my red geraniums—my bonny Scarlet Wonders?"

These red geraniums were an institution at Arden House, where, indeed, the garden grew by solemn ritual, the slow procession of the seasons producing the same procession of favourite plants, year in year out, the flowers remembered, anticipated, beloved.

In particular, Cameron loved his red geraniums. The vivid scarlet splash upon the shorn green lawn of Arden House was quite a feature of the village, and visitors would stop openly in the roadway to admire—affording Cameron a naïve and never-failing delight.

"I'm asking you," Cameron said again, "where's my red geraniums?"

Alex stood up, a short and rather stocky figure, in his shirt sleeves, his face weathered, his hands large, encrusted with dry soil. Without looking at the doctor, but keeping his gaze sheepishly upon the ground, he remarked:

"Yellow is a braw colour. You've no idea! It minds me of the yolk of an egg!" And he gave a slight snigger.

Dr. Cameron was staggered. Deans was a most respectful man, steady as a rock; he'd worked at Arden House for close on fifteen years. Drunk, thought Cameron, but somehow that didn't seem to fit. As he was in a hurry, he had no time to take the matter further. He said, very quietly:

"Get out these calceolarias, Alex. And get in the geraniums quick." Then he went out of the gate.

Yet, when he came back from his case, Alex was gone and the front bed of the lawn brimmed over with the yellow calceolarias.

That was the beginning, and soon there were growing whisperings of the strange conduct of Alex Deans. He who had been so silent and self-contained was now guilty of the wildest eccentricities. He would argue fiercely, stupidly, and come to blows about a trifle. His language, too, had taken a rude turn for the worse. Neighbours had heard him abusing his sister Annie, who kept house for him.

The climax came six weeks later, when a note arrived at Arden House from the county medical officer of health, Dr. Snoddie of Knoxhill. The message was for Cameron, and it said briefly:

"Come round at once. I want you to certify a dangerous lunatic."

It was afternoon, a grey, wet day—what Cameron called "whingey weather"—and today, in a chastened fashion, he had called it worse, for he was laid up by his old enemy, the asthma.

He was not in bed, but in his study armchair, with a tartan rug across his knees, a half-made fiddle upon his lap, and a balsam inhalation at his elbow. I was in the opposite chair, going over the morning's round which I had done alone.

"Dear, dear!" said Cameron when he had taken the note from Janet, discovered his glasses on his forehead, and read the peremptory message. "Poor Alex! I'm downright grieved about this!" And he made as though to discard the rug.

But, observing him from the doorway, Janet remarked firmly, "You're not putting one foot out of this house today."

He looked at her over his spectacles, then subsided with a wheezy sigh.

"Well, well, Janet. Say that one of us will be along presently."

When the housekeeper had gone Cameron handed the note to me.

"You'll know," he reflected, "that the law requires two independent medical reports before a man can be certified insane. Believe me, that's the sole reason Snoddie has sent for me. You'll agree that I don't often speak ill of my neighbours. But he's a man who has no use for anybody but himself." He wheezed again, and made a grimace at the fire. "And while I think of it—just watch yourself with him when you're about it. He bears you no great love since that affair with Shawhead."

Outside, Jamie was waiting with the gig. He buckled the weather-proof flap round me, and we went bowling through the drizzle to-gether. Presently, on the outskirts of Knoxhill, a row of old houses sprang out of the mist. We drew up at the end house—a house with two acres and a bit, forming a garden that reached from its gable to the embankment, land which the unhappy Deans had laboriously reclaimed and enriched.

In the front parlour downstairs the county medical officer was waiting with the rapidly mounting irritation of a self-important man who, if waiting is to be done, prefers that others should wait on him. As I came in he exclaimed:

"You're slow, sir, confoundedly slow. If you were my assistant I'd learn you to be sharper."

It occurred to me to say that I was not his assistant; but, mindful of Cameron's warning, I held my tongue.

"You know what's wanted," he went on. "I've seen the poor devil upstairs. He's quite demented. You'll have no difficulty. Let's have your certificate. I want to get away."

As I went upstairs he called after me:

70

"Hurry up, will you. I'm a busy man, and I'm going out to dinner tonight."

Alex Deans was in bed—no doubt as a measure of restraint. His sister sat beside him, her red eyes indicating that she had been weeping. Immediately I came in she rose without a word. Her silence was so hopeless, the whole atmosphere of the room so dim and tragic, that I had a momentary sense of chill. I looked at Alex, and at first I hardly recognised him. The change was not gross, it was Deans sure enough, but a blurred and altered Deans, his features coarsened in some strange and subtle way. His face seemed swollen, the nostrils thickened, the lips broad, the skin waxy, except for a faint reddish patch that spread across the nose. His appearance was apathetic, and when I spoke to him he muttered some absurd reply so slurred it was unintelligible.

"How long has he been this way?" I asked his sister.

She answered dully:

"Two days—or near enough. But before he was—just raging."

"How do you mean?"

"Nothing. . . ." She hesitated, added with extreme reluctance, "He set about me, that was all—and he used to be so kind to me."

The man on the bed stirred restlessly.

"I'll kill the lot of you," he mumbled. "You put poison on the weeds. Hand me the trowel. I maun dig . . . dig . . . dig . . . for worms!"

Silence fell upon these crazy words The words of a lunatic? Perhaps! Yet I was not satisfied. It may be that Snoddie had roused a contrary devil in me, firmed my resolution to have no preformed opinion thrust down my throat. But really it was deeper than that. In all the practice of medicine nothing is more supremely difficult than the art of diagnosis, for here the temptation is to assess the existing symptoms simply on their face value. If, for example, a patient complains of stomach distress, he is likely to be regarded as a gastric case when, in fact, the basic malady responsible for his symptoms may be something quite different, perhaps an obscure condition of the blood or of the nerves.

I have no reason to extol myself as a diagnostician—indeed, later

71

I shall reveal how lamentably I failed in this respect—yet at this moment, confronted by that case, a sense of warning, of intuition stirred in me. I lifted Dean's hand—it was dry and rough, the fingers slightly thickened at the ends. I took his temperature—it was sub-normal. I pressed the swollen, oedematous face—the swelling was firm, inelastic, and did not pit on pressure.

I thought hard, spurning the obvious solution, and all at once a light broke upon me. I had it! Myxoedema. Deans wasn't insane. He was a clear case of thyroid deficiency.

Every sign and every symptom—they fitted in, neatly, like a jig-saw puzzle. The defective memory, slow mentation, steady deteri-oration of intellect; the outbursts of irritability, of homicidal violence; the clumsy speech, dry skin, spatulate fingers, and swollen, inelastic face. There was real triumph in the completed picture.

Controlling myself, I rose. As, with great deliberation, I pushed my chair back against the wall, Annie said drearily:

"There's pen and ink on the table there, Doctor—beside the papers."

"Time enough, Annie," I answered. "I'm not in the mood for writ-ing at the moment."

I gave her a reassuring glance and went downstairs. I entered the parlour. There, in a voice purposely restrained, I told Dr. Snoddie that I could not certify the patient.

He stared at me, dumbfounded.

"Have you gone crazy, too?"

"I sincerely hope not!"

"Then why the devil won't you certify?"

"Because, in my opinion, Deans is not mad. I regard him as suffer-ing from myxoedema."

Dr. Snoddie's smooth, pink face mottled slowly to a patchy red.

"Good God Almighty! Are you setting up your opinion against mine? Haven't I seen the man? Haven't I certified him myself? He's a lunatic—a homicidal lunatic."

I kept my voice low.

"That's not my view. In my opinion, Deans is only sick in mind because he's sick in body. It would be criminal to send him to the asylum until a full course of thyroid treatment has been tried. That's why I refuse to certify. And now, as it's not my case and there's nothing more for me to do I'll say good night."

I drove home with a set face, distressed that circumstances had again brought me into conflict with this man. He was such an ignoramus that I felt sure he had not even heard of myxoedema.

As soon as we were at the front door of Arden House I gave the reins to Jamie, jumped out, and went straight upstairs. When I had told my story to Cameron he threw off his rug.

"Jamie!" he shouted. "Fetch Annie Deans here as fast as the gig will carry her."

So it happened, then, that, on Dr. Cameron's advice, Deans's sister was persuaded not to press for immediate commitment, but to give the treatment I had suggested a chance.

The responsibility was entirely mine, and I trembled lest I had made a dreadful mistake. Cameron's interest was intense. Though he said nothing, I felt his inquiring glance upon me many times in the course of the next few weeks. But I had learned from him the virtue of silence and matched his growing curiosity with stoic reticence.

One morning, however, at breakfast, I asked if I might have an hour off in the afternoon.

"What for?"

"To take a little walk," I answered dryly, "with a friend."

That very afternoon, as the old doctor pottered about the garden with his pruning knife, the gate swung open and two figures appeared. Riveted, he stood watching us approach.

"Well," I said, rather breathlessly, though I had meant to be studiously offhand, "here's your gardener back."

It was Alex—the old Alex, lean and hardy, with the familiar diffident smile. In his eyes was the look of a man who had been through hell, but the old steadiness was there, the old honesty.

"How are ye, man?" asked Cameron mechanically.

"I'm fine," said Deans shyly. "All but my hand."

"Alex has just had his hand wrung by a hundred different people," I explained. "As we came through the village, you know."

There was a pause. Cameron blew his nose hard.

"What are ye standing there for!" he said at last. "Away in to Janet and get your tea."

When Deans had gone Cameron took my arm.

Now for it, I thought. It was the moment, the great moment, when he would commend me.

Yet as we walked toward the house all that came from this dour old Scot was:

"Thank God I'll have my geraniums next summer."

But there was a rare friendliness in his voice.

# Chapter Nine

It would appear that I was rapidly distinguishing myself, "getting on fast," as they say in Tannochbrae, yet perhaps my progress was a trifle too speedy, perhaps I was acquiring too high an opinion of myself. There were moments when, in the face of my cheerful cocksureness, Dr. Cameron stroked his chin reflectively and stole a dry look at me. But if there was amusement in his eye, he masked it and said nothing.

On the day before hogmanay, a fine crisping day with a cold sparkle in the air, I was working out a Fehling's test in the little room off the surgery. Known previously as "the back room," it had, in a rush of scientific zeal, been rechristened by me "the laboratory." This afternoon when Cameron indicated that he had a case to visit in Knoxhill, I had airily remarked:

"Righto! I'll tackle the tests in the lab."

Now, with my pipe between my teeth, I watched the blue liquid in the test tube bubble above the bunsen and slowly turn brick-red —sugar, by Jove! Just as I'd suspected. Another smart piece of diagnosis.

I was interrupted by the opening of the door. Janet stood before me.

"William Duncan wants Dr. Cameron," she announced brusquely. "Young Duncan, the seedsman. Him that got married three years back and has the cottage on the Markinch road."

I looked up in annoyance—Janet, confound her, was still far

from deferential in her manner. Then, making a great show of interest in my test tube:

"Dr. Cameron's gone to Knoxhill."

"I've just told Duncan that," said Janet primly, "and he said you would have to do."

In the hall, I found Will Duncan in a state of extraordinary agitation. He stood there, hatless, without an overcoat, a scarf flung haphazard round his neck, fairly shivering with anxiety. It was the baby, he told me. Bad? Oh, yes, dreadfully bad! The little one didn't seem to get her breath, there was such a fearful whistling in her lungs, and it had come on so sudden, his wife was distracted, for Mrs. Niven, of all people, had said it was pneumonia.

I frowned. Part midwife, part nurse, part "layer-out" of the dead, waddling, interfering, wholly unqualified, the *sage femme* of the district, entrenched behind a portentous reputation for sagacity—that was Bella Niven, and every doctor in the district hated her heartily.

"I'll be along at once," I said. "You get back and let them know I'm coming."

Dr. Cameron had the gig, so I had to make the best of the two miles along Knoxhill Road on the bicycle. Not that I minded the exercise; I liked it, to be honest, but I felt it rather inglorious to pedal down the High Street with my bag swinging from the handle bars, the more so as a number of the village worthies, ensconced in the bay window of the Thistle Inn, observed me pass.

Lomond View was the name of the house, a trig little cottage standing behind a holly tree bright with bunches of scarlet berries. Though I had come fast, young Duncan had come faster. He was already at the door, panting from his run and desperately declaring:

"I've just had a word with Mrs. Niven, Doctor. She's no better, not a bit the better."

I went upstairs, and no sooner was I in the darkened room than I heard the baby's breathing; a shrill, half-whistling respiration which caught me up sharp.

Good God, I thought, there's something bad here sure enough!

76

To the mother, who stood perfectly distracted by the newly lit coal fire, I said:

"Will you pull back the curtains, please, and let me have a little light?"

Bella Niven, holding her formidable bosom against the end of the cot, interposed:

"I ordered the curtains to be drawn. Don't you know the light frets the child."

"I'm not a cat," I retorted sharply. "I can't see in the dark."

Nervously steering a middle course between her two advisers, young Mrs. Duncan went to the window. With an agitated hand she half drew back the curtains.

I bent over the cot. The baby certainly was fretful. Her cheeks were flushed, she twisted and turned, whined pathetically, clutched at the bedclothes, at her face, at everything. And through it all her breathing came and went—shrill, noisy, frightening.

I took the temperature—100°F. Then with my stethoscope I examined her chest—a difficult job, for she simply would not keep still. She twisted and turned in the semidarkness like a lively minnow in a pool. Nevertheless, there was no doubt about that breathing, it whistled ominously, a dry note, not exactly pneumonic and not pleuritic, something outside my experience—desperate, unknown. I was worried—really worried. I felt myself confronted by a most obscure disease. Was it pneumothorax, I asked myself —a rare condition I had read about but never seen? It might, yes, it might conceivably be pneumothorax, or perhaps acute oedema of the lung—but the whistling was too dry, too shrill for that. Sick children were so difficult, the very devil, in fact. If only they could talk—describe their symptoms. Abruptly I straightened myself from the cot. I was baffled, completely baffled.

As, very slowly, I began to put away my stethoscope, Mrs. Niven, with a narrowed eye, scornfully remarked:

"There's little need for all your thumping and listening. The child has congestion of the lung."

In spite of myself I began to feel intimidated.

"It's not congestion," I said—chiefly for the sake of contradicting her.

"You mean it's worse," she asserted instantly.

"The Lord save us!" whimpered Mrs. Duncan.

I turned to the frightened young mother, but Niven was upon me again before I could utter one word of comfort.

"Since you say it's not the congestion, what do you say it is?" she demanded aggressively.

I racked my brains.

"I have my own opinion," I said at last. "It's the lung!"

"The lung!" muttered Mrs. Niven, casting up her eyes. "The lung, quoth he! As if I hadn't known it was the lung the minute I stepped in this door. And what are we to do then, since you've come to the conclusion it's the lung? Am I to stand here and watch the dearie whistle herself into her beloved grave, or am I to poultice her with linseed back and front, like I wanted to do a solemn hour since if I'd had my way?"

"Don't poultice her till I tell you to poultice her," I said savagely.

"Then what . . . ?"

"Do nothing!"

I cut her off and took Mrs. Duncan by the arm.

"I must have a second opinion. This is a difficult case. Keep calm. Don't worry. I'll be back in half an hour with Dr. Cameron."

"That's the wisest thing that's been said since he put foot in this room," Mrs. Niven remarked confidentially to the ceiling.

The perspiration stood in beads upon my forehead as I went through the door. Heavens, I thought fervently, I'm glad to be out of there! But the faint whistling of the baby's breath followed me downstairs.

Crouched over the handle bars, I scorched through the gathering dusk with no thought of dignity, or the figure I presented to the village at large. I was back at Arden House in half the time it had taken me to come.

Cameron was at tea, munching hot oatcake before a cheerful fire in the dining room with the air of one untroubled by the world.

"Come away, man, come away," he cried hospitably. "You're just in time to catch the bannocks while they're warm."

I forced a smile; it was a poor attempt.

"No, thanks. I'm not minding about tea. I've a case—a bad case. Mrs. Duncan's baby at Lomond View."

"Yes?" Cameron shot me a quick, quizzical glance, then away again. "A fine stirring bairn. I brought her into the world eighteen months past. Ye know, this is a grand piece of cheese Janet's put before us. Come winter, I'm terrible fond of hot bannock and cheese to my tea. Try them, man, they go famously together."

I moved restlessly.

"I tell you I'm worried about this case."

"Tut, tut! That's not like you at all, at all. You're not the man to let a case get the better of ye! Deed! In all my born days I've never seen a man like ye to get the better of a case. Bless my soul! Ye're not serious about the Duncan bairn. Sit in and have a slice of cheese."

Under the delicate satire I coloured.

"Hang your cheese," I blurted out. "Can't you see I'm wanting you to come to Duncan's now?"

Cameron's lips twitched. Slyly he cut himself a further tiny sliver and nibbled it off the knife blade.

"Well! Well!" he said. "What's like the matter with the bairn?"

"A whistling lung."

Cameron raised his eyebrows.

"Never heard of that before."

"Then you'll hear it now," I retorted angrily. "It's got me beat. It's a pneumothorax maybe—you can hear the air whistling into the pleural cavity."

"Pneumothorax," repeated Cameron, as though the sound pleased him. "It's a braw name!" He brushed the crumbs from his vest and got up. "Umph! We'd better see!"

The gig took us to Lomond View. To my overstrung nerves it seemed as if I had spent the day tearing to and from the cottage. I followed the senior up the steps.

"Well, well!" Cameron remarked genially on the threshold of the sickroom. "What's all to do here?" His very presence soothed the air.

"I've poulticed the bairn, Doctor," whispered Mrs. Niven with a sharp look at me.

Cameron ignored her. He took a long look at the child, with his ear cocked to her breathing.

He spoke coaxingly. Then with a sure and gentle touch he lifted her out of the cot and, disdaining any stethoscope, laid his ear against her chest.

His head moved up, down, up again. He seemed almost to smile; or was it merely the play of light and shadow on his weathered face? He put the baby back to bed.

Then, for a moment he stood caressing his lantern jaw with his long, bony finger before he turned to Mrs. Duncan.

"My dear," he remarked blandly, "have ye such a thing as a hairpin in the house?"

"A hairpin?" she faltered, wondering if he had gone out of his mind or she, from panic, out of hers.

"Exactly," he reassured her. And when she fumblingly produced the hairpin he thanked her. "And now, lassie," he continued, patting her shoulder, "maybe ye'd leave us for a minute; we've something to discuss, my colleague and myself."

Half in fear, and half in wonder, little Mrs. Duncan let herself be propelled gently from the room.

"As for you, Mrs. Niven," said Cameron, in a different tone, "out you go, too!"

"I'm as well here," she answered defiantly, "to lend ye a hand. Here I am and here I'll stay."

Cameron drew down his brows in a sudden scowl, black as a hanging judge.

"Out with ye!" he hissed. "Out, ye auld bitch. And if ye don't— as God's my Maker—I'll take my boot to your big beam end."

It was too much even for the bold Niven. She quailed, and in a moment she, too, was outside.

Cameron smiled at me.

"Isn't it amazin' what can be done by kindness and what old Professor Syme called conspicuous unobtrusiveness?" Then very confidentially he inquired, "By the way, lad, do ye know what a squeaker is?"

"A squeaker?" I echoed, confusedly.

"That was what I said—a squeaker."

Nonplussed, I stared at him.

"Well!"—Cameron reflected genially—"as you don't know, I'll tell you. A squeaker is a wee thing like a button that squeaks and whistles when ye blow it. A child's plaything, ye understand; ye'll find them in crackers and suchlike party trash. And since we're speaking of children, have ye ever noticed how mischievous they can be about the age of eighteen months? They'll stuff things in their mouths and in their ears—ay, even up their noses."

As he spoke he was bending over the cot with the hairpin in his hand. Swiftly and delicately the round end of the hairpin slipped up the baby's left nostril, then out again. And at the instant the whistling ceased.

"Good God!" I gasped.

"There's your pneumothorax," Cameron remarked mildly, holding the squeaker in his palm.

The baby smiled amiably at Cameron, curled itself into a ball, and began to suck its thumb.

I turned a dull red, mumbled shamefully a protestation of my own idiocy. And, stretching out my hand, I made to take the squeaker. But Cameron with a gesture slipped it in his own waistcoat pocket.

"No, no, lad," he declared kindly. "I'll take charge of this. And if ever I see ye getting a bit above yourself—then, sure as fate, out comes this squeaker!"

# Chapter Ten

When the autumn run of salmon came into the loch, these were days to make a fisherman's pulse beat faster. Dr. Cameron well knew my ruling passion and in this season gave me many an afternoon off—from kindness of heart, no doubt, yet perhaps also because he was very partial to a slice of "brandered" grilse.

It was on one of these excursions that I made acquaintance with the strange character known on the lochside as Houseboat Tam, and thereafter I seldom went fishing without calling upon him. If I failed to do so, then Tam like as not would call on me, swimming up silently behind my dinghy and bursting triumphantly into view with a loud laugh or a friendly halloo. He would stay for a moment treading water, smiling naïvely, exchanging a word or two of news, then down would go his wet, black head, and he would glide away, striking through the water like a seal to where his old houseboat lay moored in Sandy Bay. It was here that Tam Douglas lived his solitary life, though to call Tam's home a houseboat was flattery of the first degree.

In her early days the boat had been a coal scow, plying between Levenford and Overton on the Fourth and Clyde Canal. With the finish of the barge trade she had lain for years mouldering in the mud of the Leven Estuary. In course of time a ramshackle superstructure had been added to her hull, and with a lick of paint on her sodden timbers, she was tugged up to the loch in the hope that she might be sold for a fishing bothy.

But no one wanted the old tub. Sun-blistered, wind-scoured, rain-battered, she lay deserted, forgotten, and alone in the cove named Sandy Bay. Weather had toned her first hard ugliness into something not unbeautiful. She harmonised with her background, had the look of a strange, unwanted creature that has found safe anchorage at last.

It was then that she was taken by Tom Douglas—that, was Tam's proper name! Some said Tom had got her for a pound, others for a wager he would swim across the loch—for even then Tom was marvellous as a swimmer—yet it was equally probable that Tom had simply boarded the old hulk and made her, quite calmly, his own. Nobody cared very much, and it was all so long ago no one had a note of it. The fact is that Tom was not an institution in those days. He was just a young fellow come to the loch to recover from a serious and, indeed, a most mysterious illness.

A student, was he? No one knew. And what had been the matter with him? Brain fever, some declared, contracted through overstudy for a bursary examination. But the knowing ones implied that Tom must have been "that way" from his birth. For, to speak plainly, Tom was inclined to be a little queer; simple, you understand. He was quiet and friendly, not a soul had one word against him. He was just fey or, as they say in those parts, plain wuddy. You might come on him, for instance, standing all by himself under a rowan tree, not gathering the rowans for jelly, like an ordinary body, but talking to the tree. Talking to the tree, no less! Or again, about the gloaming, you might find him on the loch shore listening to the lapping of the waves upon the shingle and smiling to himself as though he found it oddly beautiful. As if a man had never heard the sound of waves before!

He came from a place in Fife, near Kirkcaldy. But he had no folks that anyone heard tell of.

"I'm just by myself," Tom would answer, smiling, when pressed upon the subject.

He brought little money with him to Tannochbrae. And the little he had was soon gone; Tom never was any good with money. Yet he stayed on. He had come to love the place. The sweet stretch of water and wood and mountain had entered into his being, enslaved his simple mind. The loch had him for its own.

That was why he took the deserted houseboat. And in that boat he became, gradually, not Tom Douglas, but Wuddy Houseboat Tam. He lived like a hermit, cooked his own food, washed his own dishes, darned his own socks. His hair grew long, his beard unkempt. He became in course of time a character. Pleasure launches, bearing their load of tourists up the loch in summer, came to make a detour to "take in" the sight of Houseboat Tam. And Tam was proud, proud for the English tourists to take a look at him.

He would be on the deck of his boat, cutting up a cabbage for his dinner. And, as the steamer went past, like as not Tam would take care to knock a leaf of cabbage overboard, offhandedly, as though he hadn't meant it. Then, swish! Tam would take a straight header into the loch, clothes and all, and come up cool as you like with the cabbage in his mouth. The tourists loved it, especially the lady tourists, and many a good half crown came to Tam that way.

For the rest, Tam lived like a wild thing on the bounty of the loch. He was a marvellous fisher and a natural cook. A cut of fresh-caught salmon grilled on wood embers in his little galley, with a flavouring of wild thyme and parsley, was the most exquisite dish you could imagine. I had it often, and it was the finest fish I had ever eaten. In the autumn there were nuts and brambles, blaeberries and wild rasps. Tam knew all the places; he knew the roots, too, that were edible, the herbs and simples.

The winter, of course, was Tam's worst time. With ice on the water and sleet blinding down the loch in bitter squalls, Tam stayed shivering below hatches with little enough to eat for days on end. He must have suffered severely—having insufficient clothing and still less food—but no one ever heard Tam complain. He was the gentlest, kindest, humblest creature, whose little odd streaks of vanity merely made him the more lovable. He was accepted even by the pharisees of the village as part of the Creator's scheme of things. Nobody worried about him, and he worried nobody.

When I came to Tannochbrae, Tam was close on fifty years of age, yet he looked little more than thirty. The spartan rigour of his life, the constant exercise, in and out of the clean loch water, had given him the body of an athlete. Tall as a beech, muscular, upright, his skin weathered to a fine bronze, he might have stood for the statue of Poseidon. He had a striking head, with long, dark hair, a noble brow, and gentle, hazel eyes. But his tattered clothing, unkempt beard, his old canvas shoes tied on with string made him frowsy and ridiculous. To see Tam naked was to see a god. Dressed in his clothes he looked a tinker.

That first summer following my arrival was both glorious and warm. But the succeeding winter came cruelly hard, not perhaps so iron-hard as that famous winter when the loch froze over and they drove a horse and cart upon the ice at Darroch, but raw and bitter. For a whole fortnight the country lay under deep snow, and we had many patients, from the sheer severity of the weather.

Stiff work it was, getting about, with deep drifts on the roads. And there was need to get about; I made the weary drive up to Marklea, at the head of the loch, every day, and every other night, in that freezing fortnight.

On the Thursday of the second week I was snatching a cup of hot coffee in the kitchen of the Marklea Arms when the landlady casually remarked:

"You didn't see Wuddy Tam stirring about his boat, Doctor, when you drove past the cove today?"

Holding the steaming cup in both my hands—they were perished by the cold—I reflected for a minute, then shook my head. She went on:

"In the ordinary way when the weather's like this he'll win round to the back door for a drop broth or suchlike. Not charity, you understand. Tam would never take that. It's payment in kind, so to speak. For come the spring he'll leave a salmon or a dozen trout at the house and never take a penny piece for't." She paused. "But he hasna' been near us for ten days now."

"Are you worrying about him, then?"

She frowned doubtfully.

"I'm just hereaway thereaway. Maybe my notion's all wrong. But what with this awfu' frost and all, I'd an idea he might be ill. A crying shame it would be if the poor creature was stricken down with not a soul to tend to him."

I finished my coffee, pulled on my driving gloves.

"Well," I said, "I'll keep my eye skinned as I go past."

An hour later, having finished my calls, I started back on the road to Tannochbrae. I was driving myself, in a hired trap with a cob from the stables, for Cameron had taken Jamie and the gig on the Overton round. And, as I came opposite Sandy Bay, I drew up and stared across the fifty yards or so of water toward Tam's house-boat.

No smoke from the tiny tin chimney. Not a sign of life. I hailed the boat. A loud, long yell, which seemed to vibrate across the desolation of snow and blue-grey, icy water.

No answer. Nothing but stillness. And silence.

I swore impatiently. My impulse was to go on, to get back to Tannochbrae, a warm fire, and my dinner. But instinct and a sense of compunction restrained me. I leaped out of the trap, crossed the snowy shingle, and went down to the waterside. Several boats lay drawn up, boats used by the Marklea Anglers' Club and beached on this safe shore against the winter. I threw off the covering tarpaulin, chose the stoutest skiff, launched it with an effort, and poled a passage through the pack ice to the houseboat. Clambering aboard, I ducked my head and went below.

Tam lay on his narrow bunk in the tiny cabin, the atmosphere of which was frigid as an igloo. Dressed in his tinker's clothes, covered by an old rug, Tam lay on his back shivering.

"Man, man," I cried, "what's the matter that you didn't answer me?"

Tam looked up dazedly.

"I didn't hear ye. I didn't hear anything."

"How long have you been this way?"

"A week—or thereabouts," Tam muttered, his teeth chattering with ague.

"A week!" I echoed.

I stood cudgelling my brains. Tam was ill, his wretched cabin unfit even for a dog, his locker—lying open—empty of food or stimulant. His condition, moreover, made it impossible to drive him back these two snow-bogged miles to the Marklea Arms. What could one do about it? Suddenly I reached a decision.

I climbed on deck, sculled ashore, and got into the trap. Whipping up the cob, I turned into a narrow side road opposite the cove and drove up the hill to Saughend farm. In five minutes I was there, pealing on the front-door bell, asking to see the mistress of the house immediately.

For all my urgency, Elizabeth Robb was in no hurry to appear. Saughend, unlike the neighbouring crofts and steadings, was a large farm with a fine residence and ample barns. Ever since her husband Robin Robb had died, three years before, Elizabeth had managed the farm herself and, for that matter, managed it admirably. The sense of her possessions, of her own competency, added to a natural brusqueness, gave to the widow a proud and highhanded air. Yet she was a fine woman, with a full bosom, a good, honest figure, sloe-black eyes, and neat feet. On these neat feet Elizabeth was always on the move, full of life and energy; at least, since her widowhood, her energy had been relentless. In Tannochbrae they said she was turning sour; and the knowing ones—in a Scottish village there are always knowing ones—slyly adduced a reason, which was nonsense, of course, for many suitors had come after the widow Robb, or after her fortune, and had been firmly turned away.

At this moment, indeed, it looked as though I might also be shown to the door, for when in a few hasty phrases I had described the situation and put forward my plea, Elizabeth made a wry face.

"I'm not so sure about all this," she said. "We're overbusy for an upset of that kind. And we're not overfond of fusty auld tykes at Saughend."

But I was not to be put off, and in the end she allowed herself, with a rather bad grace, to be persuaded. She gave some sharp orders. Two men went back with me and carried Tam up to the farm.

"Here!" exclaimed Elizabeth, viewing Tam's dilapidated state with manifest disfavour. "Bring him upstairs! And be careful not to make a midden of my stair carpet!"

From his horizontal position, Tam gazed at her like a scolded schoolboy.

"I'm sorry." He shivered. "I'll go back to my boat tomorrow."

"Humph!" muttered Elizabeth, under her breath. "And a real good riddance of right bad rubbish. Here! Along the passage. Watch my clean wallpaper!"

And she acidly indicated the way to a good room where a new-lit fire smoked and crackled. Having made up her mind, under sufferance, to be charitable, she had decided apparently to do it in style. With the two farm hands I got Tam undressed and into bed. Then I made a more extensive examination. Finally I went downstairs to where Elizabeth waited for me in the parlour.

"It's a localized pleurisy," I announced cheerfully. "That, and exposure! Not quite so bad as I thought. He's coming round now. He ought to be off your hands in a few days. He's got a wonderful constitution, you know."

She compresed her lips with native irony.

"In the meantime I'm to drop all my work—and the Almighty knows I have plenty—in order to nurse him."

"It won't be for long," I assured her, smiling. "The minute Tam's better he'll be off like a shot. He's a shy fish. If he had his way, he wouldn't stay under a house roof for love nor money."

"Indeed!" she said with due asperity. And as that seemed to be all, I went away.

Next afternoon I called at Saughend again. Elizabeth met me at the door.

"You and your exposure," she said in a tone of just remonstrance. "Did you know that the poor man was starving? Not one bite of food had passed his lips for four days, and him with a heavy chill on him."

I made a deprecating gesture.

"Well! It's the way he lives, you see. . . ."

She cut me short.

"A crying scandal," she declared vigorously, "for anyone to live that way. And I'd no idea. Not the slightest. And him living almost at my doorstep. I've never taken any notice of the man, or I'd soon have set him right. His clothes—why, I burnt them the minute I set eyes on them! They're not fit for a human being. And, mind ye, he is a human being—ay, and a gey decent human being, if I'm a judge."

She broke off, eyeing me warily. It appeared as if she might have said a great deal more, but, with an effort, she recollected herself and led the way upstairs.

At first I didn't recognize Tam, for on entering the room I had the shock of my life. Tam was washed, shaved, and dressed in a fine flannel nightshirt. For all his pleurisy, he looked marvellous.

"Why, Tam"—I managed to find my tongue at last—"you seem better today."

"I am better," said Tam in his simple style. "She's looked after me a treat. But I think I'll get back to the boat the morn."

"You'll do no such thing," said Elizabeth Robb severely from the doorway. "You're far from better yet, you foolish fellow, and well you know it."

Tam was indeed not yet quite right—his temperature was above 100°, and there was still a faint crackle in his side.

Downstairs again, I said casually:

"By the bye, I'll not be at Marklea tomorrow, Mistress Robb, so I'll not bother to look in here till the day after."

"I beg your pardon," she said, folding her hands firmly beneath her bosom, "but you seem to forget ye're dealing with a sick man. You'll oblige me, Marklea or no Marklea, by calling at this house tomorrow without fail. I suppose, because the poor man hasna' the siller to pay you, you think you can neglect him. But I'll pay you your fee, and there's an end o't."

Next day I called again. Tam, with a large bowl of beef tea at his elbow, was well on the way to recovery.

"She's unco kind, ye know, Doctor," he remarked mildly. "But I'd better get back to the boat the morn."

Elizabeth Robb did not deign to answer. But in the front parlour afterward she addressed me quite determinedly.

"He must not go back to that awful boat until he's cured and better. He's no trouble at all, at all. He's a decent, simple chap."

Here her voice turned almost dreamy. "A most remarkable man, in fact, with not a word of harm to say against anybody. And some of the things he does say—clever, you wouldn't believe it. Do you know, Doctor, that he doesna' smoke, and he doesna' even know the taste of drink? To think that all these years he's been living like that all by himself."

A surge of indignation seemed to rise in her throat. But in a moment she went on:

"As for looks—well, you wouldna' call the Duke his master—a handsome, well-made, well-set-up man as I ever saw the like of."

Here, catching my eye upon her, she blushed, and, suddenly conscious of that blush, virtuously compressed her lips.

"You'll call tomorrow, Doctor," she concluded formally, and showed me to the door.

So I made my visit the following morning, and the next morning, and the next. And every time I came there was some fresh eulogy on Tam:

"Do you know, Doctor. . . ."

The thaw set in, the snow melted, and the green of the country reappeared.

One day when I arrived Tam was up, dressed in a good broadcloth suit, and looking solid, sensible, and well.

"That's a grand suit you've got, Tam," I declared.

"Not bad," Tam answered with his gentle, guileless smile. "It belonged to Mr. Robb. The late Mr. Robb, ye know." He smoothed the lapels approvingly. "It fits me gey well."

"Isn't it about time, Tam?" I demanded suddenly, inspecting Tam in his beautiful suit, fine laundered linen, sound boots, and air of high prosperity. "Isn't it about time that you were getting back to your boat?"

Tam looked mild and absent-minded.

"I haven't thought so much about the boat lately," he murmured. "It's pretty nice up here at the farm."

At that moment Elizabeth came bustling in, looking pleased and blooming, happier than she had done for months. She gazed admiringly at Tam.

"Doesn't he look grand?" she remarked with a proprietary air. "He's promised to come out for a stroll with me this afternoon. I want to ask his opinion about the lower Saughend field. I've a rare notion he might make a farmer yet if he went the right way about it." She gave a little conscious laugh. "Will you be calling in again tomorrow, Doctor?"

"No," I answered gravely. "There's nothing more for me to do. I'll not look back."

But I did look back. Within the month, I was best man at their wedding.

# Chapter Eleven

THE SCOTS ARE in many ways a singular people. For centuries they fought their nearest neighbours, the English, and are still a trifle hostile toward them—at least they treasure the memory of Bruce and Bannochburn as their proudest heritage. Inhabiting a small impoverished country, ridged by bleak mountains and ringed by rocky coasts against which rough seas sweep and surge, they are admittedly hardy, frugal, thrifty, resolute, and addicted to their own "usquebaugh"—a Gaelic word vilely corrupted by the Saxons to "whisky."

Yet other peculiarities, not all of which are praiseworthy, have been attributed to them, and some of these are entirely without foundation in fact. Perhaps this injustice is self-inflicted—it has been said that one of Scotland's minor industries is the export of stories pertaining to the oddity of her native sons. Be that as it may, there is one quality which is more often and more mistakenly applied to the northerner than any other: insensitivity. The general belief that the average Scotsman is a cold, phlegmatic, and unfeeling individual is a base aspersion upon the national character. During my sojourn in Tannochbrae, brief though it was, I met with an incident which brought this point home to me in an especially striking way.

One March evening, Willie Craig rang the bell of Arden House with his usual calmness.

"Good evening, Janet," he remarked in his slow, self-possessed voice. "Does the doctor happen to be at home by any chance?"

"Which of them were ye wanting to see, Mr. Craig?"

"It doesn't matter in the least, Janet. Any of the two of them'll do me fine."

"It's the assistant's night for the surgery. But I'll let Dr. Cameron know you're here if you specially want to see him."

He shook his head—slightly, for all Willie's movements were restrained and staid.

"It's all one to me, Janet, woman."

She gazed at him approvingly. Janet dearly admired a man who never got excited, and she showed him into the dining room—a special mark of favour—to wait.

Willie sat down and, putting his hands in his pockets, looked with mild interest at the fiddle hung above the mantelpiece.

He was a small, slight man of about thirty-seven, clean-shaven and rather pale about the face, dressed in a neat grey suit and a celluloid collar fitted with a black, "made-up" tie. By trade Willie was the village baker; he had his own tidy business in the High Street, where his wife served behind the counter while he worked in the bakehouse in the yard. Willie Craig's mutton pies were noted, his currant cakes second to none in all the county. But though he was well thought of, with a name for good baking, fair measure, and sound dealing, Willie's reputation in the town was hung upon a higher peg than these. Willie Craig was famous for his coolness.

"Ay, ay, a cool customer, Willie Craig," was the town's approving verdict.

When, for instance, he played the final of the Winton bowling championship on Knoxhill Green and won a deadly struggle by the margin of a single shot, folks cheered him, not so much because he won, but because of the manner of his winning. Pale-faced, unruffled, never turning a hair; while Gordon, his opponent, was nearly apoplectic with excitement. In the clubhouse afterward, Gordon, with a few drinks inside him, waxed indignant and a trifle garrulous on the subject.

"He's not human. He doesn't feel things like other folks do. He's like a fish lying on a block of ice. That's the trouble with Willie Craig. He's got no imagination!"

So Willie became known as the man with no imagination; and,

indeed, he looked stolid enough sitting there in Arden House waiting to see me.

"Will ye step this way, Mr. Craig?" remarked Janet, returning in the middle of Willie's composed meditation.

He got up and followed her into the surgery.

"Sit down," I said shortly. "What's the trouble?"

I was overworked, rushed, and in a hurry, which made my manner more abrupt than usual. But Willie Craig didn't seem to mind.

"It's my tongue, Doctor. There's something on the edge o't that bothers me a bit."

"You mean it pains you."

"Well . . . , more or less."

"Let me have a look."

I leaned across the desk and took a look at Willie's tongue. I took a good long look. Then in rather a different tone I said:

"How long have you had that?"

"Oh, six weeks or thereabouts, as near as I can remember. It's come on gradual-like. But lately it's been getting worse."

"Do you smoke?"

"Ay, I'm a pretty heavy smoker."

"A pipe?"

"Ay, a pipe."

There was a short pause. Then I rose and went over to the instrument cabinet.

I took a powerful magnifying glass, and, with the most scrupulous care, I examined Willie's tongue once again. An angry red spot stood on the edge of the tongue. A spot which was hard to the touch and, to the trained eye, full of the most sinister implication.

I laid down the glass and sank into my chair by the desk.

There were two ways open, I knew, of dealing with the situation. The first, a specious pretence of optimism; the second, to tell the truth. Reflectively I gazed across at Willie, whose reputation for self-possession I well knew. Willie gazed back at me calmly. I decided that I must let him have the truth.

"Willie," I said suddenly, "that little thing on your tongue may be something very serious. Or it may not."

94

Willie remained unperturbed.

"I suppose that's why I'm here, Doctor. I wanted to find out what it was."

"And I want to find out, too. I'll have to take a little snick out of your tongue and send it to the pathological department of the University for examination. It won't hurt you, and it won't take long. In a couple of days I'll have the result. Then I shall know whether this is what I'm afraid of or not."

"And what are you afraid of, Doctor?"

A bar of silence fell in the consulting room. I felt I must hedge. But gazing straight into Willie Craig's cool, grey eyes, I changed my mind. In a low voice I said:

"I'm afraid you may have cancer of the tongue."

That bar of silence, scarcely dispelled by those few words, vibrated and again descended, lingering intolerably.

"I see," Willie said. "That's not so good. And what if it should be cancer?"

I made a diffident movement with my hands.

"Operation."

"You mean I'd have to have my tongue out?"

I nodded my head.

"More or less. But we won't face our troubles till we come to them."

For a long time Willie studied the toes of his neat, well-brushed boots, then he raised his head.

"Right you are, then, Doctor. You'd better get on with what you've got to do."

I rose, sterilised an instrument, sprayed Willie's tongue with ethyl chloride, and snicked out a tiny fragment of the little crimson spot.

"That was soon done," Willie said.

He washed out his mouth, then picked up his hat, preparing to go.

"Let me see." I considered. "It's Monday tonight. Look round Thursday at the same time, and I'll give you the result."

"I hope it'll be good," Willie remarked stoically.

"I hope so, too," I answered gravely.

"Good night, then, Doctor."

"Good night."

95

I stood watching him as he went down the drive and into the road, carefully closing the gate behind him. I could not but admire his calm, cold courage.

But was I correct in my appraisal? The cool customer, the man with no imagination, walked along the street, his head in the air, his chin well up, his lips set.

Outwardly calm, quite calm! But inside his brain a thousand hammers beat ferociously. And in his ears a thousand voices roared and thundered. One word repeated endlessly . . . cancer.

He felt himself trembling, felt his heart thudding tumultuously against his side. As he turned into Church Street a spasm of giddiness assailed him; he thought for a moment he was going to faint.

"How do, Willie! Fine evening for the Green!" Bailie Paxton, from outside his office, hailed him across the street.

Not one man, surely, but a row of them, all waving, grimacing, blurred, and grotesque.

"A fine evening it is, Bailie."

"We'll see ye on Saturday—down at the match."

"You will, indeed. I wouldn't miss it for anything."

How in the name of God had he managed to speak?

As he moved off, a cold sweat broke upon him. The muscles of his cheek began to twitch painfully. His whole being seemed dissolved and fluid, escaping his control, defying at last his constant vigilance.

All his life long he had fought like a demon against his nerves, those treacherous nerves which had so often threatened to betray him. He had found it difficult, always—even the little things. That time, for instance, when he had won the bowling championship— so sick inside with nerves and apprehension that he could scarcely throw his final wood, yet managing to mask it with indifference—his nervous terror. But now, faced with this awful thing—oh, how could he face it? The voices blared that fearful word at him again.

He entered his house quietly, his house above the shop, which was now shut; he sat down in his chair, pulled on his battered carpet slippers.

"Ye're early back from the Green, Will," Bessie, his wife, remarked

96

pleasantly, without looking up from the pages of the local paper.

At all events, with Bessie, he simply mustn't show anything.

"I didn't bother about the Green tonight. I just took a stroll down the road."

"Un-huh! These are awful nice hats Jenny McKechnie's advertising. A new spring line. Feathers. And only five and eleven the piece. I've a good mind to treat myself to one."

Staring into the fire, he made an unbelievable effort to master himself.

"It's high time ye were buying something for yourself."

She flashed a warm smile at him, pleased by this tribute to her wifely economy.

"Maybe I will, then. And maybe I'll not. I never was one to squander money on finery. No, no. I believe in something put past for a rainy day. I'm not wanting us to be stuck here over the shop all our lives, Will. A nice bit semidetached villa up Knoxhill way— what do you say to that—in a year or two?"

In a year or two! The simple words transfixed him, like a sword thrust savagely into his breast. A year or two! Where would he be then?

He closed his eyes, fighting back the smarting, pitiful tears that rose to them. Rustling her paper, Bessie laughed.

"A lot of difference it makes to you! Ye hardened auld sinner. There's nothing on earth would put you up or down."

He went to bed early. In the ordinary way he went early enough, never later than ten, for he had to be in the bakehouse by four in the morning to see to the ovens for the first batch of bread. But tonight he turned in at nine o'clock. Yet he could not sleep. He was still awake when Bessie came to bed, although, in order that he might not have to speak, he pretended to be asleep. Lying there with tightly shut eyes, he listened in a dumb agony to all her simple, familiar movements: winding up the clock, stifling a yawn, dropping her hairpins into the tray upon the mantelpiece. Then quietly, for fear of disturbing him, she slipped into bed.

In a quarter of an hour her gentle breathing assured him that she was asleep. He lay quite still, scarcely breathing, clenching his hands

97

fiercely to control himself. The darkness of the room pressed down upon him like a pall. He wanted to cry out, to ease his tortured nerves by one wild, despairing shout. He wanted to turn to her, to Bessie, his wife. To implore her sympathy. To cry passionately:

"I'm not what you think I am. I'm not hard. I never have been hard. I feel everything, I feel it terribly. And now I'm frightened, desperately frightened—like a trembling child. There always has been something of the child in me. I've always been sensitive, always been nervous. That's why I've pretended not to be. But now I'm past pretending. Don't you hear me? Don't you understand? They think—they think that I've got cancer!"

A paroxysm of mortal agony shook him. While his wife slept in all tranquillity he thrust his hands upon his mouth to choke the sobs which racked him. His eyeballs, seared by the torture of unshed tears, seemed bursting. His ears rang with the chords of his own despair. The dark hours of night rolled over him. Not for one moment did he sleep. Not for one second did he forget.

At four o'clock he rose, put on his working clothes, and went into the bakehouse. He had hoped that the routine of the day might soothe him, distract his mind. But it was not so. As the day passed, bringing no assuagement of his suspense, he grew more desperate. Outwardly frozen, he went through his duties in the semblance of normality. He spoke, answered questions, went here and there. It was as though he stood apart, trembling, suffering, watching the figure of an automaton; an automaton which was himself. He knew now that he had cancer. Whenever he had a spare moment he went upstairs and, thrusting out his tongue before the looking glass, stared at the tiny growth, like a scarlet flower, in horror.

Comedy or tragedy? A grown man thrusting out his tongue at his reflection in a mirror. He could have laughed madly at the grotesque idea. But now he had no time for laughing. He kept looking at his tongue.

Was it worse, the swelling? Or was it just the same? A little more painful, perhaps, since the doctor had cut into it. It hurt him now when he protruded it like that. Or was that just his fancy? Strange that this little red flower should mean death. Terribly strange. But it did mean death. With a last stealthy look into the mirror he tiptoed downstairs.

That night again he did not sleep. At breakfast his wife turned upon him a mildly solicitous eye:

"You're off your food these last few days."

He protested.

"Nonsense," he said, with that frozen self-possession; and to prove his words he helped himself to more bacon and an egg. But though he ate it, he did not taste the food.

All his senses were numb now except the sense of his own condition. He was perhaps now a little mad. His imagination, working feverishly, carried him a stage further. The fact that he had cancer was accepted, proved. What was to be done, then? Operation, the doctor had said. By closing his eyes and staring into the future he saw exactly what that meant.

He saw himself in hospital in a little narrow bed; he endured the agony of days of waiting in one swift thought. Then, frowning slightly, he perceived himself wheeled to the operating theatre. The unknown terror of that place magnified its horror. What was the stuff they gave you there? Chloroform—that was it. A sickly, pungent stuff that hurried you into oblivion. But what happened in that oblivion? Sharp lancets flashed about his mouth, his own mouth. They were cutting out his tongue, cutting it deeply out by the very roots. A sob rose in his throat, choking him; and he raised his hand to his shut eyes as though to blot out the grotesque vision of his tongue, dissevered from his mouth, lying all bloody and horrible where they had cast it.

And after the operation? He would awake, of course, in that same narrow bed, an object of sympathy and intolerable solicitude. A man without his tongue. A man who could not speak, but merely mumble and mouth his words. The nurse bending over him.

"What did you say?"

And he struggling, straining, striving to tell her, to make it clear.

Oh, it was terrible, terrible, not to be endured. He lost himself in the agony of the thought. Time swung its inexorable pendulum. Wednesday night passed—it might have been a hundred years!

99

Thursday came. He had almost reached the limit of his suffering—such suffering as no one dreamed of, all locked and concealed within his soul.

After lunch on Thursday he went out of the bakehouse and walked down to the river. It was high tide, and the water, rushing past the quayside, lay but a few feet beneath him. He stared at it stupidly. One step and it would be finished, all his wretchedness, the misery of the operation and the helplessness that lay after that. The river, gurgling and sucking against the stone piers, seemed to call him.

Suddenly he heard a voice at his elbow.

"Taking a breath of air to yourself, Willie, man?"

It was Peter Lennie smiling at him.

As in a dream he heard himself reply:

"It's pretty hot in the bakehouse in the afternoon."

They stood together in silence. Then Peter Lennie said:

"I'll walk down the road with you, if you are going that way."

They talked as they strolled along the stream, little bits of gossip, petty odds and ends of a small town's news. There was no escape for Willie. He had to go on. The afternoon passed. He drank a cup of tea, then, going upstairs, changed into his Sunday clothes. His mind was made up now. He would refuse the operation. He had resolved simply to die. He knew, with sudden precognition, that the operation would not save him. Cancer came back again in spite of what they did. Yes, cancer came back, it always came back.

At half past six he told Bessie he would take a little walk. He was half afraid that she would offer to come with him, but with a smile she informed him that she was going to run round to buy her new hat. She had just time before Jenny shut the shop.

The evening was fine as he went down the street, nodding to this acquaintance and to that. He had the strange unreality of a man walking with ghostly steps to his own funeral. His tortured imagination, working feverishly, made him feel that none of these people round about were real—since none of them knew that he was nearly dead.

"Is the doctor in, Janet?"

He was saying it again, that silly, senseless phrase. Yes, he was sitting in the dining room again, staring at the silly, senseless fiddle that hung above the mantelpiece. And then once again he was in the consulting room, standing before the desk as though he stood before the judgement seat.

I looked at him a long, long time. The expression upon my face was profound and serious; then, rising, I solemnly held out my hand.

"I want to congratulate you. I've had the full pathological report. There isn't a trace of malignancy in the specimen. It isn't cancer at all—a simple papilloma of your tongue. It will be gone with treatment in a couple of weeks."

Willie's senses reeled. A great wave of joy broke over him and surged to the very centre of his being. He could have swooned from the very ecstasy of joy and sweet relief; but his pale, calm face showed nothing.

"I'm obliged to you, Doctor," he said awkwardly. "I'm . . . I'm . . . I'm real glad it's no worse."

"I hope you haven't worried these last two days," I persisted. "Of course, I'd never have let you know what I was afraid of if I hadn't been dead certain that you weren't the worrying kind."

"That's all right, Doctor," Willie murmured, with his eyes upon the ground. "Maybe I'm not the worrying kind."

That quiet, self-contained smile played over his face.

"They aye say that's my trouble, ye know. No imagination!"

Then, in his composed voice, he told me all that I have just related here.

# Chapter Twelve

It was, I think, Madame de Sévigné—a subtle and discerning woman—who first made the sage observation that no man is a hero to his valet. But Montaigne had forestalled her, less wittily, perhaps, yet with greater wisdom, when he wrote: "No man should be a hero to himself." To be honest, then, the writer who embarks upon the dangerous sea of self-revelation should acknowledge the defects of his character parallel with any merits he may possess, balance his vanities against his virtues.

Do not imagine, then, that I was the admirable Crichton of Tannochbrae, a blameless young medico who was never stupid, fatuous, or foolish. More than once I was all three. And that is why I must introduce a lady whom I shall call Miss Malcolm.

I first met Miss Malcolm at a dance, not an ordinary dance, like the Knoxhill Academy reunion or the Markinch Anglers' Social, but the annual Highland Ball, given by the President of the Society, Lord Sinclair of Dundrum Castle.

This sounds—at least for the moment—extremely grand, and, indeed, the Sinclairs were the great shipbuilding family, whose yards had outgrown and now outrivalled even the most famous shipyards on the Clyde. They were county people, connected by kinship and marriage with half the notables in Glasgow, whose tremendous estate between Markinch and Ardfillan was the pride and envy of the countryside.

Every winter, at the castle, they gave a dance—a ball, to be accurate—at which everybody who was anybody appeared. A stray

Duke often strolled in, the parliamentary member invariably was there, certainly a baronet or two, and always a flock of kilted Highland lairds, with fiery pride in their eye and nothing in their sporran. It was, in short, a function where pedigrees were flourished and the blueness of one's blood was of greater import than the strength of the claret cup.

To this affair, by way of indicating the liberalism of the gentry, were invited the least unworthy professional people of the district—the "best-thought-of" doctors and lawyers, and their wives. It came about, then, in the course of events, that a large, stiff, gilt-edged card —as full of scrolls and superscriptions as a tombstone—arrived at Arden House bidding Dr. Cameron and myself to the ball.

"Bah!" said Cameron, as he tossed it on the mantelpiece. "I'll miss my night's sleep for none of them. You can go, young fellow. My dancing days are done."

Actually, my dancing days had not begun. Indeed, my youthful struggles for existence had kept me from acquiring even the rudiments of such social graces. I therefore followed my senior's lead and protested sturdily that I had as much use for the ball as a bull for a china shop.

"Ye'd better look in, though, lad," Cameron answered in a more equable tone. "If only for the matter of policy. The Sinclairs can put many a guinea our way if they choose to think on't. Just you drop in about ten, let yourself be seen hob-nodding with his Grace." Cameron's eyes twinkled. "Sup an ice with her Leddyship, tell our Member of Parliament I thought his last speech was tripe, and then come home decent-like to your bed."

Thus I did go to the dance.

At first I did not enjoy myself; I was, in fact, uncomfortable, unhappy, and extremely ill at ease. On the wide marble staircase of the castellated mansion there was a great press of people with Roman noses and high voices, a delirious clash of clan tartans with scarlet jackets on the floor, and a strong sense of superiority in the air.

No one took the slightest notice of me. Though I doggedly called up all my democratic pride to support me, I gradually became aware of myself as a gawky youth in a badly made dress suit, borrowed for

103

the occasion from Will Duncan—an unfledged provincial doctor who knew nobody and whom nobody wished to know.

I thought of Flaubert's Charles Bovary, the doltish apothecary whom everyone ignored at the d'Andervilliers chateau, and a faint colour of shame rose to my brow. But I set myself dourly to stick it out, standing with my back to the wall in the ballroom, watching the dancing, feeling horribly lonely, trying hard to despise the petty affectations displayed before me, but despising only myself.

It was then that I discovered two friendly eyes fixed upon me. My colour deepened; but she smiled at me, and I smiled back. I felt sure I had seen her before, that Jamie had mentioned her name to me as we passed her in the main street of Knoxhill. Then I remembered. With a spurt of confidence, I went over to where she sat underneath a tall, green palm. She received me with perfect ease.

"I know you quite well," she informed me charmingly, "though we've never been introduced. But you haven't the least idea who I am."

"But I have! You're Miss Malcolm." I almost added, "the schoolteacher," but mercifully restrained myself in time. Yet she had been a schoolteacher, had taught French at St. Hilda's, that most exclusive girls' school in Ardfillan, but she had come into a little money of her own and, while quite young, had given up her profession altogether.

She smiled at me again and made room for me to sit beside her. At that, with rising self-esteem, I felt comfortable: she was pleasant, she was charming, she was somebody to talk to.

"I'm surprised to find you here," I remarked confidentially, thinking unconsciously once again of her social status, which was surely inferior even to my own.

"I'm often surprised to find myself here," she admitted. She had a delightful voice—well modulated and soft. "It's a complete nuisance. But in a sense I find myself bound to come. You see, Lord Sinclair is my cousin."

My face must have been a study. A cousin of Lord Sinclair! She was one of them, related by blood to the head of the clan, and I, poor fool, had attempted to patronise her.

"You're not dancing?" She appeared not in the least to have observed my confusion, but kept beating time to the music with her tiny, ivory fan.

"I'm such a wretched dancer," I said humbly, ashamed to acknowledge that I had not even taken a correspondence course in the art.

She smiled.

"Shall we try?"

We tried. She was a magnificent dancer, light as a thistledown, skilfully guiding my most indifferent steps, tactfully keeping me to the rhythm. And the band was splendid. After the first moments of hesitation I enjoyed the dance marvellously.

"That was grand," I said boyishly as we resumed our seats.

"What a nice way to ask me for another," she murmured. "But first you might fetch me an ice. Chocolate, please."

I dashed to the buffet and, using my elbows manfully despite the glares of the gathered clans, brought her back a chocolate ice.

She took the ice with her little smile and ate it in silence. She kept nodding to people as they swung past. I watched her with respect. Her poise really was delightful, her movements restrained and classic, without those mannerisms, those odious pretensions to gentility which one met, so often, in persons of a lower station. She was a lady. Yes, she was a lady. And she was—how could I phrase it?— she was quite good-looking. Her rather prominent eyes sparkled, the dance had brought some colour to her aesthetically hollow cheeks, she wore a charming white flounced frock—very simple and girlish. And she was not very old. How old was she exactly? Puzzled, I tried to guess. Twenty-seven perhaps; she might even be less; certainly not a day more than thirty.

I said suddenly, in a low voice:

"It's kind of you to bother with an idiot like me. Do you realise, before we met I hadn't spoken to a single soul here but the butler? And even he didn't answer me. He just drooped his eyelids at me like a bishop."

She went into a low ripple of laughter.

"That's because you don't know anybody. We must change all that."

105

She waved her spoon at a passing young man.

"Maurice! You ought to know our new physician."

In five minutes she introduced me to half a dozen men. They were not snobs, but decent fellows after all, I saw, decent fellows every one of them. I was no longer an outsider. I was one of them.

I waltzed with Miss Malcolm again. They played the "Blue Danube." It was superb.

"You really dance quite well," she said casually.

I blushed happily.

For most of the evening I danced with Miss Malcolm. She introduced me to many of the male guests, but the women to whom she made me known were—quite by chance, of course—rather too old to dance. Besides, that didn't matter in the least. It was she I wished for a partner. Our steps matched perfectly.

I had an exciting evening. I came out of my shell, was lively, gay, and gallant. I returned to Tannochbrae, not at eleven as Cameron had predicted, but at four o'clock on the following morning. Before I left Dundrum Castle I asked Miss Malcolm if I might see her home. She shook her head coyly.

"I'm staying here overnight. But you must come and see me when I get back to my house. You know where it is. In that funny old crescent behind Knowhill Park. Come in the evening when you have time. In the evening I'm usually free."

Next morning at breakfast I was fresh as a daisy and full of the doings of the night before.

Old Cameron looked at me.

"It takes youth," he observed sententiously, "to dance all night and get up next mornin' without swearin' at the porridge. Ye seem to have had a grand time."

"A glorious time," I heartily agreed.

"Ay, ay! Just so! Did ye meet many of the gentry?"

"Lots of them."

"Do ye tell me, now! That's grand, that's grand. Maybe Lord Sinclair'll be havin' ye in next time he takes the measles."

I reddened . . . that confounded reflex of an active circulation which always betrayed me.

106

"As a matter of fact," I observed loftily, "I danced most of the evening with Lord Sinclair's cousin."

"His Lordship's cousin?"

"Exactly! With Miss Malcolm."

"Miss Malcolm!" Cameron echoed blankly, then covered his amazement by falling hastily to the dissection of his grilled kipper. "Ay, ay, she is some connection of the Sinclairs'. Not a first cousin, I shouldn't say, no, no, hardly as near as that. But a nice enough body none the less."

"She is, indeed! A charming girl!"

This time Cameron nearly had a fit. He choked and spluttered, but finally coughed the paroxysm away.

"It's these damned kippers," he wheezed. "They're full of bones! What was it you were saying about Miss Malcolm?"

"Just that she was charming," I answered absently. "I must look her up one day soon."

Cameron scraped back his chair decisively.

"You're far too busy for any such damned thing. You're a working doctor, man. Not a blasted troubadour."

It was curious, in the light of that remark, how hard Dr. Cameron kept me at work during the next few days. He was so merciless that for two weeks I had scarcely a moment of leisure in which I might have called to see Miss Malcolm. At the end of that period, however, a note arrived, written on plain white paper, handmade, mat surface, deckle edges, smelling delicately of verbena.

*"I had expected you to come and see me as a friend. Now, alas! I must invoke you as a doctor. I am not quite well. Nothing serious. But a nuisance rather. Come in the evening if you can, and I shall give you coffee."*

I sniffed the note. What a charming perfume! So she was ill, poor soul, and I had neglected her shamefully. Ah, it was too bad, altogether too bad.

"There's a call for Miss Malcolm," I informed Cameron at lunchtime.

Cameron's brows jerked up, and he looked as though he might rap out an oath. But he said nothing.

"I'll do it, of course," I answered calmly.

A pause.

"I'll go round and see her. . . ."

"In the evening!" shouted Cameron. And putting down his head he began to sup his Scotch broth like a lunatic.

I admired Miss Malcolm's house the moment I entered it. Miss Malcolm's abode was—like Miss Malcolm and Miss Malcolm's note paper—charming, perfectly charming. It was not a villa—the mere word alone was too obnoxious—but a gracious old house of weathered red sandstone in a crescent with a carriage step in front, its rooms were large and spacious, and its furnishings breathed a tasteful refinement.

Miss Malcolm had travelled greatly and had picked up many bits and pieces on her travels.

"You like my painted chest? It is rather good. I got it from a funny little *Gasthof* in the Tyrol." Or: "These old candlesticks. They're Quimper ware, of course. I bought them from the dearest old peasant woman in Brittany."

Miss Malcolm was in the drawing room reclining in a long chair beside the fire. An old silver tray with Spode china and a Georgian coffeepot stood at her elbow.

"Faithless one!" she exclaimed brightly. "If I hadn't been taken ill I believe I should never have seen you again."

I protested:

"Oh, no, Miss Malcolm! I've been wanting to come round. But I've been so busy. Tell me, though, what's the trouble?"

"I think we danced together too much the other night. My heart—it's nothing, of course, a mere nothing."

Full of concern, I examined her heart. As my head bent over her, she closed her full eyes. There was not much wrong that I could make out—a faint murmur, perhaps, but no perceptible lesion. I straightened myself, addressed her solicitously:

"You must rest. That's it. You must rest for a bit. And take a little tonic. I'll make it up myself. Trust me. I'll look after you."

She thanked me, adding:

"Ever since I went climbing in Switzerland I've had a slight cardiac
108

condition. I'm perfectly strong, of course. Perfectly sound in wind and limb."

While she gave me coffee I talked to her of winter sports, at which we both agreed I would excel. The coffee was delicious—not like Janet's coffee, which was good in a homely way, but darkly aromatic, full of sensuous essences that suggested Turkey, Samarkand, the closed courtyards of the East. She begged me, please, to smoke my pipe. She adored a pipe. Then we talked of travel, of the fascinating, exotic places of the Orient, of books. She talked intelligently, provocatively, amusingly. She had read widely. Occasionally she slipped into French or German—a little phrase unostentatiously introduced.

I was not forgetful of that sweet and faithful nut-brown maid, now struggling through the final stages of her medical curriculum, who, with truth and tenderness in her shining glance, had pledged herself to me; nevertheless I gazed across at Miss Malcolm with indulgence. She was on the thin side, it is true, and her liquid, brownish eyes were too large, with specks of yellow on the eyeball and bistre shadows beneath. Her teeth, too, were rather prominent. The skin of her neck had a dry look, and her nose, from certain angles, had a queer sharpness. But she had a way of holding herself, a way of animating her features which dispelled critical analysis. She had fine, well-cared-for hands. She was elegant. She was so right, assured, well-bred. She gave me a sense of my own value, a feeling that I was lost in a wretched hamlet in the Highlands. I began, with her, to despise Tannochbrae. It was ten o'clock when I rose to go. I promised to look in without fail the following evening. As we shook hands in good-bye, I was aware of the gentle pressure of her fingers on mine.

The following evening came. And I "looked in" to see Miss Malcolm. The next evening, too, and the next. They were professional visits, she emphatically insisted—she was comfortably off, she said; she demanded to be treated like an ordinary patient, and every time, before coffee and conversation, I listened most assiduously to her heart.

About ten days later Cameron approached me in the dispensary. He hummed and hawed a little, then abruptly declared:

"You're calling pretty often to see Miss Malcolm!"

"Why, yes," I said, surprised. "She's knocked up her heart a little."

"Her heart?" Cameron echoed dryly. "Ay, ay. So they're all professional visits."

"Certainly!" I exclaimed indignantly. "Why are you looking at me like that? I've been perfectly correct toward Miss Malcolm. But if you must know, I enjoy going to see her immensely. She's got a brilliant mind. . . ."

"Are you entangled with the damned woman?" Cameron demanded violently.

I flushed to the roots of my hair.

"She's not a damned woman! She's a lady! And my very good friend."

Cameron threw up his hands.

"My God!" he groaned. "And I thought ye had sense."

Then he walked out of the room.

That evening I went round determinedly to Miss Malcolm's house. My senior colleague's attitude had made me more stubborn. I gave an extra pressure to her hand. I said how glad I was to see her. And then I took out my stethoscope and bent to sound her heart. As I did so, encouraged perhaps by my extra cordiality, Miss Malcolm lay back and entwined her arms tenderly around my neck.

"You're sweet," she murmured, "too sweet for words."

I recoiled as though a snake had stung me.

"Good Heavens!" I stammered. "You mustn't do that."

Everything in my training revolted at the idea. Conduct unbecoming in a professional respect! A man might lose his diploma, be struck off the register, for less. Panic seized me. I stared at her as she lay there with her big, brown eyes melting up at me. I blurted out an excuse and bolted from the room.

Back at Arden House I went straight to Cameron and told him everything. The old man looked at me in his shrewd and canny style.

"So you've had your lesson at last. I'll not say I'm sorry. Listen, now that you're in a condition to understand: how old do you think your braw Miss Malcolm is?"

I mumbled:

"I don't know."

"She's forty-two if she's a day! Forty-two! And she's been lookin' for a man these last four-and-twenty years. Listen! Have ye ever seen her in the mornin'?"

"No," I said feebly. "She's always asked me to come . . ."

"In the evening," Cameron acidly cut in. He paused impressively. "But if you'd seen her in the mornin' as I have, when she had the bile. . . ." And that was all.

Next day Dr. Cameron made the visit to Miss Malcolm himself. He went in the morning, and he didn't stay long. But the odd fact is that Miss Malcolm's strained heart got better instantly.

Poor Miss Malcolm! She was really a nice creature, starved of affection, a lonely spinster—and I . . . I was a blundering clod.

# Chapter Thirteen

I HAD NOW BEEN in Tannochbrae for more than a year, and although I liked the place and the people, and had moreover a genuine affection for the testy old party who employed me, with the coming of another spring I was conscious of a restive feeling, and my thoughts began to turn toward the future. Ambition still burned bright within me. I wanted to have my own home, my own practice. I was now more than ever in love with Mary, and since so many obstacles were already in the way of our marriage, I felt I must at least try to offset them with some material advantages. Could this be achieved within the narrow confines of a small West Highland village?

At this stage of uncertainty and doubt, a series of events took place which, in a singularly irrational manner, were instrumental in determining the next phase of my unimportant destiny. It all began, ridiculously enough, with a fishbone.

The fishbone was in the throat of Mr. George McKellor, and because of it, one April evening about nine o'clock I was called to the McKellor villa, which stood in its own grounds on the outskirts of the village. I found McKellor in considerable pain, although making little fuss about it. He was a taciturn man, a confirmed bachelor, with the uncommunicative abruptness of one who has made his way in life entirely through his own efforts. By profession a grain merchant, he travelled every day to his office in Glasgow, where he was a highly successful operator on the commodity markets, known to be worth a tidy fortune. Actually his home was in the city, but partly from inclination, partly also because of his business associations with the neighbouring farmers, he chose to spend the spring and summer at his country residence in Tannochbrae.

Under the bright light of the handsomely furnished dining room—McKellor had been at his solitary dinner when the mishap occurred—it was easy to locate the trouble, and with one quick stroke of the forceps I removed the offending bone, which was bedded deep down in the soft part of the gullet.

The relief was instantaneous. McKellor drew a deep breath of ease, swallowed once or twice wryly, then smiled his slow, unwilling smile.

"Must have hurt you a bit," I remarked, inspecting the jagged bone. "It's a nasty little article."

"Ay," replied McKellor reflectively. "It was hardly pleasant while it lasted. I must say I'm obliged to you for looking in so quickly." He paused significantly. "And now—I'm a man for prompt settlements, Doctor. How much do I owe you?"

I put the question aside with a deprecating smile.

"It was nothing. Just a neighbourly action to run in and tweak it out for you. We'll charge you no fee at all."

George McKellor's stare became even more shrewdly appraising, the look of a man with the money sense who has struck many a hard bargain in his day.

"Are you actually serious?"

"Certainly," I replied. "It was just a good turn I was able to do you. Perhaps some day you will be able to do one for me."

There was a silence. McKellor's expression remained inscrutable, but after stroking his square chin reflectively, he finally exclaimed:

"Sit down. I'm not minding for any more food. We'll have a drop of Scotch and a chat, you and me."

When he had poured the whisky, and we had lit our pipes, Mc-Kellor went on, noncommittally enough, yet with something compelling and confidential in his tone.

"I've heard of you, Doctor, one way and another, and it hasn't all been to your discredit." A dry smile. "I'm not given to sudden likings —no, I'm not that kind of man—but, as you say, one good turn deserves another." He paused and took a deliberate pull at his whisky. "Tell me, young fellow, have you ever heard of Roan Vlei?"

Half amused, I shook my head.

"Never," I said. "It's a share, I suppose. Anyhow, it sounds like it."

"Ay," retorted McKellor, with a grim humour. "It's a share, all right, a Kaffir gold mine, to be exact." He lowered his voice and spoke from between closed lips, as though the words were drawn from some secret fount of knowledge. "A few of us have information on the inside, over this Kaffir mine. We've formed a pool. It's in for a rise, a real big rise." Another long pause. "Doctor, I advise you to buy yourself a few Roan Vleis."

Again I laughed, pleased, yet embarrassed.

"It's kind of you, I'm sure, Mr. McKellor, but—well, that's not my line of business."

McKellor fixed me with his friendly but enigmatic stare.

"You take my tip," he said, tapping the table in emphasis. "I promise you'll not regret it." And with a solemn gesture he pushed the whisky decanter toward me.

That same night, on my return to Arden House, I questioned Cameron about McKellor.

"What kind of man is he? I must say he seems genuine."

"Ay, he's one of the best, is McKellor," Dr. Cameron replied. "A bit fond o' the siller maybe, but straightforward and honest, and his word is his bond. And, since we're speaking of money, landsakes, he's worth a pickle o't."

In spite of myself, I was impressed by this testimonial. At the outset I had not had the least intention of following the advice which had been offered me. But now the seed was sown there developed in my mind the enticing idea that here was a chance to acquire the capital so necessary for my future plans—for house, practice, and marriage alike—a miraculous opportunity which it would be folly to ignore.

The thought kept hammering, hammering away inside my head. I had a snug little nest egg of about one hundred pounds, saved since I had begun my assistantship and reposing securely in the bank. What

114

was to prevent me doubling, trebling it, perhaps turning it into a real bonanza?

I slept little that night. All sorts of golden fancies kept flashing gloriously before me, and in the morning when I rose I went directly to the telephone. McKellor, who had not yet left for the office, approved my decision.

"Right!" he said. Then added crisply and unemotionally, "You're a wise man, Doctor. Get in touch with Hamilton, my broker, in Ingram Street. He'll look after you. Mark my words, you'll not be sorry."

I had no difficulty in establishing contact with Hamilton who, on McKellor's recommendation, proved exceptionally helpful. As the sum at my disposal for investment was not large and the price of Roan Vleis rather high—they stood that morning at just under a pound per share—the broker proposed that I should operate on margin. Thus I should be able to purchase not one hundred, but five hundred shares. Who could have refused such a favour, with its prospects of greater gain? Over the telephone, the momentous transaction was completed.

The next few days passed in a state of tension and excitement. Indeed, as time went on in this prolonged suspense, I began to ask myself in a kind of anguish if I had not been overcredulous. For nothing happened! There was nothing in the newspapers, not one word from George McKellor. The stock market was as flat as a pancake, and the wretched shares stood at a few pence below the figure at which I had bought them. I chafed and worried; only my pride prevented me from rushing to McKellor's house and demanding the reason of this hopeless inactivity.

But at last, one morning toward the end of the second week, when, sick with hope deferred, I opened the *Winton Herald,* my heart gave a sudden bump. I saw that Roan Vleis had jumped a clear four shillings.

My eyes glistened and the blood went pounding through my veins. I made a rapid calculation. Overnight, I had made practically one hundred pounds. Incredible, but, oh, wonderful, simply marvellous!

115

I raced to the telephone and rang up McKellor, who was on the point of leaving for the city.

"I've just seen the news," I stammered delightedly over the wire. "It's great, isn't it? Shall I . . . shall I sell?"

"What!" McKellor's voice was calmly incredulous. "Are you gone wuddy? Sell out at the very beginning? No, no, not on your life. You wait until I give you the word. Sell at that instant, and not before." And, with a click, the receiver went up at the other end.

Flushed and elated, with my head in a whirl, I went into the surgery and tried to settle to my work. It was difficult to concentrate, and during the next few days I hurried through my cases so that I might have more time to watch the progress of my speculation.

A fascinating and profitable occupation, far beyond the humdrum routine of the practice! A great game, indeed! For now they had started, Roan Vleis rose on the market like a rocket. Up and up they went, marking a rise of several shillings each day until by the end of the week they stood at almost double their original figure. The news, which had been discreetly rumoured, was now given out with full publicity—a vein of rich ore had been struck in the mine. In consequence, everyone was rushing to buy.

Monday saw a resumption of the boomlet, bringing me fresh exaltation. I was constantly on the telephone to the stockbroker in Winton, in touch with McKellor morning and evening, kept in a perfect whirl of excitement. My original desire to sell and take a modest profit was long forgotten. Here was the chance of a lifetime to make a fortune. I had faith in McKellor, whose shrewd demeanour impressed me forcibly with the sense that I was following the right man. I went in deeper than ever. Acting on McKellor's advice, I increased my holding, buying on margin until I held not far short of twelve hundred shares in the Roan Vlei mine. My profit already stood at over seven hundred pounds, and life was wonderful indeed!

The fact that I had made this money, and made it so easily, mounted like wine to my head. I began to consider not only the legitimate objectives for which I had been striving, but the extra good things of life which riches could bring. My work suffered more and more. When not engrossed by the stock-market reports or busy

116

on telephone conversations, I kept figuring out my profits. Up and up they went. At the end of another four days they stood not far short of nine hundred pounds. Nine hundred pounds! As much as I might make in two years, slogging winter and summer, wet and fine, at the tedious round of medicine. Strung to the highest pitch of tense excitement by the money fever, I awaited McKellor's final instructions.

All this time, while my satisfaction increased, I had been conscious of a growing disapproval on the part of my employer. Once or twice he made to speak, but restrained himself. At last, however, at supper on the Thursday of that second week, when I came in late following an interview with McKellor, the old man darted a glance at me and growled:

"Late again, eh? What's come over you these days?" He inspected me with critical annoyance. "Don't stand there fidgeting, man. You're like a cat on hot bricks. You can't be still. You don't eat, either. And you look as if you can't sleep."

"I'll be all right presently," I excused myself, as I sat in at the table.

"Presently!" exclaimed Cameron. "And why not immediately?"

"Well . . . , as a matter of fact, I have something on my mind at the moment."

Cameron rose abruptly, rebuke stamped on every lineament.

"Ay," he said sternly, "I've a good idea what it is, too, and God knows I don't like it. Let me tell you plainly you're not the man you were. You're changing . . . losing your sense of values. And more. You're doing rank bad work. I'm both disappointed and dissatisfied with it." And coldly, he turned and walked out of the room.

Utterly taken aback, I sat with lowered gaze, cut to the quick by Cameron's rebuke, which I felt, under my veneer of satisfaction, to be justified. A pang of compunction took me. Was I really doing bad work? Being slack and slipshod, in order to have more time to devote to this business of getting rich? I could barely touch my supper. In a sober, chastened mood I rose from the table and went immediately to bed.

Toward six o'clock on the following morning I was awakened by

117

an early call. Stung by Cameron's remarks—they still burned in my mind—and eager to justify myself, I welcomed this summons, tumbled into my clothes, summoned the gig, picked up my bag of instruments, and set out on a long drive to Marklea.

A soft mist lay upon the loch and shrouded the forms of the budding trees. The morning was so pure and still, it struck into my heart. Though Jamie, the groom, once or twice attempted a remark, I was in no mood for conversation. I sat hunched up in my seat, silent.

Neglecting my work, I thought bitterly, between indignation and remorse; not the man I was—I'll show him!

In this frame of mind, about an hour later, I reached the whitewashed cottage home of George and Elizabeth Dallas, which stood by the lochside in a remote moorland glen, below Marklea.

Elizabeth had been stillroom maid at Dundrum Castle, a worthy, capable person, but already in her fortieth year, when Dallas, one of the shepherds on the estate, married her. The marriage had proved to be a happy one and now, rather confounding the prophets, Elizabeth was expecting a child. I had seen her several times recently at the surgery and knew that, more than anything, she wished to justify herself by presenting her husband with a son.

Attended by her aged mother, she was already in labour, although not far advanced, when I arrived. Outside, hanging about the back door, too anxious to return to his work, was Dallas. I could see him from the window of the tiny bedroom as I pulled off my coat and rolled up my sleeves. At least there was work for me to do, in plenty. And there was waiting too.

An hour passed quickly, morning merged insensibly into afternoon. The patient's pains, slight at first, became deeper and more prolonged. It was now apparent that the case would not be an easy one. Elizabeth's age, and other circumstances, her anxiety that she should do her part, that the baby should be well and healthy—all this worked against her. And her heart was not strong.

The afternoon drew in, then at last the moment came for action. Taking mask and ether, I put the poor woman, mercifully, to sleep. And that was but the beginning. A full hour I struggled through the dark ways of difficulty and danger, before the instrumental delivery was complete. And then, alas, it seemed that half my efforts had been in vain. The child came into the world pale and still. A sigh broke from the old woman.

"God save us, Doctor, the bairn's dead!"

Perspiration was streaming from my brow, and there was deep anxiety in my eyes, for the mother was herself in a serious condition. Removing the mask from her face, I applied restoratives, and at last succeeded in bring her round. When she was out of danger I turned hurriedly to the baby which lay inert and apparently lifeless, wrapped in a rough blanket, at the foot of the bed.

"Oh, dear, oh, dear," moaned the old woman, rocking to and fro in her grief. "To think it should be stillborn, Doctor. A boy, too. And her that's never like to have another."

I interrupted her harshly:

"Bring some hot water. And cold as well."

At the same time I began to apply artificial respiration to the lifeless child. When the two full basins were brought I lifted the frail, limp body and plunged it first in the warm water, then in the icy cold. Again and again I repeated the process, trying to galvanise the child by shock, using the methods of respiration in between—working desperately, feverishly, with a kind of passionate anger. I toiled and toiled until, when all seemed lost, a faint, feeble, convulsive gasp stirred the infant's chest.

A cry, as if in answer, broke from my dry lips. More desperately still I increased my efforts. Another feeble gasp and another, now less feeble, from the child . . . a little shiver, then shallow but regular respiration. Triumph swelled in me, and the old dame gave out a cry of thankfulness and joy.

"It breathes, Doctor!" she gasped. "Oh, God in Heaven, it's come to life!"

Within an hour the little bedroom, restored from its disorder, freed from suffering and sadness, was again neat and clean, the bed made up, the fire burning brightly in the grate, and the mother, pale but joyful, with the baby breathing and nestling at her breast, following all my movements with swimming eyes which tried, humidly, to express her gratitude.

Nor was the old lady to be outdone. She would not let me go until she had fed me well—a meal I badly needed—while Dallas himself, following sheepishly at my heels, wrung my hand with inexpressible gratitude again and again.

It was almost dusk when I set out on the return drive to Tannochbrae, and after seven o'clock in the evening when I reached the outskirts of the town. In the intensity of my endeavour, time had passed unconsidered. What of it? I had vindicated myself, had answered Cameron's taunt. I felt strangely rested and at peace. And yet, as the gig rattled down the main street and brought me back to the haunts of men, the mood slipped from me, and all at once, with a quickening of my heart, I thought of my Roan Vleis and how much they would have risen that day.

Impulsively I stopped the gig, and dismounting, told Jamie to go home. Proceeding on foot, I bought an evening paper at the village store.

Then, as I rapidly scanned the financial page, avid for the news that would put more money in my pocket, my eyes almost leaped from my head. Across the top of the page stretched a glaring headline: *"Bottom Drops Out of Roan Vlei Boom."*

With a sickening sensation in my breast, I rapidly read on. The report of the new vein in Roan Vleis had proved to be erroneous. The mine had struck a fault. In the course of the day Roan Vleis had slumped a full thirty shillings!

Overcome by bewilderment and dismay, I stood a moment facing this incredible disaster; then, with trembling hands, I stuck the paper in my pocket and set out at a run for George McKellor's house.

I had no difficulty in finding McKellor. Indeed, the grain merchant was waiting on me, pacing up and down the hall, glowing with ill-suppressed satisfaction.

"Come in, Doctor," he cried, slapping me on the back with unusual gaiety. "We did it this time right enough, eh?"

I stared at him aghast.

"Did it? How do you mean?"

McKellor's expression changed slowly until, quite nonplussed by my chalky countenance, he exclaimed:

120

"You've sold, haven't ye—sold like I told you?"

A pause, then I muttered:

"No, I haven't sold."

"What!" shouted McKellor in a tone of horror. "Ye haven't sold? In the name of heaven! Why, man? I rang you at nine this morning and left the message. To make doubly sure I even sent you a telegram. I told you to get out at the peak of the market before the news of the fault was made public. I told you to sell everything and go a bear on the fall. If you'd done as I told you you'd have doubled your profit."

There was another heavy silence. He was waiting for me to speak.

"I had a case"—I averted my eyes—"up at Marklea. I never had your message. You see—I've been away all day."

McKellor exploded between exasperation and disgust.

"Away all day! Didn't I tell you to keep in touch with me?" he raged. "Wasn't that more important than your miserable case?"

I did not answer. McKellor bit his lips, controlling himself with difficulty.

"You're a fine man to take trouble over," he said, turning away angrily. "It'll be long enough before I give you another tip."

I walked home slowly with a set and sombre face, all my plans, my grand ideas of riches shattered and in ruins at my feet. Dr. Cameron was seated by the dining-room fire when I went in, and for a moment neither spoke. The old doctor's eyes fell upon me as I flung myself into a chair and dejectedly poured myself a cup of tea.

"You've had a long day," said Cameron at last, not unkindly.

"Ay," I replied, and in a brief sentence I reported how the case had gone at Marklea.

"Well," said Cameron, and his tone held a hint of the old friendship, "you did right to stay there all day." He paused. "By the by, there's been an uncommon commotion while you've been away. They were trying to get you from Glasgow all morning. Something about buying and selling." He paused again, significantly. "But I had to tell them you were busy."

"Yes," I said slowly, "I was busy." And all at once a lightness came over me as I remembered the faces of Elizabeth Dallas and her husband, of the old woman, her mother, and, above all, the face of the little child as colour stole into the pallid features, and life reanimated the tiny form!

When settling day arrived I found that the brokers had sold me out the moment my margin was exhausted. Their statement showed that not only were my paper profits gone, but all my hundred pounds as well . . . at least, not quite all, for by some technicality, an arithmetical juggling with eights and sixteenths far beyond my comprehension, there actually remained of my original capital the sum of seven pounds fifteen shillings. A cheque for this amount was enclosed with the firm's compliments.

Gazing in silent bitterness at that infernal strip of paper, I was overcome by a strange impulse. I went that afternoon to the town of Knoxhill where, in the High Street, stood the establishment of a country jeweller named Jenkins. We spoke together, Jenkins and I. The cheque, to my immense relief, passed out of my hands. And a week later a christening mug was delivered to that lonely cottage on the lochside, a fine silver mug which made the eyes of Elizabeth Dallas gleam with pride, a mug which she handled reverently, and fondly displayed to the child she held so tenderly in her arms.

Upon the mug was inscribed her little son's name, *Georgie Dallas,* and, below, this odd inscription: *What money can't buy.*

# *Chapter Fourteen*

THE SCOTS—I still stoutly maintain—are an emotional people, and Dr. Cameron was, fundamentally, a sentimental man. But with this difference, shared by most of the northern race—he was not demonstrative. Any display of feeling he regarded as a sign of weakness, and one gruff word from him meant more than a score of impassioned speeches. Thus, he gave me no warning of what was in his mind until, one Sunday morning, some weeks after the incident I have just related, he looked across the Britannia-metal coffeepot as we sat at breakfast and remarked dryly:

"I find that I no longer need you as an assistant."

There was a dead silence. I had, true enough, considered the possibility of leaving Cameron, but only in my own interest. This dismissal was a different matter, and I turned pale with mortification and surprise. Then, before I had recovered from the shock, his stern expression merged into a twisted smile.

"But I could very well do with you as a partner. How about going halves with me in the practice, lad? I'll make the terms as easy as you please."

The blood rushed back into my cheeks with such violence that my head swam. He went on:

"Take a few weeks to think about it. Talk it over with your friends and"—his eyes twinkled as he got up from the table and went to the door—"with that young lady who is brave enough to be interested in you."

It was a tremendous, if unmerited, tribute he had paid me, and to this day I treasure my achievement in winning the regard of this hardheaded and high-principled old country doctor, a man who said little but observed everything, who "saw through" people with a single shrewd and penetrating glance, who would certainly never have chosen for his associate one whom he did not like and esteem. There was reason, too, in his proposal. In his own phrase, he "was not getting any younger," he wanted someone to share equally in the cares and responsibilities of his beloved practice, someone who would eventually succeed him.

My first impulse was to accept warmly, but Cameron insisted I act on his suggestion and first of all seek advice. I went, accordingly, to my former chief, Professor Stockman, whose opinion I greatly valued. To my surprise, he strongly opposed my remaining in Tannochbrae. He considered that it was not at all the proper place for me and, while in no way belittling rural practice, declared that I should be foolish in the extreme to bury myself and, he added, my talents, in a remote West Highland glen. These forcible words placed me in a dilemma. My heart told me I should stay with Cameron, my head counselled me to leave him.

While I was in this state of indecision, winter took a last vile fling in a burst of abominable and atrocious weather. It snowed and rained, snowed again, then rained on top of that, until the roads were almost impassable with slush and mud. Wicked going and weary work it made for us. My costume day after day was heavy boots, leggings, and the thickest ulster in my wardrobe. Sleep became a luxury. Pleurisy, pneumonia, and every form of chill and congestion ravaged the countryside.

It was the worst time of all the year, when to work a busy, scattered practice was little better than slavery in its crudest form. And yet, perversely, the very torture of this treadmill inclined me to remain. How could I desert the old man at such a time?

Late one January night I stamped into the dining room after a particularly killing day, tugged off my boots and leggings, drew on my soft slippers, and sank into a chair. With a sigh of incredible relief I relaxed for a moment before the blazing fire, then silently accepted the bowl of steaming broth which Janet, having heard me come in, brought through from the kitchen. Outside, the wind howled and scuffled in the darkness, battering the hailstones against the windowpanes like a fusillade of icy shot.

"Please God," I thought, with a little shiver, "I'll not be out again tonight." And, standing on no ceremony, I supped the scalding soup as I sat there by the fire.

Half an hour later Cameron came in, equally worn out, his gaunt, weather-beaten features pinched with cold and fatigue, his figure bowed a little, his whole aspect utterly fagged. He came forward slowly and stretched out his hands to the fire, while the steam rose from his damp clothing. A silence of sympathetic understanding linked us, the knowledge of common endeavour, of work done in the face of difficulty and hardship. Then Cameron, with a long expiration of his breath, nodded to me, went to the sideboard, poured out some whisky, added a little sugar, then marched to the fireplace and picked up the little kettle which always sang there upon the hob. With an eye which thanked Providence for the small mercies of life, he smacked his lips and cannily mixed some toddy. But, alas, just as Cameron gratefully raised the steaming brew to his lips, the phone bell rang.

"Dammit to hell," muttered Cameron, lowering his toddy untouched. We both listened apprehensively, fully conscious that the cursed bell might mean a summons into the icy darkness of the night.

Two minutes of waiting; then Janet came in, her eyes falling, not upon me, whose duty it usually was to take the night calls, but upon Cameron himself, and in Janet's face there was a genuine reproach.

"It's from Mr. Currie, of Langloan," she announced, with a baleful shake of her head. "They've been expecting you all day long"—pause—"and now they want to know if you're coming at all." Crossing her arms upon her bosom, Janet gazed at the old doctor like a schoolmistress sorely put out by a favourite pupil.

Cameron groaned. Then, for all his casehardened imperturbability, he let out another heartfelt oath.

"The de'il dang me for an idiot! What on earth was I thinking of to forget Neil Currie? And me passed his very door twice!"

I was silent. I well knew the misery of missing a call in the rush

125

of the day's work and having to retrace weary steps to make good the oversight. Quickly I swallowed the last of my broth and reached again for my boots, when Janet, interposing, stopped me with a gesture.

"It's no use your goin', Doctor. They're fair upset at Langloan. It's Dr. Cameron or nobody."

At this information, so stoically conveyed by Janet, Cameron's lined face took on a deeper shade.

"Dang my bones!" he exclaimed, seriously distressed. "Neil thinks I'm neglecting him."

He put down the glass on the mantelpiece and buttoned his coat resolutely.

"Let me go," I protested. "You're absolutely dead-beat."

"Dead-beat or no," said Cameron, "I'm going. Neil will never be satisfied unless I show face myself."

"I'll send round for Jamie and the gig," exclaimed Janet practically. "It'll not take more nor five minutes to get him back."

"No," growled Cameron. "Jamie's worn out, and the beast's half foundered. It isn't more nor a mile to Langloan. I'll just step there myself. I'll be there and back in no time."

In spite of my attempts to dissuade him, he had his way. Neil Currie was one of his oldest friends, a member of the Anglers' Club, a prominent man in the village, and at present laid low by a bad attack of jaundice. Turning up his coat collar, he braced himself to the bitter wind and left the house.

Somehow, hearing the whistling of the wind outside, I was not easy in my mind. And, indeed, when, an hour later, Cameron returned it seemed as though my anxiety were justified. The old man was blue to the ears and completely exhausted. Nevertheless, he wheezed triumphantly:

"I think I've smoothed out that affair. I explained to Neil how it happened. For heaven's sake, don't let me forget to see him in the morning."

As he stood by the fire he coughed sharply, and abruptly, a moment later, remarked:

126

"I think I'll get upstairs."

But when halfway to the door he pressed his hand to his side and took a quick breath.

"Dod!" he exclaimed. "It catches me here right enough."

I rushed to his assistance, blaming myself now in grim reality. Ignoring his protests, I got Cameron upstairs to his bedroom, helped him out of his clothes and into bed. Once there, he seemed better and thrust aside my offer to examine him. But he did not mind when I dosed him with hot toddy and quinine. I waited in the bedroom until he fell into a restless sleep. I hoped that he would be fit again by morning.

But next morning Cameron was far from well. When I went in at six o'clock I found him flushed, fevered, breathing rapidly, and tormented by a short, suppressed cough. This time I was not to be put off. I carefully sounded his chest. There was no doubt about it. Cameron had pneumonia, lobar pneumonia, and he himself was aware of the fact, for, gazing at me with distressed yet quizzical eyes, he gasped:

"The right lung, isn't it?" And at my silence: "Well, it seems I'm in for it this time, sure enough."

Confronted by this emergency, I marshalled all my forces to meet it. Without hesitation, I telephoned Linklater's, the wholesale chemists in Glasgow, who also conducted a local medical agency. Through them I obtained a locum tenens—a raw Inverness youth named Frazer, who arrived early that same afternoon.

Keyed to a high tension, I put the fear of God in Frazer, deputed to him the surgeries and the outlying work. Then, rushing through my own cases with all possible speed, I devoted the remainder of my time entirely to Cameron.

I realised only too well that there could be no immediate and spontaneous cure. In that era we knew nothing of the wonder drugs, of sulphanilamide, penicillin, and the other antibiotics which, as by a miracle, can cut short the worst pneumonic lesion, which have reduced the mortality rate of that once dreaded disease by 85 per cent. Then, for nine to ten days, lobar pneumonia "ran its course," each

127

day showing a steady deterioration in the patient's condition, until the crisis came, bringing liquefaction to the solidified lung, benign though belated relief.

Thus the task before me, and one to which I gave myself with passionate intensity, was to pull Cameron through these fateful days. I felt I would succeed, too, for Cameron, despite his pain and discomfort, was alert and cheerful.

"Don't look so annoyed wi' me, man," he declared, with an attempt at humour. "It's a grand opportunity ye're havin' to observe how sickness makes the most impatient man behave."

I smiled an acquiescence I was far from feeling as I punched up the old doctor's pillows, then measured out his medicine. I looked round: the fire was burning cheerfully in the grate, the draught screen in position, the windows open at the top, the room ordered, and fresh and airy. The nurse from Knoxhill stood by the foot of the bed, trim and competent, ready to anticipate Cameron's every want. Everything was being done, and everything would be done, I thought grimly. I must get Cameron through—I must, I must!

In this fashion for the first three days all went smoothly, and the condition ran a normal course. But on the fourth day, with alarming unexpectedness, my patient took a sudden turn for the worse. As I read the sick man's temperature and felt his running pulse, I steeled myself to betray no anxiety; but underneath, my heart throbbed with a sudden fear. I redoubled my attentions. All that night and the following night I sat up with Cameron, making every effort to stem the ominous advancing tide.

But on the sixth day Cameron was definitely worse; he coughed up a quantity of dark prune-juice mucus, and tossed through long, sleepless hours that night. Accordingly, on the seventh day, with a heavy heart, I telephoned Dr. Greer in Glasgow, and asked him to meet me in consultation. Greer, one of the best-known medical specialists in the west of Scotland, was an authority on pulmonary diseases. He arrived that afternoon with due precision and, in his unhurried, methodical way, which even in this extremity I could not but admire, probed every aspect of the case. Afterward, he was

128

kind in what he said to me, agreeing with my diagnosis and treatment, but alas, far from reassuring. When pressed for an opinion he shook his head.

Cameron, he said, pursing his rather full lips, was over sixty years of age, and worn down by years of arduous exertions. Under the toxins of the pneumonococci his strength had failed considerably, and more than that, he seemed now to offer little resistance to the malady. There was a definite breaking down of the blood cells and also involvement of the left lung—double pneumonia. He could no more than urge me to continue the measures I was taking: to press the injections of strychnine, to resort to oxygen when necessary, to try to stimulate the patient's powers to fight back against the deadly march of the disease.

When Professor Greer had gone, I stood for a moment alone in the sitting room, realising the truth of what the specialist had said—that Cameron was failing utterly to maintain his earlier aggressive stamina. At the thought I pressed my hand to my brow, overcome by an insupportable feeling of wretchedness, recollecting at the same time all that I owed to him. The memory of his kindness, affection, and goodness rushed over me in a kind of agony.

The eighth day came without a shadow of improvement. Though I doubled the efforts at stimulation, using strychnine, brandy, oxygen, even ether; though I battled frantically to arrest the growing weakness of the sick man, it was useless. The old fighting quality, which had been so characteristic of Cameron, was finally extinguished. He lay passive on his pillow, with half-shut eyes, breathing jerkily into the glass funnel through which the pure oxygen gas bubbled from its metal cylinder. He could not rouse himself to take nourishment. He had ceased to respond to his medicine, and my murmured words of exhortation and encouragement fell on deaf ears.

By this time it had become generally known throughout the village how dangerously ill was their old doctor. All day long messages and tokens of sympathy kept pouring into the house from the town and the surrounding district. There came also every conceivable form of country delicacy, accompanied by expressions of the sincerest good will. Straw covered the road in front of the house. And Janet moved about on tiptoe in her felt slippers, with desolation on her drawn face.

Then came the ninth day, pregnant with fatality. All afternoon I sat by the sinking man, watching Cameron's strength ebb away under my very eyes. Never shall I forget that still cold winter twilight. Evening came, and with the falling dusk it seemed as if the mantle of death descended and hung above the enfeebled figure in the bed. Cameron was perfectly conscious now, and almost placid. Weakly he turned his head, an indication that he wished to speak.

"No use, lad," he whispered; "it's all up with me this time."

Unable to reply, I clenched my hands until the nails bit into my palms. Violently I shook my head. But Cameron's eyes were already closed. . . . It was the end.

How long I sat there, in that silent room, I cannot tell. Janet came and went. There was the glimmer of a candle. Then, from without, through the still and frigid air, came the slow tolling of the steeple bell.

Three days later the old doctor was buried in the village churchyard. I had never heard him speak of his relatives, but now there appeared at the funeral, from a remote northern town, two nephews and their wives. They descended in apparent grief, in reality like wolves upon the fold.

Nothing was sacred to them in their avaricious possessiveness, from the dead man's bankbook to the clothing hanging in his bedroom cupboard. They fingered and ferreted, poked their way into every corner of the house, interfered with Janet, with the patients, even hinted that I was pocketing the fees. But they were, of course, his legal heirs. Within the month the practice had been sold and the incoming man had taken over.

I was pressed by many people to remain, to set up in opposition to the new doctor, with Janet as my housekeeper, but with Cameron gone, the appeal of Tannochbrae was finally extinguished.

I left silently, one winter morning, from the Junction station, the wind-swept platform desolate as on the day of my arrival, yet no more desolate than was my heart. Indeed, such desolation as now possessed me induced a mood of utter recklessness, linked to a crying need of tenderness. Gone now were all practical considerations. I sought out Mary who, having passed her last examination, was living with her parents in a pleasant country villa some twenty miles from Glasgow. Abruptly, I took both her hands in mine.

"Mary," I said, "I have no position, no prospects, and no money; in fact I'm thirty pounds in debt. I can't even offer you the barest pretence of a home. As you know, I'm a Catholic—a damn bad one, I'm sorry to say—and you are a fairly strict Protestant. Also I'm quite sure your family consider me an irresponsible blackguard—and perhaps with reason. It all sounds hopeless, but we love each other, I know we can get along together, and I'm sure I can get some sort of job straightaway. So will you marry me, quickly, without fuss, one day next week . . . and take what looks like a very long chance?"

She did not speak, not a single word, but I read her answer in the swift tightening of her grasp, in the quivering brightness of her dear and steadfast eyes.

# PART TWO

# Chapter Fifteen

LATE THAT JANUARY afternoon, an ordinary young man in a new store suit and a pretty young woman wearing a dove-grey dress sat tightly holding hands and gazing with fixed intensity through the window of a dingy third-class compartment in the almost empty train labouring up the Rhondda Valley from Cardiff. All day long, after our wedding, my wife and I had travelled from Scotland, changing at Carlisle and Shrewsbury, and the final stage of our long journey to South Wales found us strung to a state of increasing tension at the prospects of beginning our life together in this strange, disfigured country.

Outside, a grey mist was swirling down between the black mountains which rose on either side, scarred by ore workings, blemished by great heaps of slag on which a few mangy sheep wandered in vain hope of pasture. No bush, no blade of grass was visible. The trees, seen in the fading light, were gaunt and stunted spectres. At a curve of the line the red glare of a foundry flashed into sight, illuminating a score of workmen stripped to the waist, their torsos straining, arms upraised to strike. Then the searing vision was swiftly lost behind the huddled top gear of a mine.

Darkness had fallen, emphasising the strangeness and remoteness of the scene when, some minutes later, the engine panted into Tregenny, the end township of the valley and the terminus of the line. We had arrived at last. Gripping our suitcase, I leaped from the train and helped my bride to alight.

At the station exit we paused, disappointed in our expectation that one of the colliery officials would meet us, depressed by the blurred and huddled aspect of the town, made up of ugly rows of miners' dwellings, interspersed with tin chapels and taverns, set between high dumps of pit refuse, beneath a pall of fog and smoke. What a prospect, I thought, with sinking heart. Where, oh where, now, were the fresh green glens and heather-clad moors of Tannochbrae?

As we stood there, not knowing our way, a loud hooter sounded and squads of miners began to come off shift from the pithead. Dark, sallow fellows they were, grimed with sweat and coal dust, each with a tiny oil lamp fixed to the peak of his cap. Approaching one of them, I asked to be directed to the doctor's house. He stared at me, then broke into a wild torrent of Welsh, not a word which was intelligible to me. Another responded in similar fashion. But at last we found a lad who understood our inquiry and who kindly led us to our lodging, which, to our consternation, we discovered to be no more than two sparsely furnished rooms in an ordinary collier's cottage. As we arrived we were greeted by a stream of dirty water sluiced from a tin bath through the side door.

The woman of the house was short, heavy, and black-haired, her thick eyebrows joined by a tuft, and a mole on her long upper lip. While perfectly civil, her welcome was not effusive. She introduced herself as Mrs. Morgan, showed my wife the bedroom upstairs and the few amenities provided by the kitchen, indicated that water came only from the outside well and that such toilet facilities as existed were confined to the back yard. Then she left us to ourselves.

"Well," I remarked, with false brightness, "it's not too bad."
"No, dear."
"And at least we'll be together."
"Yes, dear."
"But I must say," with a rush of indignation, "I can't see where their damned comfort comes in."

The advertisement in the *Lancet,* inserted by the Tregenny Coal Company, which had brought us at short notice to this outlandish spot, had promised the company's incoming medical officer not only remuneration at the rate of 500 pounds per annum, but also what was pleasingly described as "comfortable living quarters."

Facing each other across the worn stretch of linoleum, chilled by the rickety furniture upholstered in wax cloth, by the thin frayed curtains, the burst armchair, the sickly fern on its mottled bamboo stand, by this pinchbeck atmosphere of a fourth-rate boardinghouse, all so different from the picture painted by our glowing fancy—which, indeed, had envisaged Wales as a land of fruitful pastures and cosy cottages, in short, a perfect paradise for two—we exchanged a wan and tremulous smile. Then, observing a door which I felt might lead to an additional apartment, I tugged it open. Immediately, with a frightful clatter, there fell from a cupboard, not a skeleton, which might have proved diverting, but a score of empty whisky bottles left there by my predecessor, who, we learned afterward, had drunk himself into delirium tremens. This final shock proved too much for my poor wife. Her nerve gave way completely; she sat down on her suitcase and burst into tears.

In such an emergency there was only one remedy—food. We had eaten nothing but a few sandwiches all day, so, as nothing seemed likely to emerge from the kitchen—the silence in the back regions was abysmal—I took my wife's arm and led her out.

There were no restaurants in Tregenny—only an idiot would have sought for them—but on our passage from the station I had perceived a vulgar caravanserai of a type which, in my impecunious student days, I had frequented with pleasure and profit: in brief, a fish and chip shop.

In this establishment, which was warm and steamy, filled with the rich odours of frying fat, of fish fresh from the pan and patrons still black from the pit, we found a table. Our supper, served on the bare boards, was, as I had fully expected, hot, savoury, and satisfying—experience had taught me that where workingmen eat the food is usually good—and when we had consumed it, life seemed less complex, definitely rosier.

"I wonder should I go down to the company's office and report."

"You'll do no such thing. We've had a long, tiring journey. You're going straight back to bed."

137

Sudden realization of the implications of these words, uttered purely in a spirit of maternal protectiveness, caused my wife to blush, but she added, bravely, in a practical manner:

"At least it's a good hair mattress. And I saw that the sheets were freshly laundered."

"Darling," I murmured romantically, ignoring the fat Welsh cook, who between fries was watching us from behind the counter and picking her teeth with a hairpin, "you are without question the sweetest, bravest girl in all the world. Just think of it. You could have married someone who would have given you all the comfort and luxury you're accustomed to . . . a honeymoon at Monte Carlo, the Italian lakes, Florence, Capri. But no, out of the goodness of your heart, and against your parents' wishes, you marry me, a pauper, let me tear you from the bosom of your family, from your lovely home, from the life you had planned for yourself, practically under false pretences, for this . . . this goddamn dump. Forgive me, dear, I know I promised not to swear. But just wait, darling. I'll make it up to you. I'll be a success for your sake. . . . No, don't take your hand away, I don't care if the waitress is listening. . . . I'll be rich, famous, the top specialist in Harley Street. And although we can't be in France or Italy tonight, I promise my love and adoration will make up for it. Ah, dearest, tonight. . . ."

"Hey, mon, be you the new doctor?"

My rhapsody, so lyrical, so inane, was cut short by the abrupt appearance through the swing door of a sturdy, broken-nosed little man with a face which seemed tattooed, so seamed and pitted was it with tiny bluish scars. He wore a leather skullcap on his round, cropped head and carried a safety lantern in his hand.

"Sorry-like to fetch you, Doctor, bach," he went on, when I had answered in the affirmative, "but they do want you at t'pit."

It was annoying to be disturbed, yet I drew at least some slight comfort from this official recognition of our arrival. I escorted my wife across the street to our lodging, told her I would be back in half an hour, then set off with my new friend.

His name, he told me, was Rhys Jones, and for thirty years he had worked underground, beginning as a pony boy and rising gradually to his present position of shot-firer. When I asked him why I had been summoned, he replied, in the tone of one long accustomed to hardship and disaster, that a man had been injured underground, that we must go down to aid him.

We reached the colliery yard, crossed a network of rail tracks glistening under flares, and went into the first-aid room where, in silence, Jones handed me a battered surgical bag. Then, turning, he conducted me to the shaft head where, beneath the winding gear, the iron cage stood waiting for us. We entered. As the gates clanged, he gave a signal; then before I could draw a breath, the cage dropped like a plummet, with sickening velocity, nine hundred feet into the depths of the earth.

At the bottom we drew up with a jerk. Leaving the cage, we emerged into a sort of vaulted cave, roughhewn and dripping with water, from which there gave off a series of tunnels. Along one of these tunnels my companion led the way.

Never before had I been down a mine. Indeed, except in the remote distance, I had never seen a colliery and knew no more of the mining industry than the lump of coal which, without a thought as to how it had been won, I placed upon the fire. Now, however, as I toiled after Jones, who had set a fast pace, along this low, dark, dripping tunnel, bent double to avoid bumping my head—and even so I had twice already almost decapitated myself on rocky projections from the roof—I began to realise something of the rigours of a miner's life.

Every few minutes Jones drew me aside into little safety niches while, with a rumble and a roar, a train of metal tubs conducted by men stripped naked to the waist thundered past, missing us, it seemed, by inches.

"Aren't we nearly there?" I asked, as we reached a steeper incline.

"Nay, mon," he answered. "T'face is two miles from the shaft. Takes us forty minutes to reach it."

Nine hundred feet beneath the surface of the earth, in a tiny burrow two miles from the sole exit to free air—a horrible claustrophobia attacked me, a constriction of my throat and chest, I had to fight to keep my head. Though I flattered myself on my physical fitness, now I was gasping for breath and sweating profusely in the humid, dust-charged air. Ignoring my halfhearted protests, Jones relieved me of the heavy bag as, turning off the main level, we entered a branch tunnel cut from solid rock, not more than three feet high, indeed of such restricted dimensions that we had to crawl forward on our hands and knees. The bed of this jagged conduit was awash with running water—Tregenny, I afterwards learned, was a "wet pit"—so that in my inexpert progress I was soon wet to the waist. My God, I thought to myself, this is where men work, toil for long eight-hour shifts, hacking and hewing the coal from the narrow and difficult seams, day after day, through boyhood, manhood, the prime of life, yes, even to old age—a lifetime spent in this troglodyte existence, and all this for a wage which barely keeps body and soul together.

Presently, we arrived at the coal face and here, succoured by the undermanager and three of his mates, lay my patient, flat on his back, pinned by a heap of debris. When he had briefly greeted me, the undermanager spoke to me, aside, in a low voice. They had been shot-firing to bring out the coal and through a fault in the stratum the blast had undercut, bringing down masses of broken stone and leaving a great insecure ledge overhanging the cavity beneath. Not only was the injured man caught in the fall, but at any moment the entire roof, a hundred tons of solid rock, might cave in.

Although the manager's voice was steady, it held an unmistakable urgency. With a hurried glance at that hanging tombstone overhead, I crept up to the trapped miner. His left leg, mutilated and useless, was hopelessly gone—as though pulped by some gigantic press—and so irretrievably wedged that he could not be moved an inch. Only one course was open: an immediate amputation below the knee.

The thought appalled me. The baleful prediction of my student days had come to pass, and I knew by this time only too well my lack of skill as a surgeon, or at least my limitations in that bold and delicate art, which demands a special coordination of mind, heart, and hand it has never been my good fortune to possess. But now, fearful though I might be, there was no drawing back. I opened the first-aid bag, slit away the tattered clothing with a pair of curved scissors, and bared the mangled limb. I saturated the mask with ether. My patient was still conscious.

"I'll get you out of this," I whispered, with a confidence I did not feel. "Just breathe in and forget about everything."

When he was under the influence of the anaesthetic I propped the bottle against his side, tightened the tourniquet, pulled on a pair of rubber gloves, picked up the knife, and in a strained silence, having swabbed the knee with iodine, made the first incision.

There was no time for finicking—it was neck or nothing. Lying flat on my stomach under that low and pendant roof of rock, I worked like one possessed, shaping wide flaps, methodically clipping on the artery forceps one after another, cutting down to the bone. Then I reached for the saw. But as I did so there was a cracking sound, a fragment of stone detached itself from the roof and fell upon the container of ether, smashing the glass to fragments, flooding every drop of anaesthetic upon the ground.

I swore despairingly. But it was impossible to stop. At frantic speed I went through the bone, and began the ligatures. The under-manager, with his eye on the cracking roof, kept urging me to greater haste. I slipped in two drainage tubes, made good the last internal sutures, and started, with deep stitches, to sew up the skin flaps. As I threaded my needle for the last time I suddenly looked round and caught the injured man's dilated eye fixed strainingly upon me.

"Ye've made a fine job of it, Doctor, bach," he whispered from between his clenched teeth, "though I only saw you do the hint end of it."

He had been out of the anaesthetic, and watching me, for a full five minutes.

As they pulled him clear of the undercut and laid him on the stretcher his eyes were still fastened upon me. He tried to speak again. Instead, he fainted. And, indeed, I almost gave way also, for no sooner had we started back on our slow and painful passage to the shaft, than fifty paces back of us, with a final rending crepitation, the entire rock ceiling fell in.

141

We reached the surface at two in the morning, and to me, at least, the stars had never seemed brighter. There was no ambulance. We carried our patient on the stretcher to his home, and there, aided by the district nurse, I worked over him until he had begun to recover from the worst symptoms of shock. Dawn was breaking when I finally reached our lodging. Heavens, I thought dizzily, as I let myself in, what a way for any man to spend the first night of his honeymoon!

# Chapter Sixteen

---

FIRST IMPRESSIONS of a place often prove misleading—but in this instance they showed a melancholy accuracy. No mining town can ever be a thing of beauty, and Tregenny was certainly, in the local idiom, a "rough shop." The community's existence was centred in the mine, and as the little Tregenny Coal Company, though highly rated for integrity and fair dealing, was not a rich concern, operating at a disadvantage in wet, narrow seams where the coal was of indifferent quality and difficult to "win," and as, moreover, the mining industry in general had, at this period, lapsed into a slump, it was inevitable that local conditions should be bad, with a complete absence of those amenities which one normally expects in a civilised country.

There was no hospital, no ambulance, no X-ray apparatus. The sanitation would hardly bear looking into—one shuddered at the thought of future epidemics. The houses were damp and in poor repair, many without water, others with washing facilities only at the scullery sink. In such an environment medical practice could hardly conform to the more romantic traditions of the profession.

The company did its best by providing a doctor for the miners and their families, but, inevitably, the standard of men attracted to such an appointment was lamentably low. Thus in recent years Tregenny had seen an irregular coming and going of raw youngsters fresh from college, older practitioners unaware of what they had "let themselves in for," licenced apothecaries with quasi-medical degrees, and, worst of all, a draggled succession of "dead beats,"

143

doctors who had failed elsewhere, fallen into disrepute, or even been struck off the register for professional misconduct. Such unfortunates usually try to hide and eke out a living in some forgotten corner of the world. Our predecessor, poor fellow, was a habitual drunkard who was removed finally to Cardiff Infirmary in a state of alcoholic coma.

Small wonder, then, that our arrival caused no commotion, that our welcome was both chill and apathetic. Yet beneath their dark and upright dignity, the people were, at heart, warm and kindly. The Welsh are capable of generous impulses, and once their distrust of strangers is overcome, they can be intensely hospitable. My conduct of that first case—for which, forced upon me as it was, I actually deserved no credit—had created a favourable impression, and while still gazing at me askance, people began to wonder, hopefully, if they had "got a half-decent chap" at last. The manager, Dai Lewis, called at our lodging and went out of his way to be civil and obliging. He sent us, with his compliments, a load of firewood and coal from the pit head so that we should at least be warm. And Mrs. Morgan, our landlady, unbent so far as to hang clean curtains in our sitting room and even promised to teach my wife how to bake a batch of that noted Welsh delicacy—raisin griddlecakes. This short, dark-visaged woman had lost her husband in a pit disaster some years before and now harboured within her bosom deep strains of melancholy—a reserve quite different from that of Dr. Cameron's Janet, whose silences had an ironic quality and who, beneath her firmness, seemed always to be struggling against laughter.

I was now in the thick of my practice, consulting morning and evening in the crowded surgery near the pit, until the walls sweated and the air was choked with the steam of damp bodies. Miners with beat knee, nystagmus, chronic arthritis, sprained and lacerated limbs. Their wives too, and their children with coughs, colds, and colics— all the minor ailments of humanity. Those patients who were more seriously ill I visited in their homes—a round which usually occupied four or five hours each day. Despite handicaps and shortages, or perhaps because of them, it was worth-while work. My amputation

144

case was making an admirable recovery. Alone in the village, with no other physician for miles around, I felt a queer pride in my responsibilities, a rising exultation in the hope and promise of the future.

In other ways, however, Tregenny was unquestionably grim. There was no social life, no means of entertainment, not even a cinema. My wife and I both loved the country and were used to long rambles together through woods, fields, and meadows. Here, however, shut up in this narrow valley, hemmed in by the smeary blackness of the wasteland, it was impossible to escape to verdant pastures. In fact, that very colour, green—nature's own sweet tint—was something we never saw in all the monochrome of drab Tregenny. At times this sense of being buried, far down in this swart cleft of the mountains, was singularly oppressive. But we were young, healthy, and absurdly in love. We also had a sense of humour which enabled us to laugh at the deficiencies and oddities of our existence. In brief, we were happy.

Every afternoon, when I was free, we went to the pit stables to see the old ponies. These little animals, true Welsh moorland ponies, sturdy and shaggy-maned, had, most of them, spent all their working lives in the mine, pulling the long heavy trains of tubs, loaded with coal, from the face to the shaft bottom. Years in the darkness of this underground existence—for while in use they were never brought to the surface but always stabled underground—had rendered most of these patient and willing little creatures almost completely blind. Now, infirm and aged, they were unfit for further service. But Lewis, the manager, was a humane man, who would have none of that hateful practice, existing at many mines, that crime of sending worn-out animals abroad to Belgium or Holland, there to be sold and slaughtered in the knacker's yards. Instead the ponies were housed and fed, let out in the yard when it was sunny, allowed to end their days in peace.

We got to know them all—Nigger, Gingersnap, and Taffy were our special favourites. And how they loved the carrots and lump sugar which we never failed to bring them! After such a *bonne*

145

*bouche* they would lean their old heads out of the stall and, reaching out blindly, rolling their opaque old eyes, try to lick us all over with their moist, rubbery tongues.

Occasionally we were joined at the stables by the person who had become our most intimate friend in this carbonaceous wilderness. She was the district nurse, a middle-aged woman who became especially dear to both of us. And since her history is one which merits consideration, I might perhaps anticipate events and recount it now in its entirety.

Olwen Davies was only twenty-five when, fresh from her hospital training course, she was appointed visiting nurse to the district of Tregenny. Her lodging, comparable to ours, was a cold and sparsely furnished room in Chapel Street, and her reception was equally chilly. Nevertheless, Olwen threw herself enthusiastically into her work, walking in all weathers over the bleak mountain trails, visiting the sick, tending the few patients who appeared at the bare, simple dispensary provided by the rural board.

The company doctor at that time, old Dr. Gallow, was slack and incompetent. He gave her no help whatsoever. In the face of continued discouragement, the young nurse had to fight down a temptation to resign.

Toward the end of her first summer a sharp epidemic of enteric fever struck Tregenny. When Olwen went to Dr. Gallow, hoping for instructions to combat and confine the epidemic, she received a surly rebuke. These outbreaks were no rarity in the village; what in heaven's name could one do but physic the sick and endure the visitation?

Aroused, the young nurse took up the challenge. Collecting samples of water from the various wells—one of which she felt sure must be polluted—she took them to the health offices in Cardiff. Forty-eight hours later an official telegram arrived announcing that the typhoid infection had been traced to a well at the foot of Gower Street which supplied the lower part of Tregenny. Immediately, on orders from the colliery manager, the well was sealed.

There was something of an outcry at such "interference" on the part of the young nurse; some of the chapel deacons protested that she had far exceeded her authority. But the proof of the pudding is in the eating of it. No new cases of typhoid appeared, in record time the epidemic was confined, and Olwen, going about her work, felt the tide of public esteem flow slowly but surely toward her. No longer was she greeted with dark looks and hostile silences. The people opened their doors to her, and their hearts. Presently the children on their way to school ran across the street to greet her, miners returning from the pits grinned at her, old women detained her by the fireside with a cup of tea and a new-baked cake.

Then, at the end of that year, a great event took place: a local committee made her a present of a three-speed, all-weather bicycle. It cost the good people of the township no slight effort, for times were bad in the valley, many of the pits working half shift, and the pennies and sixpences that made up the subscription were desperately scarce. But its worth to Olwen, freed now from the drudgery of tramping her daily ten-mile round, was inestimable.

It was on this same machine, now far from new but still sturdy and serviceable, as she came to meet me on the amputation case, that I first saw Nurse Davies. She was a tall, solidly built woman of forty-seven then, her figure buxom, her face mature. But there was a steady frankness, an ardour in her clear grey eyes that bespoke a sincere and earnest soul. Many times when confronted by a situation beyond my experience—and, obliged as I was to undertake, on hope and a prayer, cases which would have made a Harley Street specialist blanch (this was no infrequent occurrence)—I found reassurance in her presence. Perhaps it was the way she had of standing at the bedside, of handing an instrument or a dressing, of murmuring encouragement when I was obviously in doubt and of rewarding me with a quiet glance of approval for anything well done.

Often in the midnight hours as we worked together in the cramped attic of a broken-down dwelling, fighting to save a human life, I marvelled at her fortitude and patience. At the pit head, when summoned for a surface accident, thanks to her indispensable bike she was usually there before me—calm, cheerful, and courageous. Most laudable of all was the work which she had done in opening, on her own initiative, a clinic for the children and aged people of the township, and which she held, every day, in a room rented, and paid for, by herself. It was this unconscious selflessness which, above all else, sounded the keynote of her character. Her thoughts were of others. She was never too busy to speak an extra word of sympathy, or too tired to rise at night for an urgent call.

She was no conventional saint. She enjoyed a cigarette with her coffee and, in later years, a glass of oatmeal stout. In a town of many chapels, she rarely went to church. Too busy, was her smiling excuse. Yet in all our association I never once heard her speak ill of anyone. She was not a clever woman, yet she possessed a priceless fund of common sense and an instinct of resourcefulness which never deserted her. Upon one unforgettable occasion, when the current failed in an isolated cottage during an emergency appendectomy and I, in the sudden blackness, stood helpless, she slipped outside, returning with a brilliant light by which the operation was successfully completed. It was her electric bicycle lamp.

That old black bicycle, it really seemed a part of her! When our vigil in the night had ended and she had brewed me a restoring cup of hot, strong coffee, she would nod a brisk good-bye and pedal back to her lodging beside her clinic. To tease her, I pretended to believe that she was, and would be all her life, geared to those inexorable wheels.

Often I wondered why she had never sought out a better position. The nurses with whom she had trained had all "got on"—indeed, one of them had recently been appointed matron of a great new hospital in Liverpool. When I read of this in the *Medical Journal*, I could not help remarking:

"You should have had that post. It's just what would have suited you."

"No." Nurse Davies raised her eyes steadily to mine and smiled her quiet, generous smile, without a trace of jealousy or rancour. "I'm not much good at managing people, and a bit rusty on surgical technique. I'm much happier, and a lot more use, careering around this old place."

One morning before breakfast as I was dressing, Mrs. Morgan came rushing to the bedroom, in a state of agitation contrasting strangely with her usual composure.

148

"Mr. Lewis wants to see you, Doctor. . . . It's Nurse Davies."

The colliery manager was downstairs. He looked at me from beneath drawn brows.

"You haven't heard?"

I shook my head, gripped by sudden alarm.

"She was biking to a case last night . . . out Blanethly way." He spoke with compressed lips. "A pylon had blown across the road. She ran smack into it in the dark. Lay all night in the wind and pouring rain before the men coming on day shift found her." A long moment of silence, then he added: "I think her back is broken."

Horrified, I snatched up my hat and coat, set off with him at once. As we hastened up the street together his profile was fixed and rigid.

"You didn't know, Doctor," he broke out suddenly, gazing straight ahead, "that years ago I asked her to marry me. But she wouldn't have me. Too bound up in her work." He paused. "Ay, devoted, devoted to her work."

At her lodging, whither they had taken her, I made a prolonged examination. Two of the lower spinal vertebrae were fractured, there was neither sensation nor power of movement in the lower limbs—a total paralysis. Serious, too, was the intense occipital headache of which she complained. A lumbar puncture produced some alleviation of this pain; then we carried her to the station where she was placed on a double mattress in the guard's van of the forenoon train for Cardiff. Lewis and I went with her, and three hours later she was in the city infirmary.

Back in Tregenny we waited for news. At first it was doubtful that she would survive. Then came word of a series of operations, long and complex—nothing is more protracted than surgery of the spine—and for hours she was upon the operating table. Afterward, weeks in plaster of Paris, massage, electrical therapy. Finally, the devastating verdict—it had all been in vain, she would never walk again.

The weeks went past. We had a new nurse now, a young probationer, who worked well enough on the district. But there her activities ceased—the clinic, which had been Nurse Davies' special charge,

149

was not reopened. And here more than anywhere was the old nurse missed.

One afternoon, as I passed the disused room in Chapel Street I drew up short. Was it fancy, or merely an illusion springing from momentary recollection, a sudden memory of the past? I had thought I heard her voice. Instinctively I threw open the door. Then I saw something which made my heart turn in my breast.

There, in a wheel chair, her hair turned completely grey, bent a little, much thinner, her paralysed legs covered by a rug, but still in her uniform, was the old district nurse. Surrounded by her patients, children mostly, she steered herself skilfully about the room, whirling the spokes of her mobile chair with a practised touch. Motionless, I stood in the shadow. When the last patient left the room she had barely time to spin round before I went forward and clasped her hands—those worn, capable hands that had served the needs of others for so long.

"Nurse Davies . . . Olwen! You're all right."

She gave me her rare smile.

"Why not? Can't you see . . . ? I'm back at work"—her smile deepened—"and still on wheels!"

# Chapter Seventeen

A WET AND DARK December night. The wind howled down the narrow valley among the scattered rows of houses, driving the rain against the window panes and scouring the deserted streets in hissing gusts. The shops were long since shut, and only a bleary gleam came through the blinds of the Tregenny Arms.

When I had finished my last round I came in, soaked to the skin, tired as a beaten dog, utterly dispirited. It was one of those days when I cursed the fate that had brought me to Tregenny. I was, I told myself bitterly, no selfless altruist, no saint, like poor Olwen Davies, no fond and fervent martyr in the cause of suffering humanity. And after eleven months in this dismal place, lost amidst the black Carmarthen mountains, doing my own dispensing in the ramshackle surgery, walking interminable distances since I could not afford a gig, I was beginning to feel that I had the worst end of the bargain. The place itself, less from drab ugliness than from its queer and unearthly detachment, was utterly foreign to me. There seemed, indeed, in the very air of this remote village a queer sense of unreality and superstition which grew upon one like a ghostly fantasy. Many of the people were friendly now, yet beneath the surface strange currents ran, and depths existed that I could not plumb. They were secretive, fiercely religious. On Sundays hymns came sounding from the chapels, Zion, Bethel, Ebenezer, and Bethesda, so loud and passionate the very mountains appeared to take the chanting up and echo it to heaven.

At such moments, the air vibrating with atonement, redemption,

151

and salvation, cynicism was no armour; one felt, almost with a thrill of fear, the presence of the supernatural.

I had little heart that night for supper, although my good wife, seeing me depressed, urged me to it. After a mug of hot cocoa and a mouthful of bread and cheese, I flung myself into bed, bone-weary, praying that I would not be disturbed. I fell into a heavy sleep.

The faint whirring of a bell half awakened me. On and on it went, so damnably insistent it would not let me be. Still dazed with sleep, I fumbled in the darkness and took up the telephone receiver beside my bed. A woman's voice spoke instantly, but from a far way off.

"Come at once, Doctor. Come to Evan Evans' house by Ystfad."

I groaned.

"I can't possibly get up to Ystfad tonight."

"But you must come tonight, Doctor, bach. . . ."

"Who are you?"

"I am Evan Evans' wife. And my daughter is very ill."

"I'll come in the morning, I tell you."

"Oh, no indeed, you must come now. For God's sake, Doctor, you must come now."

I could have sworn aloud—of all the miseries which afflict the weary and overworked doctor, a night call is the worst. But against my own inclination, the pleading, the pitiful urgency of the voice persuaded me. I dropped the receiver, lay for a moment collecting my scattered wits, then I rose, tumbled into my damp clothes, and picked up my bag.

Outside the rain had ceased, but the wind was high and bitter cold, driving dark scuds of cloud across an icy moon. The mountains rose in wild and haggard majesty upon a scene so starkly desolate that instinctively I shivered and drew my scarf about me. I knew—at least, I thought I knew—what lay before me: a five-mile walk toYstfad, which stood halfway up the ridge of Penpentre, the highest peak in that rugged chain. And as I stumbled along the broken mountain road, with time for reflection, I began to recollect a vague story of this man, Evan Evans, whose wife had called me out.

It was little enough I had heard, and in this uncommunicative spot might well have been less. Evans had lived, at one time, in

152

Tregenny itself, where he had been an outstanding member of the small community. He was not a highly educated man, yet he was respected and prosperous, the owner of the snug little "outcrop" pit known as Tregenny No. 1. But one day, by some unhappy chance, a dispute had arisen between himself and the main Tregenny Coal Company concerning the matter of a wayleave underground. The question was negligible, even trivial, but Evans was a violent man, especially when what he termed "his rights" were questioned. The dispute became a quarrel and then a lawsuit. Evans lost his suit. Immediately he took it to appeal. He lost his appeal. Burning with resentment, he took it to a higher court. Again he lost. And so the process was continued until finally, beaten and despoiled, his money dissipated, his colliery sold above his head, he had retired, a warped and ruined man, to a forsaken house on the mountainside by Ystfad, which had long lain empty and desolate. There he had remained for years hating and avoiding his fellow men, perhaps a little crazy from his misfortunes, until he had become an almost legendary figure. He guarded his seclusion jealously, but in the autumn evenings he might be seen, a dim, gaunt figure, shooting the wild snipe on the ridges, and sometimes at night he would gallop his pony along the moonlit summit, wildly, as though he rode against the world.

This was Evans, then, so far as scanty rumour had brought him to my notice, and after a journey which seemed unending, I reached his lonely house at last. Large and rambling, adjoined by a huddle of outbuildings, it was, whatever its history in better times, now a gloomy and dilapidated barracks. Not a glimmer of light was visible as I trudged up the narrow path, and no sound broke the universal stillness but the remote hooting of an owl. I pulled the bell. There was no answer. I stood for a moment listening, and hearing nothing but that distant, mocking owl, then with a sudden rush of impatience I battered my fist against the heavy door.

Immediately there arose a furious barking of dogs, and after a long delay the door was opened by an oldish woman in a dingy black dress and shawl. While she peered at me with a frightened, hooded face that seemed as heavy, and as pale—by the lantern she held—as a bladder of lard, two hounds skulked about her heels, showing their

153

teeth and growling at me. Annoyed by this reception, I pushed past her through the hall and into a large stone-flagged room, barely furnished and badly lit, that seemed half kitchen and half parlour. Here my eyes fell at once upon a young girl who lay, unconscious, wrapped in blankets, upon a horsehair sofa beside the fire. Beside her, bowed in an attitude of heavy watchfulness, sat a gaunt and powerful man. His physique was, in fact, tremendous—six foot six he must have stood when his great, wasted frame was raised erect. He was in his shirt sleeves, wore rough grey knickerbockers and no shoes, and his air of general disorder was heightened almost to the uncouth by a mane of iron-grey hair which fell in tangles about his head. He might have been fifty-five years of age. He was Evan Evans without a doubt.

So intent was his scrutiny of the sick girl, he did not hear me enter, but as I heaved my bag upon the table, he swung round with alarming suddenness, his eyes glittering in his dark face with such wildness that I was fairly taken aback.

"What do you want?"

He spoke thickly, with a husky intonation, and I thought at first he was drunk. I answered with as much moderation as I could muster:

"I'm the doctor. If you step aside I'll have a look at the patient. She looks pretty bad."

"Doctor!" He repeated the word with a kind of brooding wonder. Then the blood flooded his brow. Though he did not raise his voice, an indescribable menace filled it. "I won't have any doctors here. I won't have anybody here. Get out. D'you hear me, get out."

His manner was formidable in the extreme, yet a sense of real indignation sustained me. I thought of my trouble in answering this call, my weary walk through the darkness, and this boorish treatment at the end of it. I said hotly:

"You're crazy to talk like that. Your daughter is seriously ill. You've only got to look at her to see it. Don't you want me to try to help her?"

He winced when I said that and darted toward the sofa a furtive glance in which there was a sudden and almost piteous fear.

154

"I don't trust doctors," he muttered sullenly. "Not for my daughter. I don't trust anyone."

Silence in that strange and barren room. What was there to be done? I glanced toward the woman, who stood in mortal terror by the doorway, her hands clasped weakly upon her breast. I presumed that she had shot her bolt in summoning me against her lord and master's will. No further help could be expected there. Only one course seemed likely to succeed. With a set face I moved to the table and picked up my bag in the pretence of leaving.

"Very well. If your daughter dies you know who is responsible."

For a moment he remained motionless, clenching and unclenching his fingers, his cheek twitching indecisively, his gaze filled with the conflict between his hatred and his fear. Then when my hand was almost on the door, with a sobbing breath that seemed torn from his great chest, he cried:

"Don't go. If she's bad like you say, you better look at her."

I came back slowly and, advancing to the sofa, knelt down and examined the patient. She was older than I had imagined, about eighteen years, and despite the coma which held her, there was in her slender immaturity a strange, uncared-for beauty. A sudden pity seized me. She was so helpless here in such surroundings, thrown on the mercy of such incompetent parents. She moaned when I moved her gently. Her skin was burning to the touch, but showed no signs of rash. Her lungs were clear; her heart gave no evidence of murmurs or friction. I was puzzled as to the cause of the infection. And then I saw the faint but dusky swelling behind her left ear—acute suppurative mastoiditis. When I had made quite sure I turned to Evans.

"You ought to have sent for me days ago."

"It is only a blast," he muttered, using the local idiom for inflammation. "We have used goose grease and bran poultice. I am after fetching leeches tomorrow from the lake by Penpeoch. She will be better then."

"She will be dead then."

His jaw dropped and his gaunt cheeks turned bone-white. He stood before me like a man paralysed. The woman, glancing from my face

155

to his, wrung her hands together and set up a wild wailing in Welsh.

"Look here, Evans,"—I spoke vehemently in my effort to convince him—"you must understand me. The whole of this mastoid bone is filled with pus. Unless it is opened up and drained it will break through the skull into the brain. You know what that means. If we don't do something at once, your daughter has about six hours to live."

He reached out to the wall as if for support. His great frame seemed to shrink into itself. His eyes never left my face. At last he moistened his lips.

"Is that the truth?"

"What earthly reason have I for lying?"

A short silence. I saw his jaw clench with a sudden and painful spasm.

"Do it then"—he paused—"she must get better."

He said no more, yet the glitter in his eyes, which remained fastened on me, was unmistakable. I saw his delusion—that the hand of every man was turned against him. He was trusting me against his will because necessity and fear compelled him. And, at a sudden thought, a thrill of apprehension shot through me. I had persuaded him to let me operate. What would happen if I failed?

But there was no time to dwell on this reflection, not a second to lose. I opened my bag, laid out my instruments and dressings, prepared two basins of carbolic solution, then between us we lifted the patient, a slight burden, onto the bare wooden table. The pungent odour of the anaesthetic rose into the smoky air.

The light, a glaring oil lamp, held by Evans, was atrocious, the conditions unimaginably bad. As my first incision slit up the puffy skin behind the ear I realized that I had to make only one slip, one single error of judgement, and I would penetrate, fatally, the lateral sinus of the brain. I worked by a kind of instinct, and through it all painfully conscious that the wild eyes of Evan Evans were bent upon me. I was down to the bone now, the delicate bone of the skull. With a small gouge I cut into the antrum. The tissue offered more resistance than I had expected from necrotic bone, and there was no trace of pus. Was there no pus after all? Slowly, I went deeper, and deeper

156

still. And then, when I felt I must surely pierce the dura into the very cerebrum itself, a heavy bead of pus welled up through the spongy cells.

Hurriedly, I took a spoon and cleared out the pent-up matter, then carefully scraped the cavity, washed it with antiseptic, packed it with iodoform gauze. Quickly, quickly, I finished the work. Five more minutes and the patient was back upon her improvised bed, breathing quietly and deeply, as if asleep. Her pulse was stronger and a better colour tinged her skin. I was convinced that, free of the morbid centre of infection, with her healthy young constitution, she would recover.

As I packed my bag, filled with that sense of achievement which comes on rare occasions to the long-suffering general practitioner, the feeling of having justified oneself, of having succeeded against long odds, I threw a look at Evans. He stood by the table where, during the past hour, he had remained immobile and inarticulate, watching me. I noted that the sullenness was gone from his dark face, which now wore a singular embarrassment. I said briefly and with grim triumph:

"She'll do now."

He did not answer for a minute; then he muttered:

"Yes, indeed; she does look better."

I could see that he was rent by a new emotion—gratitude. And somehow at the sight of him there, with his great dangling hands and his troubled brow, my anger died. He was so deeply affected by the prospect of his daughter's recovery. And in a milder manner, nodding toward the woman of the house, who had at that moment taken a chair by the bed, I said:

"One thing you mustn't forget. You owe it to your wife for asking me to come."

His sombre eyes followed mine in complete bewilderment.

"I do not understand. That is Gwynneth, our servant." He added, "She can't speak English—only Welsh."

I stared at him.

"But, man alive," I expostulated, "don't you know that's how I got the call? She telephoned me to come here."

157

He gazed at me wonderingly.

"There is no telephone here. Nor for miles by here."

One glance convinced me that he spoke the truth. My head reeled. I faced him dizzily.

"Good God, don't you realise that your wife begged me to make this call? She spoke to me this very night. Do you hear me? I asked her who she was. She told me plainly that she was your wife."

He flushed darkly and, towering above me, raised his clenched fist. I thought he was about to fell me to the ground. Then with a great effort he mastered himself.

"You don't know about my wife." He broke off, his injected eye searching my startled face, then with a sobbing cry: "Haven't they told you it happened . . . because I wouldn't have a doctor . . . ? She died in this room five years ago."

I wish I might end the incident of this astral telephone call, this message coming so dramatically from the great beyond, on an eerie note of mystery. I should then receive many letters of appreciation from my spiritualist and crystal-gazing friends, from theosophical groups, and other bodies dedicated to the occult. Alas, my veracity compels me to record the truth, which I learned shortly afterward.

Evans' daughter had a solitary friend, a woman who knew the family's tragic history, knew also that the girl was desperately ill, and who, taking her courage in her hands but disguising her identity lest Evans should find her out, had at the last moment resolved to act, and put a call through in the name of Evans' wife.

She was the switchboard operator on the Tregenny telephone exchange.

# Chapter Eighteen

TIME WAS FLEETING—days, weeks, and months—and I was getting nowhere. In the first flush of my enthusiasm I had promised my darling wife—although now I did not use this term of endearment when her efforts at Welsh cooking made me dose myself with bicarbonate of soda and groan that she was slowly poisoning me—I had promised her, I repeated, riches, position, a house in Harley Street, and, if I recollect correctly, a villa on the Mediterranean. And here we still were, plodding along, trying to save a little money—a depressing state of affairs under any circumstances—never "getting out of the bit," as the Scots say, still buried alive in these wretched mountains. I chafed, used many strong words, and applied for many situations, all without avail. Then, one memorable day, I burst in with a letter.

"We're leaving. At the end of the month."

My partner in distress gazed back at me, wide-eyed.

"Leaving! But I'm just getting to like it here."

Was there ever so perverse a woman, trying to convince me that she had nobly settled down? I restrained myself.

"You'll like it better where we're going. It's a much finer job."

I handed her the letter. It was from the secretary of the Medical Aid Society in a neighbouring valley of Tredegar, offering me a post as doctor to the society. The salary was only slightly more than I was now being paid, but what caught the eye and made the pulse bound was the fact that a house—a real house—was included in the

terms of the appointment. Her nobility melted before such a temptation: she could scarcely bear to wait.

We remained long enough to enable the company to secure another
doctor—Dai Lewis was a sad man to see us go—then, packing our
few belongings into a borrowed truck, we took leave of the manager,
of Olwen Davies, and of melancholy Mrs. Morgan, climbed in beside
the driver, and set out over the high ridges for our new home.

Tredegar was a colliery town, too, but it was trim and clean and set
on the verge of still unspoiled hill country. There were several decent
stores, a public library, and—one could scarcely believe it—a town
hall where moving pictures were shown twice a week.

The little house to which my wife had looked forward was stoutly
built of red brick, with a gabled roof. Standing in a wild patch of
garden beside a clear mountain stream spanned by a wooden bridge,
it was appropriately named "The Glen." It seemed almost a mansion
after the two rooms we had previously occupied, and although her
brief but close association with me no longer permitted her to claim
to be a saintly character, she thanked Heaven sincerely for the blessing of at last having a place of her own. To such an end the labour
of moving in was as nothing—she greatly enjoyed getting things
into shape.

Also, there was plenty of interesting work for me. Under the
medical-aid scheme which had engaged me, all the miners paid a
small weekly contribution to the society and were entitled thereby to
free medical treatment for their families and themselves. In actual
fact, this scheme can definitely be regarded as the foundation of the
plan of socialised medicine which was eventually adopted by Great
Britain. Aneurin Bevan, the Minister of Health, who was mainly
responsible for the national project, was at one time a miner in
Tredegar, and here, under the local aid organization, the value of
prompt and gratuitous treatment for the worker was strongly impressed upon him.

There is certainly virtue in the scheme, but it also has its defects,
of which the chief one, in Tredegar, was this—with complete carte
blanche in the way of medical attention the people were not sparing,
by day or night, in "fetching the doctor." In a word, the plan fostered

hypochondriacs, malingerers, and those obnoxious "hangers-on" who haunt a doctor's surgery in the hope of obtaining something—spectacles, crepe bandages, cotton wool and dressings, even a Seidlitz powder—for nothing.

My real invalids were numerous, but I had also to deal with the other sort. There was one hale young woman who lay in bed all day long, and insisted on being visited, in the belief that she was consumptive—an *idée fixe* which no amount of argument could dispel. Many of the old-time miners affected the symptoms of nystagmus and beat knee, occupational diseases which entitled them to a pension, and as they were adept at what was known as "swinging the lead," they sometimes succeeded in confusing me. Also there were cases where the imagination held even greater sway upon tissues and mechanism of the body. I had in those early weeks a most remarkable example of that rare medical condition—pseudocyesis. This was a childless woman, aged forty, eminently respectable and married for fifteen years, who suddenly decided that she was pregnant and who, therefore, developed every sign and symptom of the condition. She had morning sickness, capricious appetite, typical breast changes, swelling of the abdomen, and, of course, amenorrhoea. Nothing could convince her that the condition was a pure neurosis. I could only repeat Lord Asquith's famous phrase: "Madam, we will wait and see." And, indeed, at the end of nine months, though she laboured greatly, she only brought forth . . . wind!

At first I was conciliatory toward such cases, but soon my patience wore thin and I developed a brusqueness which would have pleased that master of invective whose "Dammit to hell" had so often resounded in the cottages of Tannochbrae. On one occasion, at two in the morning, I was routed out, dog-tired, to see an old woman who, when I entered her room, exclaimed from her comfortable bed: "Oh, Doctor, Doctor bach, I cannot stop yawning." At which I glared at her and, as I made for the door, replied over my shoulder in broad Scots: "Then shut your b—— mouth!"

We had come in the month of October, and winter was soon upon us. Then, indeed, the going became fairly rough. Our finances were still so straitened that a car was out of the question, and I

161

would tramp miles through the snow in leggings and oilskins, carrying my heavy black bag. It was a relief when, for fifty pounds, I was able to purchase a secondhand motorcycle. Unfortunately this machine, bought through a seductive advertisement in a Birmingham paper extolling its beauty and speed, proved to be a heavy twin-cylinder racer with a huge exhaust and no kick starter. How often, panting and sweating, did I push this brutal contraption halfway along the road before it suddenly flamed and exploded into action. Yet once in motion, it went like the wind.

This was a time of great happiness. Our simple furnishings came from the local store, our rugs were certainly not from Persia, nor were our pictures from the best galleries, yet we had both pride and comfort in our small domain. On the cold nights we sat before our blazing fire—coal was plentiful and free—reading, talking, arguing. We had tremendous arguments. Unbelievably, my wife's cooking improved. She even revealed herself as a skilful gardener, raising tulips and noble hyacinths in the tiny glassed-in porch of the house.

Many sunny days came that winter, and when we were free to explore it we found a wild beauty on the high, bare heath which stretched far and away above "The Glen." A breeze always blew there, intoxicating as wine, which made me misquote Walt Whitman: "There's a wind on the heath; when I feel it on my cheek I want to live forever." For miles under the racing clouds one would be lost in the exhilarating vastness of this primitive moorland, cut only by a few sheep tracks—then suddenly, breasting a crest, we would see the little town with the colliery headstocks far beneath, and would sit down to rest and to pick out, with pride, the toylike house which was our home.

Much of our outdoor leisure was spent up there. We took prodigious walks, gathered, "whinberries" for deep-dish pie in the summer and in the fall, borrowing the colliery undermanager's gun, I went out after the snipe which wheeled and darted and always seemed to elude me.

In my medical knowledge I was progressing steadily, making friends among my patients and, at the cost of a few humiliations, learning that I did not quite know everything. The chief doctor of the district, Dr. Davies, was not only a highly skilled physician, with several exclusive London diplomas, but a brilliantly successful surgeon as well. When he consulted with me over a difficult or serious case, rolling up in his large spotless chauffeur-driven limousine while his younger colleague arrived on foot or on that execrable mud-spattered machine, often he differed, in the kindest manner, yet with authority, with my diagnosis.

After such interviews I would sit all evening, grinding my teeth, muttering invectives against my worthy superior. Then suddenly I would jump up. "Damn it all, he's right and I'm wrong. It *was* t.b. meningitis, and I should have spotted it days ago. I know nothing, absolutely nothing, but I will—I tell you I will!"

To my audience of one, knitting sedately on the other side of the fireplace, this might well have seemed a natural pique, soon to be passed over and forgotten. But no, I was in dead earnest. Davies had shown me my limitations; I knew I should never progress until I had overcome them.

I could sense my spouse wondering how this quest of knowledge would reveal itself. And soon she knew, for presently there began to arrive at "The Glen" a succession of large crates which at first sight looked as though they might contain interesting articles like new sheets or table linen or a set of dinner china (which she badly needed), but which, under my vigorous assaults with the hammer, revealed nothing more exciting than dozens of large, thick, and horribly abstruse-looking medical textbooks. Not having enough spare cash to purchase the books, I had joined the library of the Royal Society in London—in fact, it looked as though the entire library now were here, and it was only the beginning.

Now, every night when I came in from my eight o'clock surgery, I sat down before these books. Often, after a punishing day's work, I was so weary I could scarcely keep my eyes open. But with relentless determination—a grim strain strangely incompatible with my mild and amiable disposition—I forced myself to study, often reading until one o'clock in the morning.

After several months it became necessary for me to put in some practical work in biochemistry. The nearest laboratory was in the

Health Department of Cardiff, more than fifty miles away. But this did not deter me. I applied to the secretary of the Medical Aid Society for four hours off duty on Thursday afternoons, and when this request was granted I departed every week on my motorcycle for the distant city. By making the journey at breakneck speed, I could secure two full hours in the laboratory before returning to my evening surgery.

It was misery, not for me, but for my poor wife who had a ghastly premonition that I would kill myself on that winding valley road. These afternoons became a nightmare for her, and as six o'clock drew near she would sit with her eyes on the clock, her ears straining for the sound of that infernal exhaust. Quarter past six . . . then half past. . . . At last, when she saw herself already a widow—young, no doubt, and interesting, but still desperate with grief—a shattering roar would make her gasp with relief.

I would enter, dusty, covered with methylene blue and Canada balsam, but in the highest of spirits and usually bearing a small gift which I had brought her from civilization—a certain kind of coffeecake which she was specially fond of, or, more rarely, since I rather liked the coffeecake myself, a bunch of violets. How pleased she was by such consideration, how gay were these evening reunions!

Of course, neither of us realised in the slightest the craziness of my project, which was to take no less than three major postgraduate degrees to supplement my M.B., Ch.B.: the M.D., the M.R.C.P., and the D.P.H. of London. For a practitioner commanding the expert teaching and highly technical resources of the great hospitals and universities, this constitutes a formidable enterprise, in which the average failures are more than 75 per cent. For an overworked colliery assistant, equipped only with borrowed books, prepared by no more than a few hasty dashes to a provincial laboratory, the thing was surely an impossibility.

I shall never forget the wet and windy day on which I departed for London to sit the examinations, nor the pessimistic bulletins, each gloomier than its predecessor, which I felt obliged to send home during the ensuing week. It is a strange contradiction in my character that, despite the confidence which sustains me during months of effort, the actual test of that effort finds me dispirited and hopeless. All my striving, my frenzied efforts, my almost hysterical outbursts seemed far away and done with. My brain was inactive, almost dull. I felt that I knew nothing. Indeed, when I began the written part of the examination, which was held at the College of Physicians, in Trafalgar Square, I found myself answering the papers with a blind automatism. I wrote and wrote, never looking at the clock, filling sheet after sheet, until my head reeled.

I had taken a room at the Museum Hotel, a modest establishment where I had stayed during the war on my first visit to London. Here it was extremely cheap. But the food was vile, adding the final touch to my upset digestion, and literally doubling me up with a bad attack of dyspepsia. I was compelled to restrict my diet to hot malted milk. A tumblerful of this innocuous beverage in an A.B.C. tearoom in the Strand was my lunch. Between my papers I lived in a kind of daze. I did not dream of going to a cinema, a music hall, or any other place of amusement. I scarcely saw the people in the streets. Occasionally, to clear my head, I took a ride on the top of an omnibus.

After the written papers the practical and viva-voce part of the examination began, and I was more afraid of these than anything which had gone before. There were perhaps thirty other candidates, all of them men older than myself, and all with an unmistakable air of assurance and position. The candidate placed next to me, for instance, a man named Harold Beaumont whom I had once or twice spoken to, had an Oxford B.Ch., an out-patient appointment at St. Bartholomew's, and a consulting room in ultrafashionable Brook Street. When I compared Beaumont's charming manners, immaculate professional attire, and obvious standing with my own provincial awkwardness I felt my chances of favourably impressing the examiners to be small indeed.

My practical, at the South London Hospital, went, I thought, well enough. My case was one of bronchiectasis in a young boy of fourteen, which, since I had met this condition in my practice, was a piece of good fortune. I felt I had written a sound report. But when it came to the viva-voce my luck seemed to change completely. The "viva" procedure at the College of Physicians had its peculiarities.

On two successive days each candidate was questioned, in turn, by two separate examiners. If at the end of the first session the candidate was found inadequate, he was handed a polite note telling him he need not return on the following day. Faced with the imminence of this fatal missive, I found to my horror that I had drawn as my first examiner a man I had heard Beaumont speak of with apprehension, Dr. Maurice Gadsby.

Gadsby was a spare undersized man with a pigeon chest, a tremendous "ha-ha" manner, and a beribboned monocle in his small, severe eye. Recently elected to his Fellowship, he had none of the tolerance of the older examiners, but seemed to set out deliberately to confuse and confound the candidates who came before him. Somewhat to my surprise, he greeted me, repeated my name several times, then demanded:

"Are you Richard's younger brother? Dick was at Cambridge with me, you know."

When I confessed, reluctantly, that I had no brother, he was plainly disappointed—indeed, almost aggrieved. He inspected me through the monocle.

"Were you at Cambridge?"

"No, sir."

"The other shop?"

"What shop, sir?"

"Oxford, of course."

"No, sir."

"Then what university?"

"Glasgow."

A hollow, devastating silence. He did not deign to comment but, with a supercilious lift to his brows, placed before me six slides. Five of these slides I named correctly, but the sixth I could not name. It was on this slide that Gadsby concentrated with all the contempt of one to whom the mere mention of a Scots university was almost obscene. For five minutes he harassed me on this section—which, it appeared, was the ovum of an obscure West African parasite—then languidly, without interest, he passed me on to the next examiner,

166

who was none other than Lord Dawson of Penn, Physician to the King.

I rose and crossed the room with a pale face and a heavily beating heart. All the lassitude, the inertia I had experienced at the beginning of the week was gone now. I had an almost desperate desire to succeed. But I was convinced that Gadsby would fail me. I raised my eyes to find Lord Dawson contemplating me with a friendly, half-humorous smile.

"What's the matter?" he asked, unexpectedly.

"Nothing, sir," I stammered. "I think I've done rather badly with Dr. Gadsby—that's all."

"Never mind about that. Have a look at these specimens. Then just say anything about them that comes into your head."

Dawson smiled encouragingly. He was a handsome, fair-complexioned man of about sixty with a high forehead and a long, humorous upper lip masked by a cropped moustache. Though now perhaps the second most distinguished physician in Europe, he had known difficulties and sharp struggles in his earlier days when, coming from his native Yarrow, he had encountered prejudice and opposition in London. As he gazed at me, without seeming to do so, he could not but observe my ill-cut suit, the soft collar and shirt, the cheap, ill-knotted tie, above all, the look of strained intensity upon my serious face, and it may have been that memories of his own youth came back to him, instinctively enlisting his sympathy on my behalf. He nodded encouragingly as, with my eyes fixed upon the glass jars before me, I stumbled unhappily through a commentary upon the specimens.

"Good," he said as I concluded. He took up another specimen—it was an aneurism of the ascending aorta—and began in a companionable manner to interrogate me. His questions, from being simple, gradually became wider and more searching in their scope, until finally they came to bear upon a recent specific treatment by the induction of malaria. But, opening out under his sympathetic manner, I answered well.

Finally, as he put down the glass jar, Dawson remarked:

167

"Can you tell me anything of the history of aneurysm?"

"Ambroise Paré," I answered, and my examiner had already begun his approving nod, "is presumed to have first discovered the condition."

Lord Dawson's face showed surprise.

"Why 'presumed'? Paré did discover aneurysm."

I reddened, then turned pale as I plunged on:

"Well, sir, that's what the textbooks say. You'll find it in every book—I myself took the trouble to verify that it was in six." A quick breath. "But I happened to be reading Celsus, brushing up my Latin —which needed brushing up, sir—when I definitely came across the word *aneurismus*. Celsus knew aneurysm. He described it in full. And that was a matter of thirteen centuries before Paré!"

There was a silence. I raised my eyes, prepared for kindly satire from His Majesty's physician. Decidedly he was looking at me with a queer expression, and for a long time he was silent.

"Doctor," he exclaimed at last, "you are the first candidate in this examination hall who has ever told me something original, something true, and something which I did not know. I congratulate you."

I turned scarlet again.

"Just tell me one thing more—as a matter of personal curiosity," he concluded. "What do you regard as the main principle—the, shall I say, the basic idea which you keep before you when you are exercising the practice of your profession?"

There was a pause while I reflected desperately. At length, feeling I was spoiling all the good effect I had created, I blurted out:

"I suppose—I suppose I keep telling myself never to take anything for granted."

"Thank you, Doctor. . . . Thank you very much."

A few minutes later I went downstairs with the other candidates. At the foot of the stairs beside his leather-hooded cave a liveried porter stood with a little pile of envelopes before him. As the candidates went past he handed an envelope to each of them. Beaumont, walking out next to me, tore his open quickly. His expression altered; he said quietly, with impeccable good form:

168

"It would appear I'm not wanted tomorrow." Then, forcing a smile, "How about you?"

My fingers were shaking. I could barely read. Dazedly I heard Beaumont congratulate me. My chances were still alive. I walked down to the A.B.C. and treated myself to a double malted milk. I thought tensely, "If I don't get through now, after all this, I'll—I'll walk in front of a bus."

The next day passed grindingly. Barely half the original candidates remained, and it was rumoured that out of these another half would go. I had no idea whether I was doing well or badly: I knew only that my head ached abominably, that my feet were icy, my inside void.

At last it was over. At four o'clock in the afternoon I came out of the cloakroom, spent and melancholy, pulling on my coat. Then I became aware of Dawson of Penn standing before the big open fire in the hall. I made to pass. But Dawson, for some reason, was holding out his hand, smiling, speaking to me, telling me—telling me that I was now a Member of the Royal College of Physicians.

Dear God, I had done it! I had *done* it! I was alive again, gloriously alive, my headache gone, all my weariness forgotten. As I dashed down to the nearest post office my heart sang wildly, madly. I was through, I had done it, not from the West End of London, but from an outlandish mining town. My whole being was a surging exultation. It hadn't been for nothing after all: those long nights, those mad dashes down to Cardiff, those racking hours of study. On I sped, bumping and cannoning through the crowds, missing the wheels of taxis and omnibuses, my eyes shining, racing, racing to telephone news of the miracle back home. But no, some latent dramatic instinct made me hold things a little longer in suspense. Instead of the full, effusive message I had planned, I sent simply a brief wire asking my wife to come at once to London . . . no more than that curt command. She obeyed, fearing the worst, expecting to find me sick in hospital, perhaps on the verge of suicide. I met her at Victoria Station, tense and pale, with a dreadful glitter in my eye. Then I smiled and hugged her. Gave her thus, holding her tight, the incredible news, blatantly assured her that we were already on the way to Harley Street.

How good life seemed at that moment! How wonderful to share this joy with one so deeply loved! At first neither of us could speak; then we both started to talk at once. I crowded her into a taxi, whirled off to the Savoy. We celebrated recklessly, my dyspepsia forgotten, on a seven-course spread; went on to a George Edwards musical comedy; then to a champagne supper at the Café Royal, from which we emerged in a state of such sublime elation that the very pavements danced and swayed beneath our feet. We were both exhausted when, late the next evening, we reached the clear cold air of our mountain village and once again saw, under the high vault of heaven, the calm and reassuring stars.

# Chapter Nineteen

SOME EIGHT WEEKS later, on a crisp December morning, I came out, before breakfast, to the front porch, of "The Glen." The little town lay tranquilly before me, and as I gazed at its familiar outlines, the thought of our impending departure gave me a pang of regret. For three years now we had lived in Tredegar. Here we had really taken up the yoke of married life, here our first child had been born. The work which I had done might not rank high in the social or professional scale. I didn't wear a frock coat and a stiff collar, but more often than not leggings and hobnail boots. I usually walked straight into my patients' houses without knocking. I had no bedside manner to speak of, and could discourage a malingerer with the rudest adjectives. Yet I had made many friends among the miners and officials of the surrounding collieries. They never directly paid me fees—as I have explained, my quarterly cheque came from the society—but always at Christmas I received evidence of their regard in a host of homely presents. There would be a couple of ducks or chickens from one, a print of fresh butter from another, a hand-tufted rug from a third . . . nor should I neglect to mention old Mrs. Griffiths, whom I had almost (but, to be honest, not quite) cured of her rheumatism, and who hobbled across the bridge on New Year's Eve to offer us her blessings and a fine fat goose.

There was a quality in this gratitude which moved me profoundly —something which went deep down to the very roots of life. Then why should I be leaving? Most of my classmates at the University had already settled down permanently in steady provincial practices.

Alas, in me the urge to move forward was not to be denied. The previous month I had handed in my resignation—in another ten days we should be gone.

Suddenly, as I stood there, regretful, yet feeling my heart lift up at the prospect of new adventure, I heard a faint and distant concussion, less an actual detonation than a vibration of the air, as though a great harp string had been plucked by a giant hand, behind me. It came from the neighbouring valley, lasted only for a moment, then vanished, so slight, so swift to come and go, it seemed of little consequence. Yet to one acquainted with this district, surrounded by so many mines, it had an ominous significance, and I listened intently, anxiously, for a confirmation of my fear. Nothing happened, however, and a few minutes later I went in to breakfast. But I had barely begun my first cup of coffee when I heard a hooter sound the alarm, six long blasts—and almost at once the telephone rang. It was George Conway, secretary of the Medical Aid Society. Briefly he told me that a disaster had occurred in the Ystfad Colliery at Pengelly across the mountain, they had sent out a routine call for aid. Would I go over at once?

Hastily, I swallowed a few mouthfuls of food, finished my coffee, and set off across the ridge on my motor bike. It was no more than two miles by mountain track to Pengelly, and I reached the village in less than five minutes. Yet already the news of the calamity was travelling through the narrow streets. Doors in the terraces were open, men and women rushing downhill toward the colliery. As they ran, more ran with them. They ran as if they could not help themselves, as if the pit had suddenly become a magnet drawing them irresistibly toward it.

When I arrived, five hundred men and women had gathered on the outskirts of the pit yard, and there were more outside. They stood in silence, the women mostly in shawls, the men without overcoats. It had been snowing here and their figures were very black against the white snow. They stood like some vast chorus, massed in silence under the clear sky. They were not the actors in the drama, but they were of it none the less.

Eight o'clock had just struck when I pushed my way into the pit

172

yard and entered the wooden colliery office, where a number of the surface crew, all in their working clothes, were collected. The mine manager, Dai Jenkins, whom I knew well, was there with his deputy, Tom Lewis, looking at the crowd. As I entered the deputy was saying:

"Will I have the yard gates shut?"

"No," answered the other. "Have a fire lighted in the yard, a large fire. It's cold for them standing there, and God knows they may stand long enough."

In the pause which followed I asked what had happened. At first Jenkins did not seem to hear, then, turning upon me his strained and harassed gaze, he told me that water had broken into the pit from the old workings. Both main shafts were flooded and both morning shifts, sixty-one men in all, were entombed. They were waiting for the first rescue party to bring heavy pumping equipment from the emergency centre at Gilfach. They could not tell how things were underground, having lost all contact with the trapped men. They could only wait for the moment, until the rescue party arrived. As he spoke, more people came crowding into the office—two of the underviewers, a young inspector of mines, another colliery manager from further down the valley, and a party of volunteers from the neighbouring colliery. There was no confusion, no babble of voices, but an attitude of such deep gravity it filled me with foreboding.

Suddenly, in the midst of this tense expectancy, the mine telephone whirred—not the public-service instrument upon the manager's desk, but the wall attachment of the colliery system which communicated only with the underground workings. Instantly, there was a mortal silence, then, in three strides, Jenkins was at the phone. He spun the little handle violently, lifted the receiver.

"Hello, hello!" Then his face paled, he half turned to the other: "My God . . . it's Roberts."

At first I did not understand. Then I realised, with a contraction of my heart, that a voice, the voice of a man not yet dead, was rising out of the dark tomb of the flooded mine, fleeing in despairing hope over waterlogged wires to us, on the surface, two miles away.

"Hello, hello." Jenkins was listening now, he listened for three minutes with strained intentness, then rapidly, in a hard clear voice, he began to speak. "Listen to me, Roberts, bach. You must make for the old Penygroes shaft. You can't come out this way—both shafts are water-sealed, and it may be days before we clear them. You must travel the old workings. Go right up the slant. Break through the frame dam at the top east side. That takes you into the upper level of the old workings. Don't be afraid of water, that's all in the bottom levels. Go along the road, it's all main road, don't take the trenches nor the right dip, keep bearing due east for fifteen hundred yards until you strike the old Penygroes shaft."

A thick, roaring noise came over the wire, audible in the room, and Jenkins' voice rose feverishly to a shout.

"Do you hear me? The rescue party will meet you there. Do you hear me?" But his words were lost as a water blast tore out the wires and left the instrument dead in his hand. He let it fall—it swung dangling, while he stood there, bowed, motionless. At last, wiping his brow, he revealed to us what Roberts had told him.

The first shift underground had been working their heading in the usual way, drilling and shot-firing to bring down the coal. But Roberts, the undermanager, after the last two shots, found a thin trickle of water coming from the middle of the coal face. There appeared to be no pressure behind it, but it had a bad smell of blackdamp; he knew it was not virgin coal water, and he did not like the look of it.

Immediately the men began to "tub" the water—to try to get rid of it by letting it through the pack walls on the low side of the drawing road. Meanwhile, Roberts felt it his duty to warn the second shift of twenty-three men working further underground, two hundred yards up the branch. He started off and had almost reached the other face when he heard a terrific bang. He knew it was an inrush. He had expected trouble but nothing so sudden or terrible as this. Instinctively, he turned back, but after going ten yards he saw the water rushing down the main haulage, roof-high, in a great swell of sound. The gas thrown back by the rushing water extinguished his lamp but as he stood, petrified, for ten seconds in the sounding darkness, he knew that the men of his first shift, all of them, were drowning, or already drowned, in that frightful flood. The speed

174

of the water was ferocious, its volume that of a tidal wave. On and out it swept, reached the pit shaft, spouted and cascaded, swirling the bodies of the first shift in a backlash, at pit bottom, drowning the ponies in their stalls there. As fast as one might think, the water had risen in the two main shafts, sealing the pit absolutely and preventing all access to the workings from the surface.

The suddenness of the calamity was unbelievable and deadly, but Roberts and his mates on the second shift were still alive. They were at the top of the slant and the inrush went away from them. They were altogether twenty-two men and a boy of fourteen, standing together without speech—they knew enough to make them silent. But Roberts had recovered himself—long familiar with the mine, he remembered a return airway through which he might lead the party to a higher level. Starting off, he found the airway, began to crawl along it, on his stomach, followed by the others. But before he had gone thirty yards, he felt himself turning sick and sleepy, and hurriedly he ordered his men back. The airway was full of blackdamp, carbon monoxide driven from the old waste workings by the water, and Roberts knew then that every escape road was blocked. Trapped in the high dead end of the branch, the water and blackdamp rising steadily about them, they had perhaps half an hour to live. It was then, in this last extremity, that Roberts had remembered the telephone.

When Jenkins finished speaking—and his account, terse and technical, was briefer by far than the explanation I have given here—for a full minute no one said anything. Then, in an even voice, Mr. Deakin, the mines inspector, broke out:

"If they get through to the old workings there's just a chance."

Jenkins nodded, turned to his deputy.

"Take ten men and go to old Penygroes shaft. Make an inspection —as quick and complete as you can. Find out the condition of the shaft. Then hurry back to me."

Meantime three trucks had rolled into the yard bringing the pumping gear, and the manager left the office to start off its erection. It would take hours to complete this heavy task, and I sensed that Jenkins had little faith in it. All his hopes were centred in these old

175

workings which honeycombed the deep, surrounding strata. If only they could be penetrated we might reach the trapped men.

Alone in the office, I now telephoned George Conway in Tredegar, giving him the facts of the disaster, asking if I should stay on duty at the pit. The secretary endorsed my desire to remain, indeed he insisted I hold myself, from now on, at Jenkins' disposal—Dr. Davies would take over my practice until further notice.

As I rejoined the group outside, the deputy came back from the old Penygroes shaft. There was rubbish and blackdamp in the shaft, he told Jenkins, a man lowered on a crab rope had come out pretty sick, but he believed the shaft could be cleared of gas and stowing in twenty-four hours.

Immediately, then, the necessary gear was assembled, and leaving the pump erection at the main headstocks to proceed, a party of picked men led by the manager and his deputy went out across the troubled ground toward the old shaft. Following the instructions I had been given, I went with them. It had turned colder and a few thin snowflakes began to fall, trembling gently out of the unseen sky.

The disused shaft lay in a wretched place of wasteland known as the Common, all hummocks and subsidences from the network of tunnels underneath, now covered with snow and swept by a bitter wind. Small wonder they called it "troubled land." Here they began to fit headgear, winding engine, and a fan.

In spite of the fire in the pit yard nearby, everybody had left the yard and stood gathered at the Common. They stood well back from the riggers who were raising the headstocks, working fast and hard.

Within three hours they had fitted headgear, steam winding engine, and fan; then they began to free the shaft of blackdamp. When the gas was finally cleared out, a fresh relay, standing ready, went in and started to remove the stowing which blocked the road into the waste. These men worked fast, so fast that they were clearing the stowing from the main road at the rate of six feet an hour. There was more stowing than they had thought. But the relays launched themselves in waves, they battered into the obstruction, there was something frantic and abandoned in their assault. It was more than

176

human progress; as one relay slipped in another staggered out.

"This road runs due west," said Jenkins to the inspector. "It ought to take us pretty near the mark."

"Yes," the other answered, "and we ought to be near the end of that damned stowing."

All day long this work went on, and by midnight the relays had cleared one hundred and forty feet of the old main road. Two hours later they broke through into clear road, into an open section of the old waste. A loud cheer rang out, a cheer which ascended the shaft and thrilled into the ears of those who still waited on the surface.

But there was no second cheer. Immediately beyond, by the light of torches, it was seen that the main road ran into a dip or trough which was full of water and impassable.

Dirty, covered with coal dust, wearing no collar and tie, the inspector stared at Jenkins.

"Oh, my good God!" he said hopelessly. "If only we'd known this before."

Jenkins remained unmoved.

"We must expect difficulties. We must blast a new road above the trough."

There was something so sternly inflexible in the manager's words that even the inspector was impressed.

"My God!" he said, exhausted to the verge of collapse. "That's the spirit. Come on, then, and we'll blast your blasted roof."

They began to blast the roof, to blast down the iron-hard whinstone into the water so that the trough might be filled and a road established above water level. A compressor was brought down to supply the drills; the finest diamond drill bores were used. The work was killing. It proceeded in darkness, dust, sweat, and the fumes of high explosive. It proceeded in a sort of insane frenzy. Only Jenkins remained calm. He was there, the motive, the directing force. For a full eighteen further hours he did not leave the Penygroes shaft. Yet he ordered the others to take some rest.

Emergency cots and blankets had been brought into the long "lamp room" in the pit yard, and here, with the inspector and other

177

officials, I stretched out and got six hours' sleep. Fresh from this res-
pite, the inspector pleaded with Jenkins to knock off.

"Take some sleep, for God's sake. You're killing yourself."

But the manager shook his head. All that day, and the next, he
snatched only an odd half hour on his office couch.

The whinstone blasting was proving incredibly difficult, an almost
insuperable task. As the hours moved on, with only the slowest
progress, insensibly hope began to fade. Nothing was said, but the
expressions of the rescuers reflected a growing desperation.

On the evening of the third day, Jenkins told me to spell off for
the night. As I passed through Pengelly on my way home the streets
were deserted, every door closed, not a single child at play. Many of
the shops were shuttered. A still agony lay upon the terraces, the
stillness of despair. From opposite ends of the street two women
approached. They were friends. They passed each other with averted
faces. Not a word. Silence: even their footsteps silenced by the
snow. Within the houses the same silence. In the houses of the entombed men the breakfast things were laid out upon the table in
preparation for their return. It was the tradition. Even at night the
blinds remained undrawn.

I returned to the pit early next morning. They had lowered the
water level in the main shaft—not the Penygroes shaft—sufficiently
to allow divers to descend. The divers had to contend with a maxi-
mum head of eighteen feet of water in the levels. In spite of this
they fought their way along the levels as far as the fall. They made an
arduous, exhaustive search. No one knew better than they how useless this search would be. All that the divers found was thirty-eight
drowned bodies.

The divers came back. They reported the absence of any living
soul. They reported that at least another month would be required to
dewater the levels completely. Then they started to bring out the
bodies: the drowned men, roped together, dangling out of the mine
into the brightness of the day they did not see, laid silently on stretch-
ers, and given to their womenfolk in that snow-trodden yard.

Everything now was concentrated on the approach by Penygroes.
Yet any hope that remained seemed forlorn. It was fully realised

that the men unaccounted for might never have reached the waste. Moreover, eight days had now elapsed since the date of the disaster, and it was a slender chance that these men might still be alive. Nevertheless, in a fresh frenzy of endeavour, efforts above the trough were redoubled. The rescuers spurted, strained every nerve. Six days after blasting was begun the last charge was fired, they broke through and regained the old main roadway beyond the trough. Exhausted but jubilant, the rescuers pressed forward. They were met, sixty paces due west, by a complete fall of whinstone roof. They drew up hopelessly.

"Oh, my God!" the inspector moaned. "There might be a half mile of this. We'll never reach them, never. This is the end at last." Utterly spent, he leaned against the whinstone rock and buried his face in his arm.

"We must go on," Jenkins said with sudden loudness, and a note of hysteria in his voice. "We must go on."

At that moment, when all seemed lost, a faint, unearthly sound was heard in that unfathomable darkness, an almost ghostly tapping: tap, tap . . . , tap, tap . . . , tap, tap, tap, tap, like a weak tattoo beat out upon a tribal drum.

"For God's sake, listen . . . ! Can't you hear it . . . ? The jowling."

Jowling is the name given to that method of signifying one's position by striking the rock face with a hammer; many men have been saved by jowling their rescuers toward them. Everyone stood stock-still, with straining ears. Feebly, wearily, as though by one long since exhausted, the tapping was repeated.

"By God, you're right," cried the inspector. "They're there . . . , close to us . . . , just through the rock. They hear us."

"Stand back, behind there," shouted Jenkins through cupped hands.

A final wild blaze of effort, then, with a rending crash of whinstone, we were through, through to the imprisoned men.

There they lay, huddled together, with their backs against the branch wall, silent and spectral forms, clothed by their own comradeship, a few guttered-out pit candles at their feet.

But they were alive, every man of them; yes, the boy was alive as well, crying softly to himself as we came forward.

179

They were all too weak to stir themselves, nor would I permit them to be moved until I had administered to each one a pint of strong bouillon laced with brandy, glucose solution, and a hypodermic of strychnine.

"They'll recover, Doctor?" Jenkins asked anxiously.

"Yes . . . , every one of them."

Slowly, carefully, we brought them out. News of the rescue had preceded us and as we came forth to the surface there arose in a great volume of sound, soberly, yet spontaneously, swelling to the sky from the huge congregation assembled on the troubled wasteland of the Common, that favourite Welsh hymn, "O God, our help in ages past."

It was a moment of emotion that rent the heart, a sight I shall never forget. Yet through it all, the triumph of achievement, the gladness of reunion, one could not forget the thirty-eight coffins, ranged in the hall of Emmanuel Chapel, not a hundred yards along the street. The mass funeral was held the day before we left Tredegar. I attended it. A sad leave-taking of the valleys of South Wales. Yet it brought home to me, who from custom had perhaps grown heedless and indifferent, the endless hazards faced by these brave men.

Years later, in a famous London club, a plump, pink-cheeked habitué, having finished an excellent dinner and a pint of burgundy, was standing, newspaper in hand, his back to a glowing fire, holding forth to a little coterie on the damnable iniquity of the current miners' strike.

"Another sixpence an hour," he complained. "There's no satisfying these cursed blighters. What the devil do they want?"

"Only the right to live!" I interposed mildly.

I was a new member at the time and should certainly have held my tongue. Instead, I told of this disaster, and of these thirty-eight "cursed blighters" who had no further need of those extra six pennies an hour which their comrades had dared to claim.

# PART THREE

# Chapter Twenty

LONDON IN SPRINGTIME: could anything be more fascinating, more enchanting for two people who had never before been there in that delicious season? Against the azure sky the outline of the city—shops, houses, churches, towers, and temples alike, crowned majestically by the dome of St. Paul's—stood clear and glittering in the balmy air. The Thames, sparkling in the sunshine, glided beneath its graceful bridges. In Kensington Gardens, where well-dressed children trotted beside proud, bestreamered nannies, the lilacs and pink chestnuts were blooming around the statue of Peter Pan. On the Serpentine, pleasure boats splashed and circled. Throughout the West End, in Piccadilly, Bond Street, and Mayfair, overstuffed with the loot of cities, with gold and silver, jewels and precious ornaments, with silks and costly stuffs, exotic fruits and flowers, the fashionable throng paraded elegantly. The windows of the most exclusive clubs, fronting St. James's were filled with loungers, ogling the pretty women, toying with the finest coronas, betting thousands of pounds on Goodwood, Ascot, and the turn of a card—egad! The King, God bless him, was in residence; they were changing the guard at Buckingham Palace, changing money in the Bank of England, changing their winter underwear for fabric of a finer weave. Soon, in the warm dusk, open landaulettes would purr softly toward the smart restaurants, bearing to the ballet, to the opera, to all the theatres, dark handsome gentlemen in evening dress, with lustrous ladies in low-cut gowns. And we, yes, we were part of all this gorgeous, this glittering parade. . . . Was it not truly wonderful!

In the third floor back of a seedy Fulham Road boardinghouse, facing the gasworks and the blank brick wall of the local tube station, my wife and I exchanged a ghastly smile. Surrounded by cheap luggage, by a litter of clothing and soiled baby's napkins, plunged in despair at our vain attempts to find a practice and deafened by the yells of our first born, we were endeavouring to heat his evening "bottle" on a methylated spirit stove. Never was there an infant so contrary at feeding time, so allergic to any but one variety of food . . . bread. He adored the product of the baker and would bury his toothless gums on the driest crust, with the drooling voracity of an aged cannibal battening upon the choicer cuts of roast missionary. Good sweet milk, however, he abhorred—the very sight of it drew from him ear-splitting protests.

At last, after many struggles, he was fed, tucked into his portable cot, and, with the help of his thumb, asleep. And his mother and I, facing each other over an impromptu meal of sardines and crackers, laid out on a suitcase covered with newspaper, discussed our situation in subdued whispers.

"If this goes on," I brooded, "we'll be selling matches in the streets."

For six weeks now, while our small capital dwindled, we had been seeking a suitable practice which we might purchase in this great city, something which would give us a foothold on the ladder of success. It was not, as we had so optimistically fancied, an easy task. True, the various agencies which specialise in the transfer of medical "good will" supplied us freely with fulsome particulars of practices for sale. We would set out together with high hopes to view the prospect. But after five minutes' conversation in a shabby waiting room, my spirits would fall, and, making an excuse, I would quickly get away.

"Another dud," I would grunt. "His books are cooked, his surgery was empty, and did you smell his breath?"

We had never imagined that there were so many alcoholic or broken-down doctors in London, or so few houses that were not dingy and damp, with cavernous basements and attics like mousetraps. Naturally it would have been different had we been in a position to disburse thousands of pounds for a high-class connection with a fine Queen Anne house in Wimpole Street. But, alas, our limited means made our choice a restricted one.

The week before we had thought ourselves fortunate in finding a charming little house and practice in Chelsea. The doctor was charming too, an agreeable, if rather silent, gentleman with quite the Harley Street manner, and the price he asked was absurdly low. I was about to leap joyfully at the opportunity when a streak of native caution caused me to take the long journey to Tavistock Square and make inquiries at the Medical Association headquarters. I returned to my wife with a pale face.

"My God, what an escape! Our charming friend comes up on trial next month for criminal abortion. All his patients have left him! He's certain to be struck off. And may get penal servitude as well!"

Small wonder, then, that I had now begun to be acutely anxious. And it was with an air of gloomy scepticism that I took from my pocket the latest communication from the agents and handed it to my wife.

"This came in at noon. It doesn't match up to our rosy dreams. But if you can believe him, it seems promising enough."

An elderly practitioner, Dr. Herbert Tanner, who had the excellent F.R.C.S. degree, wished to retire. His practice was in Bayswater, a rather run-down quarter given over to boardinghouses, but very near the best residential districts of the town. At one time the income had been considerable, but, owing to the incumbent's advancing years, it had lately somewhat fallen off. The doctor's residence was included in the sale.

We went there early next morning. The house was a rather severe terraced dwelling painted battleship grey, but occupying a corner lot, on a bus route—an excellent site for attracting casual patients—and, although narrow and old-fashioned, it had not too many stairs. We approved of Dr. Tanner, too—he seemed, like his practice, honest and sound.

Unfortunately, the price asked by the good doctor, while a very fair one, proved more than double the amount of our small capital,

185

scraped together with great difficulty during the previous four years. Our hearts sank. Now that we seemed fated to miss this opportunity, it took on new attractions.

"Nothing like it will come into the market for months," I groaned, at my wits' end, as we took the bus back to our lodging. "You know the junk we've been looking at. Oh, if only we had that extra cash."

Unlike the best heroines of romantic fiction, my wife had no jewels to sell, and at all her consoling suggestions, in my state of tension, I snapped her head off. How forbearingly, then, as ever, did she suffer my irritation! And finally she brought out what was, in truth, a far more sensible plan than anything I could have conceived.

"Why don't you go down and explain our position—make a clean breast of it to Dr. Tanner. Say that, if he gives us time, we'll pay him everything."

I glared at her and at our unfortunate infant, whom she was holding on her knee and endeavouring to nourish with a bowl of pap, which, naturally, he was dribbling all over his face. Then suddenly my expression altered, as though all at once I saw her as a wise wife and a beautiful mother, fondling the most priceless babe in the world.

"I believe you're right." I took my hat and went out.

Herbert Tanner was something of a character—a doctor of the old school, a gaunt, clean-shaven, ruddy man of seventy, with a thatch of white hair and bushy white eyebrows above rather fierce eyes. He spoke his mind to his patients, stood no nonsense from anyone, and had once fought a husky cabby outside the surgery for ill-treating his horse. It appeared a stiff job to ask a favour from such a man.

Yet it proved amazingly easy. Dr. Tanner had taken a liking to us —or perhaps we flattered ourselves and it was merely pity! He found in me some resemblance to his only son, also a doctor, who had been tragically killed in action in the war. In answer to my stammered explanations he remarked quite simply that he was prepared to trust us. He would accept our amount down and the balance could be paid quarterly out of receipts.

When I told my wife the news, she wanted to rush out and fall on the old man's neck. "There *are* good people in the world," she exclaimed. This one kind action, this chance freely and generously offered to us, held more inherent goodness than all the fine words and phrases, more than all the sermons we had ever heard.

Within a month the transfer was completed, Dr. Tanner had moved out to a rural retreat in the Cotswolds, and we, with palpitating hearts, had moved in.

"It's all or nothing now," I barked, as I lay flat on the floor tacking down the consulting-room carpet. "We've staked everything. We've got to succeed or we're finished."

It is my defect to feel things intensely and express them perhaps too forcibly, yet at that moment the new sense of responsibility, of strain and impending struggle, which suddenly supplanted our earlier jubilation, thoroughly justified my remark. We had put down every penny we possessed, our house was only half furnished; in brief, our very survival depended upon our ability to make good.

At first no patients came at all, and we began to wonder fearfully if the old doctor's clientele intended to repudiate us utterly. Then, toward the end of the third day, the surgery bell rang. Sitting biting my nails, in a new swivel chair (not yet paid for), I jumped up as if I had been shot and bolted toward the door. Half an hour later I returned to my wife, pale but triumphant, and gloatingly displayed three shillings and sixpence in my perspiring palm.

"My first London fee." My voice actually shook as I transferred to her the pitiful yet momentous coins. I added ravenously, "Go out like a good lass and get some chops. And bring a loaf of brown bread for the brat."

For months the uphill struggle continued. Winter came, and I had never known one so desperately cold. On our lovely Tredegar uplands we had revelled in the deep snow and thrilled to the clear arctic blue of the burnished sky. Here there was sleet, slush, and poisonous yellow London fog, which penetrated everywhere, making one cough continually, piercing the marrow of one's bones. Our waterpipes froze, then burst, flooding the basement, turning the kitchen into a swamp.

My wife had no help whatsoever, did all the housework and the cooking, attended to our son, admitted whatever patients came to the house, even made up the medicines and stock solutions required. Often the endless stairs from basement to attic got the better of her, and she would pause, her hand to her side, and gasp out something in language picked up from me and, alas, far, far removed from those prayerful invocations with which she had once thought she might convert the heathen.

If only it hadn't been so cold, so beastly, so damnably cold! Except for a gas fire in the consulting room, we used no heating in the house at all. Going to bed at night, we dressed up in all our warmest clothes, as though for a polar expedition; then, for the look of things, put our pyjamas on top.

Even in my first assistantship in the Rhondda we had lived better. Then we were always sure of a blazing fire and a hot meal. Now, more often than not, we had neither. All our small receipts seemed consecrated to paying off the drug bill and the quarterly obligation, looming ahead, to Dr. Tanner.

We ate infrequently and only the cheapest kinds of food. How well do I remember coming in, fagged—less with work than anxiety —and sitting down to a dish that we were all sick of. "This muck again," I would mutter. "What kind of doctor am I? Is nobody ever sick in this part of town?" More often than not, however, I would begin to eat silently, having first glanced across at my wife. "Have you had your milk?"

Yes, she was supposed to drink milk, for on top of all this worry, we cared for each other more than ever, and she was again in that state euphemistically known as "an interesting condition"—in fact, our second son was due to appear, and in truth did appear, in about three months.

# Chapter Twenty-one

THAT FIRST YEAR in Bayswater, marked by much hardship and by an intensity of purpose which never for a moment relaxed, was as great a martyrdom as that suffered by the early Christians. But by keeping our sense of humour and laughing off our trials and discouragements we managed to survive. And it was wonderful when the tide gradually turned and began, vigorously, to flow our way.

It is true that I worked desperately hard. To attain a particular objective, one must give everything, offer unsparingly the sum total of one's capabilities—and in these twelve months I did not take a single half-day's holiday. Yet I must admit that good fortune had its part in our ultimate success. I was lucky to make friends with the policeman on point duty, a good Scot by the name of Sergeant Blair, who got me many a useful fee for casualty work; and with the proprietor of the neighbourhood chemist's shop, who often sent along customers who had asked to be "recommended" to a good doctor. Nor must we forget a certain native shrewdness which secured for me an entree into many of the private hotels which are so numerous in Bayswater.

Summoned in the middle of the night to some poor waitress, or cook, or scullery maid, who was sickening with influenza, or perhaps (this happened more than once) had surprised her unsuspecting employer by developing labour pains, in short, the kind of patient whom few of the other doctors wanted, I would get out of bed, treat the unfortunate woman like a duchess, visit her every day for a month,

189

and finally wind up with several of the guests of the hotel in my waiting room.

"Doctor, you did such wonderful things for poor Sarah Jones, I wonder if you could help my gastritis."

And Doctor did, of course—there was nothing I would not, or could not, put my hand to, and everything that I attempted seemed to come off. A growing reputation is a thrilling, tingling tonic for the struggling practitioner. Instead of sitting chafing, waiting for patients to arrive, the entire day seemed too short for fulfilment of the demands made upon me. As though this were not enough, an event occurred which must surely have been arranged by a benevolent Providence.

Late one November evening, as the mist swirled up from the Thames and the traffic of the busy street was stilled, the night bell rang. I had not yet turned in, but was sitting up in my dressing gown, trying to master an abstruse article on diabetic metabolism in the current number of the *Medical Journal*. I answered the bell myself. When I opened the door the haloed light of the street lamp revealed a young maidservant, hatless, coatless, and in a breathless panic of agitation. Her mistress, Mrs. Arbuthnot, at No. 5 Palace Gardens, had taken poison. She had run for the family doctor only to find that he was away from home. Would I, for God's sake, come at once?

There is an instinct, or it may only be experience, which permits the long-suffering practitioner to determine, in one illuminating and heartsearching glance, the nature of a call. And in the open countrified countenance of this little maid, in her sincerity, her obvious distress, even in the neatness of her simple uniform, I saw, despite that ominous word "poison," nothing but what was good. Without a word I took up my emergency bag, which stood ready on the hall table, hailed a taxi that was crawling past in the fog, and bundling into it, still in my dressing gown, told the driver to make all speed toward Palace Gardens.

Within four minutes we were there. Number 5 was a small but handsome flat, solidly furnished in the Victorian style, with warm carpets, rich velvet curtains, and spotless antimacassars on the horsehair armchairs. In the bedroom, collapsed on the old-fashioned brass bedstead and quite unconscious, was a fragile little old woman in a lace nightgown. Upon the bedside table were two bottles of medicine, exactly similar in size and shape: the one an obvious bismuth stomach mixture marked "One tablespoonful as required"; the other, dark blue in colour and bearing a scarlet label: "The Liniment. Poison. Not to be taken."

Little imagination was needed to deduce what had happened: the old lady, falling asleep, had felt a twinge of indigestion, had reached drowsily—forgetful of the presence of the other bottle—for a dose of the palliative mixture, had mistakenly swallowed a portion of the lethal liniment.

This, indeed, as I afterward learned, was the exact explanation, but at that moment, with the patient *in extremis,* there was no time to dwell on theories. The old lady was almost gone, the pulse a mere flicker in her slender wrist. But what was the poison? Useless to telephone the chemist and turn him out of bed to hunt through his file of prescriptions. I must decide instantly. The fixed, dilated pupils, that dry flushed skin, the injected eyeballs and fluttering heartbeats suggested one thing—belladonna—a supposition partly borne out by the greenish colour and sickly smell of the liniment. Now belladonna, prepared from the leaves of *Atropa belladonna* collected when the plant is in flower, is a powerful depressant which, acting through the vagus nerve, paralyses the respiratory centre in the brain. Already my patient had begun to gasp convulsively. It must be belladonna . . . , yet . . . on the other hand, there were at least six other deliriant narcotics which could produce the same effect. Well—I must risk it. Quickly I passed a stomach tube, blessing the practice in Lochlea Asylum which had given me skill in this difficult art, and washed out the old lady's stomach with a solution of saline. Next I pumped into her 15 milligrams of diamorphine hydrochloride, perfect antidote to the atropine alkaloid which is the deadly element in belladonna, yet toxic enough in its own right, if my diagnosis was wrong, to ease her quietly to a better world. Anxiously I studied her, awaiting the result. At first I thought she was gone.

191

Instead, however, she began to breathe better, the pulse strength-ened, after about fifteen minutes she sighed, opened her eyes, and looked glassily at me.

"Young man," she murmured, "what are you doing in my bedroom in your dressing gown?"

Then she tried to go to sleep again. But we would not, by any means, permit her to do so. All night long, despite her pleadings, the little maid and I marched her up and down the apartment, pausing only at intervals to dose her with black coffee well laced with stimu-lant. When morning came the effects of the drug had worn off, and in about a week, despite the apparent frailty of her constitution and her advanced age—she had long since passed her seventieth year—she made a complete recovery.

Firmly resisting my ethical attempt to return her to the care of her own doctor, whom she characterized—tartly and, I fear, unjustly —as a gouty old fool, who could never be found when wanted and was always rushing off to Harrogate to drink the waters which, she averred, should have been more properly reserved for his patients, she adopted me as her physician, insisting that I visit her every day. Thus began my acquaintance, ripening quickly to deep friendship, with one of the most remarkable old ladies I have ever known.

Of Spanish extraction—her maiden name was Mina da Costa —she had been born in Buenos Aires and had married, of all people, an adventurous expatriate Scotsman. Much of her life had been spent in Mexico, where her husband had managed, and finally owned, a large silver mine near Asunzolo and where, indeed, during the revolution of 1917, while resisting an attempt of the mob to take over his property, he had been fatally shot. But she had lived everywhere, travelled, in later years, to every corner of the globe, to countries as far apart as India and Brazil, climes as different as Persia and Peru. She had wintered in Nice, in Cairo, attended the opera at Vienna, the festival at Bayreuth, the races at Longchamps, viewed the bullfights of Mexico City and Madrid, assisted in her own *caseta* at the Easter *feria* in Seville. One year she spent the spring on the slopes of the Andes; the next, under the scented cherry trees in the shadow of Fujiyama. A complete cosmopolitan, she had spent lavishly, and even now, restricted physically and, to a certain extent, financially, small, shrunken, with sharp little features and fragile bones, she still maintained her cheerful, worldly outlook, and in her bright, birdlike eye there burned, with a kind of humorous irony, the determination to continue to enjoy her life to the last gasp, to pave her footsteps to the grave with thoroughly mundane intentions.

Every morning she took *The Sporting Times,* known to initiates as "The Pink 'Un," and lighting a cigarette after her breakfast of coffee and *croissants,* she cocked an eye through the smoke and studied it intently. Then, having reached a decision with the help of Ruff's *Turf Guide,* she went to the telephone and bet a few shillings with her bookmaker. Thereafter, she might have an appointment with her hairdresser, or if the weather was fine she would hire a hansom from the adjoining mews—never a taxi—and go for a drive in the Park. In the afternoon she usually played bridge at a neighbouring club. On her way home she bought the evening newspaper and scanned the race results with an excitement which, while pleasantly stimulating throughout the day, now reached its peak. If her horse had lost she said something which was not polite, beneath her breath, in Spanish. When it won, she had a glass of champagne at dinner, always an admirable meal, sent in hot from a neighbourhood hotel and served, on fine porcelain and old silver, by the little maid.

Many times she invited me to share this repast with her. And afterward, over a liqueur, smoking her evening cigarette, she would talk of the past. There was in her, apparently, not a shred of sentiment. In contrast to those patients who profusely, often tearfully, voiced their gratitude, then left the district without paying their bills, she never thanked me for having saved her life, as I undoubtedly had done. Indeed, she preferred to tease me for having appeared, half undressed, at midnight in her bedroom—implying, of course, that my intentions had been strictly dishonourable. But one day when I called, she handed me in silence a small tissue-wrapped package. It was an exquisite gold cigarette case, inscribed with my monogram, the phrase *Recuerdo de Mina,* and the date *30:4:29—*

I have at this moment looked at it to refresh my memory—on which I had first been called to her. When I attempted to express my appreciation, she mockingly brushed aside my halting words.

"Don't thank me, Doctor. Thank a horse named Maiden's Prayer, which just paid me ten to one. By the way, my son got back from Europe yesterday. He wants to know you. May he visit you next week?"

A few days later Manuel Arbuthnot called upon me. He was a man of about forty, short and suave, with brilliant dark eyes, smooth olive complexion, glossy black hair, and a definite inclination toward embonpoint—he lived, I learned later, in perpetual conflict with his figure. Dressed in dark broadcloth of perfect cut, his linen immaculate, a pearl in his sombre grey tie, he conveyed an impression of perfect elegance, a trifle overpolished perhaps, yet restrained by impeccable good taste. His manner was perfect, too, yet beneath his urbanity I could sense a cool, impersonal proficiency. Without seeming to do so, these glittering, slightly hooded duellist's eyes were taking me in, appraising my character, the quality of my consulting room, perhaps even judging, to a penny, the price of the curtains which hung behind my desk.

Such a man, son of such a mother, might well be expected to follow some bizarre pursuit, and I was not surprised when he informed me that he was head "buyer" for the West End *maison* named Brunelle's. At that time I had, needless to say, slight knowledge of the extraordinary world of the *haute couture,* yet no one who perused the daily news sheets, no matter how cursorily—and my breakfast glance was often hasty in the extreme—could possibly have missed that word Brunelle or have failed to appreciate, if he gave the matter a second thought, the premier importance of this establishment as a purveyor of the latest modes to many of London's most fashionable women.

Manuel said nothing of this; indeed, his visit was brief. He spoke a little of his recent business trip to Paris, where he had been viewing, and buying, the new season's modes for his house, thanked me politely for my attention to his mother, then rose to go. As he left me at the front door he handed me, with an almost imperceptible bow, his card. At least, I fancied it to be his card until, a moment later, I discovered it to be the address of a firm of tailors: Sandon and Company, 12 Savile Row. Involuntarily, I burst out laughing, but it was not a particularly merry laugh—I felt that my recent visitor was rather too cold a customer for my taste, and that his gratitude had been expressed in a somewhat peculiar form.

However, I had reason to regret this hasty judgement, for presently there arrived at my surgery, bringing their national health insurance cards and requesting to be placed upon my panel, a number of the staff of Brunelle's—seamstresses, messenger girls, and *vendeuses*. Then came a bevy of those glamorous creatures who acted as mannequins for the house and whose function was, of course, to sell fantastically costly creations, in which they themselves looked ravishing, to women no longer young, fighting a perpetual battle with sagging tissues and expanding waistlines. Of these beautiful models I remember—if only because of the help they gave me— Helena, with her black lustrous eyes, blooming underlip, and glistening teeth; Genevieve, who was tall and willowy, moving with undulating grace; Eloise, an ash blonde with eyes clear as agates and a fair, perfect skin; and Madeleine, petite and dainty as a woodland nymph. Despite their exotic appearance, these girls were at heart simple and natural. Indeed, it was astounding to discover that each, behind that exquisite façade, that air of sophisticated hauteur, had the same fundamental aspiration—to get out of satin and sequins, of guipure and brocatelle, to marry a decent man, settle down, and have children. The truth is, of course, that they were all continually plagued and persecuted by that type of "man about town" who believes his charm irresistible and who seeks to force it upon pretty and unprotected girls. When they discovered that my interest in them was confined to curing their coughs and colds—I was too settled in my home life to be tempted by exterior distractions—they were quick to accept me as a counsellor and confidant, and to recommend me, not only to their friends, but also, with due discretion, to their clients.

This was a tremendous benefit. A doctor is not permitted to advertise—it is the process of recommendation which does the trick.

195

Thus calls began to come in, at first gradually, then with increasing frequency, from parts of London outside my own district, and far superior to it in social standing. I went to South Kensington, to Knightsbridge, to Mayfair, entering these fine houses in the beginning with great timidity, then with confidence, and finally with that assurance which springs from the knowledge of one's success.

Most of these patients were women, many of them rich, idle, spoiled, and neurotic. A young doctor with a Scots accent and a string of "good" degrees, strongly recommended by one of Manuel's young lovelies, was a distinct novelty, regarded with the curious interest they might bestow upon a species of new lapdog. Yet I was no lapdog, being quick to realise that in order to succeed with such patients the utmost firmness was essential. I was firm, I was stern. I bullied and commanded, I even invented a new disease for them—asthenia. This word, which means no more than weakness or general debility, became a sort of talisman, which procured my entry to more important portals. At afternoon tea in Cadogan Place, or Belgrave Square, Lady Blank would announce to the Honourable Miss Dash —eldest daughter of the Earl of Dot:

"Do you know, my dear, this young Scottish doctor—rather uncivilized, but amazingly clever—has discovered that I'm suffering from asthenia. Yes . . . , asthenia. And for months old Dr. Brown-Blodgett kept telling me it was nothing but nerves."

Having created a disease, it was essential to produce the remedy. At this time the system of medication by intramuscular injection was coming into vogue—a process whereby colloidal suspensions of iron, manganese, strychnine, and other tonic medicaments were introduced to the patient's blood stream, not by the mouth, but through the medium of the hypodermic syringe. Later on, this technique was largely discounted as being in no way superior to the old-fashioned method of oral administration, but at that moment it suited me to perfection.

Having diagnosed asthenia, it was noticeably thrilling for my patient when, in a sombre voice, my manner modelled upon that of Proust's Dr. Dieulafoi, whose autocratic demeanour at the bedside subdued even the Duc de Guermantes, I declared:

"Madam, I fear I shall be obliged to submit you to a course of injections."

"Oh, really, Doctor?" with acute interest.

"Yes, madam. Your condition demands most drastic treatment."

"Yet you will cure me, dear Doctor," in some agitation.

"I guarantee it, madam. But two courses may be necessary."

Injections for asthenia were now as much the mode and as eagerly sought after as Manuel's new spring gowns. Again and yet again my sharp and shining needle sank into fashionable buttocks, bared upon the finest linen sheets. I became expert, indeed, superlative, in the art of penetrating the worst end of the best society with a dexterity which rendered the operation almost painless—my standard preamble being, "I assure you, dear lady, this will cause you no inconvenience"—and which increased my reputation by leaps and bounds.

Strange though it may seem, the results of this complex process of hocus-pocus—and I was, I assure you, a great rogue at this period, though perhaps not more so that many of my colleagues—were surprisingly, often amazingly, successful. Asthenia gave these bored and idle women an interest in life. My tonics braced their languid nerves. I dieted them, insisted on a regime of moderate exercise and early hours. I even persuaded two errant wives to return to their long-suffering husbands, with the result that within nine months they had other matters than asthenia to occupy them.

For one who had hitherto been struggling in a middle-class surgery for driblets of five shillings and even half a crown, this turn of events was a godsend, a lifesaver—in brief, immensely profitable. My treatment would never have been deemed worth while had I not charged for it an appropriately exorbitant fee. Where pence had previously been my recompense, guineas now poured in—a golden stream.

Why should I be hypocritical and pretend that this financial victory was not gratifying to me? It brought many pleasant things in its train. Presently our obligation to Dr. Tanner was fully discharged, the house repainted and properly furnished. There was a neat maid to open the door, and a nice nurse to take the children out for after-

197

noons in the park. I had at last been persuaded to patronise Manuel's tailors, had been put up for a good club, escaped occasionally for an afternoon's golf, and I made my visits in a new Austin coupé.

Often I would pause, and in a kind of daze, wonder at the circumstances which had brought us all this . . . and, we hoped, though dubiously, heaven too. A little old woman had, by mistake, swallowed a lethal dose of belladonna liniment, and I, called in by chance, had been fortunate enough to save her. The rest had followed, like ripples spreading outward, farther and farther, when a stone is dropped into the still waters of a pool. Ah, yes, I was riding upon the crest of these wavelets. Had I not reason to be pleased with myself?

Nevertheless at the back of my mind I was conscious now and then of a vague dissatisfaction as the character of my practice changed. More and more I was preoccupied by my "high-class" patients, less and less by the ordinary working people who came to the side door. While I enjoyed the sweets of prosperity and revelled in the sense of fulfilled ambition—nothing is more thrilling to the Scot than the knowledge that he is "getting on"—I could not but contrast the work I was now doing with the work I had once done.

The climax came one afternoon when I stepped out of my consulting room for a cup of tea, very well pleased with myself having just conducted to the door a new patient—an erect, military-looking man with a coppery complexion and a moustache.

"Do you know who that was?" I inquired smugly of my wife.

She shook her head.

"Sir ——— ———, C.B., I.C.S." I mentioned a name prominently before the public of that day. "I'm getting the men now as well as the women. He was recommended to me by his wife."

"What's wrong with him?"

"Not much," I chuckled. "Touch of liver. Anglo-Indian, you know. He's going to have a course of injections at five guineas a time. Think of it. When we started here I had to sweat like the devil for a miserable two and six. And now, five guineas for three minutes' work."

She did not answer, but, in silence, poured me another cup of tea. Something in her reserve nettled me.

"Well, what about it? Don't you think I deserve some credit?" I smoothed the lapels of my well-cut Savile Row suit. "After all, I've come a long way from the days when I tramped up the miners' rows in dirty oilskins and hobnail pit boots."

She looked me straight between the eyes.

"I think I liked you better in those hobnail boots. You thought more of your cases and less of your guineas when you wore them."

I reddened to the roots of my hair. I wanted to blast her out of the drawing room—"Damn and hell, there's no satisfying you!"— but I surprised myself by keeping silent. Then after a long pause, I mumbled:

"Perhaps you're right. . . . Mustn't ever forget those days. . . . They were well worth while."

# Chapter Twenty-two

"IT'S THE MOTHER SUPERIOR to see you, sir."

Katie, our dark-eyed Irish maid from Rosslare, made this announcement to me in a voice hushed with awe. In Westbourne Grove, quite near, set back from the street, there stood a quiet grey building, the convent of the Bon Secours nuns. Occasionally one heard from it the soft chime of the Angelus bell. Otherwise it was quite unobtrusive, and one rarely saw signs of life within.

But "on the district," that network of poor slum streets and alleys surrounding Portobello Road and Notting Hill Gate, it was a different story. The order of the Bon Secours was not enclosed. On the contrary, its members, as their name implied, had pledged themselves before God to succour the needy, the destitute, and those unfortunates, outcast from society through their own misdeeds or the wrongdoing of others. Many times I had come across these good sisters, always two of them together, walking swiftly, with lowered gaze, on some errand of mercy, through mean and darkened streets which were scarcely safe by day and downright dangerous by night. These devious passages which opened off the Portobello Road—itself a narrow channel choked by stalls and hucksters' barrows, lit in the evening by naphtha flares, crowded with the riffraff of the city, all pushing, jostling, and shouting—were well known to the police as the resort of pickpockets, thieves, mobsters, and worse. Many of the houses were dens of iniquity, and evil things were done there. I always dreaded a call to this locality, and on several occasions, before I was recognised as a doctor, I had missed disaster by a hairsbreadth. But the good sisters seemed to go there without hesitation and apparently without fear.

In my waiting room I found the Reverend Mother standing by the window, a tall, slender, distinguished figure, supremely graceful in her dark sweeping habit and spotless white coif, and, despite the coarse serge of her robe, of an elegance which at once informed me that she was French. She turned as I entered, revealing a pale, delicately modelled face, the nose long and straight, a noble brow, pressed by its circlet of linen, luminous eyes in which, however, there burned a fire of energy and purpose.

"I am Mother Cécile, Doctor. I have meant so often to call upon you, for I have seen you occasionally in church. . . . Such an excellent example to everyone."

At this tribute to my piety, wholly unwarranted, betraying such ignorance of my true character, I had the grace to be confused.

"And since you are the only Catholic doctor in the neighbourhood," she went on, "I have come to ask a favour of you. Up until now we have been attended by Dr. Collins of Eldon Road. But he is getting old now, and it is a long way for him to come, a great hardship. I wondered, therefore, if we might regard you as the doctor to our convent."

"Why . . . , yes . . . ," I stammered, uncertainly.

"I warn you, it is often hard, unpleasant work. . . . As you know, we go out to cases on the district. Then, we are very poor. We could not afford to pay you a large fee."

"Oh, I should want no pay at all," I exclaimed with great nobility.

Quietly, she inclined her head, rather disappointing me by failing to acknowledge my magnanimity with effusive thanks. Instead, she said simply:

"You will be doing it for God, Doctor. And perhaps, if it is convenient, you could come with me this afternoon to Notting Hill Lane. There is a girl there, Lily Harris, who needs our help."

Cornered, realising that I must put off the golf game I had arranged, I answered with mixed feelings:

"Yes . . . , of course."

At three o'clock, then, I went with Mother Cécile to Notting Hill

Lane, and there, in a single tenement room, we found Lily Harris. She was not more than twenty, pretty, with brown hair and hazel eyes, dressed in a tight black skirt and cheap fancy blouse. Her face was pale, disfigured by a faint rash, her lips drawn tight together, her expression holding something sullen and suppressed. She looked at me in a hard way when I told her to open her bodice so that I might examine her. Some minutes later on the stair landing, confronting the Reverend Mother, annoyed at being dragged into this situation and, above all, at missing my golf, I spoke with brutal frankness.

"You told me it might be unpleasant, and it is. She has syphilis. And she's pregnant."

Mother Cécile did not flinch. She answered quietly:

"I thought as much."

And she told me that Lily, once decently employed in a florist's shop, had fallen in love with one of the district's worst characters, a man named Sivins, pickpocket and race-track tout, who had twice been in prison for robbery with assault. For some months she had lived with him; then he had tired of her and put her on the streets. Yet still he exercised over her that power which belongs to men of his type, and, though beaten, degraded, and abused, she continued to bring him her earnings as a common prostitute.

Back in the room I told Lily, abruptly—for admissions of this disease were always difficult to arrange—that she must be removed at once to hospital. But if my manner lacked sympathy, Mother Cécile, by her sweetness and gentleness, made ample atonement. As I watched her console the unhappy girl and, while holding her close, tenderly wipe away her tears, I thought of those aristocratic women who, in the Middle Ages, tended and kissed with holy humility the running sores of lepers.

That same evening, I succeeded in getting a bed for Lily in the Euston Lock Hospital and, glad to be relieved of this responsibility, imagining, quite mistakenly, that I should never see her again, I promptly forgot about her. Yet I could not so easily escape from the gentle yet insistent exactions of Mother Cécile. If by chance

202

my good wife had begged of Heaven that I might lose something of my sin of worldliness, here, surely, in this spare, elderly, austere French gentlewoman was the answer to her prayer.

Having lured me to the fold, Mother Cécile called upon me for her poor and her nuns quite mercilessly, and quite without remuneration, "all in the service of the good God," as I somewhat sourly reminded her. Yet the more I knew her the more I grew to love her. She was a cultured woman and possessed both dignity and beauty. There was high breeding in the fine bones of her face and in her wide gentian-blue eyes. Her constitution was not robust, but she never complained, and though pale with fatigue, impelled by a kind of inward fire, she forced herself on.

As our friendship deepened she gave me, occasionally, a cup of tea in the convent parlour—a frigid little room, with bare boards waxed till they shone, where she conducted the business of the order. And there, one day, my gaze lit upon a small framed photograph which stood upon her desk.

"What a beautiful scene!" I could not help exclaiming.

"Yes, it is beautiful." Her eyes followed mine to the picture of a great château, white and castellated against a forest of giant beeches with a sweep of terraces and formal gardens running down toward the lakes. "It is the Château d'Anjou."

"I've heard that name before. It's historic, surely. Do you know it?"

"Oh, yes," she answered mildly, and at once changed the subject, but not before I had realised that the Château d'Anjou had been her home.

One morning, some two months later, I received from the Lock Hospital the official notice of Lily Harris' discharge. As I had expected, and fortunately, her baby had been stillborn. But Lily herself had now a clean bill of health—she was completely cured.

I put the paper in my pocketbook and, at the end of that week, when I went to the convent parlour for my usual cup of tea, I handed it to Reverend Mother.

"There!" I exclaimed. "Now say 'thank you' to your servant of God."

To my surprise, she did not answer. Then she smiled sadly, a smile which held all the pathos of experience, all the pitiful, compassionate knowledge of human weakness.

"Doctor . . . , when Lily left the hospital . . . the first thing she did was to return to Sivins . . . , and now . . . she's back again on the streets."

"Oh, no . . . , no!"

"It's a common experience for us." She bent her head. "Souls are not won so easily. . . ."

"She can't possibly love that scoundrel."

"No . . . , I would say rather that she hates him. He gave her a dreadful beating when she came back. . . . At the same time there's a horrible fascination . . . , a kind of dominance. . . ."

"What shall you do?"

"We must go on trying . . . , hoping . . . , and praying."

Toward the end of the following month, at my evening surgery, when most of the patients had gone, I saw, seated, a stiff and upright figure in a bedraggled little hat and buttoned-up raincoat. It was Lily Harris. She came in and in silence removed her blouse, revealing a large burn, of the second degree, reaching partly down her back, roughly dressed with oil and a torn square of cotton.

"When was this done? Last night by the look of it." Observing her wince I made an impatient sound with my tongue. "You should have come sooner."

"How could I?"

I glanced at her intently, beginning to dress the raw and blistered skin.

"How did you do this?"

"Spilled a kettle of boiling water on myself."

"Nonsense. You don't carry the kettle on your back."

She made no answer, but shut her lips tighter, keeping her wounded gaze upon the floor. I knew then how it had happened.

"Why don't you leave him, Lily?"

She shook her head numbly and there was fear now in her eyes.

"It's no use. He'd get after me somehow." She added, "He was waiting for me when I came out of the hospital."

For the first time I felt truly sorry for her. Frequently, in plays and novels, I had seen, romanticised, the woman of the streets. It was, in fact, a feature of this era, if not to glamourise the courtesan, at least to portray her as an interesting and exciting type. But Lily. . . . I looked at her with a heavy heart.

"Come again and have that wound dressed," I said. "And let me know . . . at any time . . . if I can help you."

She did not come again. But ten days later, about five o'clock in the morning, while it was still dark, a small boy came running to my house.

"Lily Harris wants you." And as soon as he had given the message, he bolted.

In twenty minutes I had reached Nottinghill Row. I entered Lily's room. And there I drew up, chilled by what I saw. Crouched in a corner, with a face like chalk, was Lily. Spread-eagled on the bare floor, with a dried trickle of blood at his nostrils and a purple bruise in the centre of his brow, was a man. One glance at the burly, sprawling figure, the mottled face, the slack lips fallen awry, was enough—he was dead.

I knelt by the body, sickened by the stale smell of liquor from the gaping mouth, and ran my hand over the skull; the scalp was unbroken, but behind, in the region of the occiput, I could just make out the thin serrated edge which grated on pressure. I thought quickly: struck on the forehead, fell crack on the back of his head, fracture of the skull at the opposite pole.

My eyes searched the room; yes, there at Lily's side was a heavy poker with a large round knob. Rising, I walked over to her.

"What made you do it, Lily?"

She did not seem to hear me. Like a beaten animal she crouched there, her upper lip twitching, her arms huddled about her bosom.

I put my arm across her shoulder, repeated the question.

She looked up at last, dully. After a long pause she said:

"I tried to leave. . . . He wouldn't let me."

Only eight words—but enough.

Silence.

I took the poker, wiped it carefully with a strip of gauze and laid

205

it back upon the fender. Then I turned to Lily and spoke slowly, so that every word might sink into that shocked and shrinking mind.

"Go to Mother Cécile at the convent. Go there at once. And say nothing . . . , absolutely nothing. That's all you've got to do."

When she had gone I went to the nearest telephone booth and called up my point-duty friend, Sergeant Blair of the Camdenhill police. When he arrived I was kneeling by the body, my hand upon the dead man's heart.

"You're too late, Sergeant," I said regretfully. "I thought you might have given me a hand—but he passed away just before you came through that door."

"What's wrong, Doctor?" asked Blair.

"A stroke!" I announced decisively. "He came home in liquor, had a seizure, and fell bang on his brow. That's how I found him. He kept muttering, 'I fell down—I fell down,' right to the last—poor fellow!"

"Poor fellow!" Blair echoed sardonically. "Don't you know who this is? Chuck Sivins . . . , one of the worst lags in the city. I'm not sorry to see the end of him. Well, it was a sudden call, and him in drink. But I always said he would come to a bad end."

I stood up, spoke casually.

"I'll give you the certificate tonight, Sergeant, at six o'clock. There's no need of an inquest. I'm quite satisfied."

That evening, in the surgery, I made out the death certificate, "Cerebral haemorrhage," in a clear round hand. As I wrote, I thought grimly—I'm giving a false certificate, concealing a crime. . . . I'm making myself a criminal by this act, I could be struck off the roll if I were found out, chucked into prison. I blotted the slip carefully, handed it over to Blair.

"Have a drink, Sergeant, before you go."

"I don't mind if I do, Doctor."

We had a glass of Scotch together. The big sergeant drank his neat, wiped his moustache with the back of his hand, and put on his helmet.

"By the way, Doctor," he remarked mildly, at the door. "At the station, we were just saying how lucky you were on the spot when this took place. We don't know how you got there . . . ," suddenly his expression broke—"and the inspector says to tell you we don't propose to inquire. Goodnight, Doctor. All the best."

In the summer of that year Lily Harris left for Canada, with a number of other young women, bound for domestic service in the Dominion. Mindful of Mother Cécile's words, I had no great hopes of her. But again I was wrong. Some eighteen months later I received from her a brightly coloured picture postcard of Niagara Falls. She had married a young farmer and was settled, happily, in the wheatlands of Saskatchewan.

When I showed the card to Reverend Mother she gazed at me gravely.

"You see, Doctor dear, you really have been the servant of the good God."

To that I replied, somewhat irreverently:

"I hope, one day, He won't forget to let me have my fee."

# *Chapter Twenty-three*

As TIME WENT ON I came to know the convent well. How can I describe the peace of this little citadel of goodness—quiet, ordered, immaculate, with its tiny courtyard garden shaded by two lime trees, placed in the very heart of the great and bustling city. In crossing its threshold one entered a world of brooding and mysterious tranquillity. The chapel was small but of singular beauty, the interior panelled in unpainted wood, the altar of rose marble, surmounted by a large plain crucifix. The candles flickered and shed a soft radiance on the brass doors of the tabernacle and on the white flowers on either side. Against the walls, the Stations of the Cross showed vaguely, and dim, too, were the black figures of the nuns, kneeling in silence, which is felt nowhere so intensely as in a convent church, a stillness which might flood the pure in heart with a delirious ecstasy of calm and joy, but which, at this stage of my life, always pierced me with a stabbing remorse. Then, indeed, I was conscious, although perhaps incompletely, of a lack of purpose in my existence, of a void which no amount of five-guinea fees could fill. I realised that there were certain vital questions and inner promptings which I was evading, throwing conveniently into the discard of the future, and at such moments, filled with self-dissatisfaction, I would swear passionately to reform, a resolution which, unfortunately, once I returned to the diversions of the outside world and the exciting rush of practice, I failed lamentably to carry out.

Despite my lack of virtue, I became friendly with all the good Sisters, who did their best for me by offering the one gift that was theirs to give—prayer. They were of all nationalities. Mother Cécile was, of course, the one who had captured my heart. Yet I loved also old Sister Josephine, stout and voluminously robed, with myopic eyes, reduced by steel-rimmed spectacles, the mistress of novices; and the cherry-cheeked Belgian sister, Marie Emmanuel, who controlled the kitchen, and was always smiling; nor must I omit young Sister Bridget, pale and hollow-cheeked, from Limerick in Ireland, afflicted, poor child, with tuberculosis of the lungs, whose sad yet calm blue eyes revealed to me her knowledge that she soon must die.

But if these good sisters had earned my affection, it was Sister Caterina, the Italian nun, who caught and held my hand. Black-haired and saffron-skinned, with visionary yet intelligent sloe-black eyes, Caterina was a pure romantic, a throwback to the past, who had her being exclusively in quatrocento Italy. Her knowledge of this period was encyclopaedic, and when we had the opportunity to talk together she would tell me how the Della Scala dynasty arose in Verona and the Estensi in Ferara, how Ravenna had fought Padua, and Lucia defeated Florence.

Then she would talk of the Renaissance painters: Pinturicchio, the saintly Fra Angelico, Fra Bartelomeo, a little less holy, alas; then Michelangelo, lying on his back for seven years to paint the ceiling of the Sistine chapel; and Raphael, poor fellow, misled by a bad woman, La Fornarina, but decorating the loggia of the Vatican, just before his untimely death.

There were the sculptors too, and the great architects, Donatello and Brunelleschi, constructing the dome of Santa Maria del Fiore, and the great Bramante, studying the Pantheon and Constantine's basilica, the better to design St. Peter's. And, of course, the poets, Cavalcanti, Lapo Gianni, and Dante, whom she would quote by the hour. Then came the saints of sunny Italy—she knew all of them, all the good deeds they had done, the miracles they had performed. Familiar with all the mediaeval legends, she had also, I fancy, a vivid imagination which, I assure you, did not diminish the interest of her stories. Of these there remains vividly in my mind one which might, perhaps, better acquaint you with Sister Caterina than any description I could give of her. I can still hear her warm yet dreamy voice as she began: "*Di un monaco che ande al servizio di Dio.*"

Over two hundred years ago, in a remote country district in southern Italy, there lived two boys who were inseparable companions. Mario, clever and self-assured, son of a prosperous landowner, was the leader. His faithful follower was Anselmo, not very forward at his books, whose father was the village cobbler.

As the two roamed the countryside, Mario would discourse gravely upon his future. His pious parents had destined him for the Church, a prospect which did not displease him, since he was of a ceremonious disposition and had often been fired by the dignity and splendour of the ritual. In particular, he aspired to be a great preacher. One day, as the two boys lay among the vines on a sun-bleached hillside, Mario exclaimed:

"Truly, I would give much to have the gift of tongues."

Anselmo looked at his friend with loyal and loving eyes, and mumbled:

"I will pray, Mario, every day, that you may have that gift."

Struck by the incongruity of the remark—for Anselmo was not noticeably devout—Mario burst out laughing. In condescending affection he threw his arm across his companion's narrow shoulders.

"*Amico mio,* I am deeply obliged. But, all the same, I think I shall study rhetoric."

In due course Mario entered the abbey of the Capuchins. For a few lonely months Anselmo hung about the village. Then, unable to bear the separation, he followed his friend to the monastery where he became a lay brother, a servant of the Order, carrying out the menial duties of the house. The difference in their spheres kept the two friends apart, but at least Anselmo was under the same roof as Mario, and as he laboured in the fields, tended the animals, or scrubbed the refectory floor, he was able to exchange a speaking glance, even a few words with his beloved comrade.

In the fullness of time, Mario was ordained. On the eve of Easter Sunday, when he was to preach his inaugural sermon, as he passed through the cloisters a shadowy figure lay in wait for him.

"Good luck, Mario . . . ! I shall be there . . . and praying for you."

Next morning, when Mario mounted the pulpit, the first person he saw, immediately beneath him, squeezed against a pillar in the corner of the nave, gazing up at him with ardent and expectant eyes, was Anselmo.

Encouraged by that silent tribute, Mario gave of his best. It was a spirited sermon; few better had been heard in that old monastery church. And it was followed, at intervals, by sermons of greater fluency and power, sermons which stirred the members of the chapter and brought tears of pride to the eyes of the lay brother, always pressed in obscurity against the pillar beneath the pulpit.

Gradually, Mario's fame as a preacher grew. When invitations came for him to preach at other churches in the province his Superior bade him accept, and since it was the custom that none should journey unattended from the abbey, he readily acceded to Mario's request that Anselmo should accompany him.

The years passed, and together these two travelled throughout the length and breadth of Italy. Inevitably, preferment came to Father Mario. He was made preacher in ordinary to the king, finally Lord Bishop of Abruzzo. Here, in his episcopal palace, Bishop Mario lived in lordly style. Flattered by society, sought out by princes of the Church, courted by nobles, he had become a power. His figure was turned portly, his bearing dignified. Now, indeed, he barely deigned to notice that submissive, ever-willing little brother who, though grown bowed and shrunken, still served him with self-effacing docility, tending with loving care his splendid vestments, polishing his jewelled shoe buckles, brewing to perfection that cup of French chocolate which broke the episcopal fast.

But one Sunday, as he preached, Bishop Mario was conscious of a vague deficiency in his surroundings. It was an odd, unsettling sensation, and, gazing down, he became aware that Anselmo was not in his accustomed place. Taken aback, the bishop paused for a moment, and had difficulty in picking up the thread of his discourse. Fortunately, the sermon was nearly over. At its close he hastened to the sacristy and demanded that Anselmo be sent for immediately.

211

There was a pause. Then an old priest quietly answered:

"He died a quarter of an hour ago."

A look of shocked incredulity came into the bishop's face as he was told:

"For months he has been suffering from an incurable complaint. He did not wish to trouble Your Grace with the knowledge of it."

A wave of sorrow welled up within Mario, but sharper than his grief was that strange sense of personal deprivation.

In an altered voice he said:

"Take me to him."

Silently, he was led out behind the stables to a small, bare, narrow cell where, on the straw-covered plank bed, wrapped in his worn habit, lay all that was left of Mario's boyhood friend.

The bishop seemed to meditate. Could it be that he weighed against this naked poverty the grandeur of his own apartments? He glanced inquiringly toward the priest.

"This is where he lived?"

"Yes, my Lord."

"And how . . . how did he spend his days?"

"My Lord Bishop," said the old priest, looking surprised, "he served you."

"But beyond that?"

"My Lord, he had little time to spare. But every day, in the garden, he fed the birds from his own platter. He spoke often to the little children at the palace gates. I fear he fostered a crew of beggars at the palace kitchen. And then . . . he prayed."

"Prayed?" as though the word was strange to him.

"Yes, my Lord, for a lay brother he prayed prodigiously. And always, when I asked him why, he would smile and whisper, 'For a good intention.'"

The bishop's expression was inscrutable, but a knife was striking at his heart. Yet if he had not properly appreciated Anselmo's worth, if his manner toward him in these last years had been haughty, he could not stay to reproach himself. He must leave immediately for Rome, where in St. Peter's he was to preach before a gathering of archbishops.

On the following day when he slowly ascended to the pulpit, the vast basilica was crowded. It was an honour long anticipated, a glowing moment in his proud career. But when, in the bated hush, he began to speak, the dullest platitudes issued from his lips. He could read the surprise and disappointment in the congregation. The sweat broke upon his brow. He glanced beneath him, but those rapt eyes were no longer in the shadow of the pulpit. In confusion, Mario hurried through his discourse. Then, hot with shame, he left the precincts of St. Peter's.

Deeply injured in his pride, furious that he should have permitted so imbecile a fancy to disconcert him, he set to work to prepare his next sermon with meticulous care. That he, the Bishop of Abruzzo, the greatest preacher in Italy, should owe it all to a dull, obscure lay brother. . . . Why, the thing was madness! And yet, when he came to deliver the address the words were lifeless. This ruinous obsession went on, from bad to worse, until one day Bishop Mario broke down completely and had to be assisted from the pulpit. To those who helped him he turned and muttered, brokenly:

"It is true. . . . He was the substance. . . . I am the empty husk."

His physicians agreed that he had been working too hard, was in need of a change; and, that he might more readily regain his health and powers, a visit to the high Pyrenees was proposed. But Mario demurred. He preferred, instead, to go to the monastery where he had been ordained, where Anselmo had first come to serve him, where indeed, the little lay brother now was buried.

There Mario spent his time in seclusion, walking in solitary meditation in the garden of the abbey, visiting every day the shady graveyard beneath the olive trees. A great change had taken place in him—the fleshy arrogance had melted from him, his manner was subdued. One afternoon the Prior came unexpectedly upon him kneeling beside Anselmo's grave. As Mario rose the Superior placed his hand upon his shoulder.

"Well, my son. . . ." He smiled, between deference and affection. "Do you pray that eloquence may be restored to you?"

"No, Father," Mario replied gravely. "I ask for a greater blessing." In a low voice he added, "Humility."

213

# Chapter Twenty-four

---

IF I FOUND in the convent a pleasant oasis of virtue, the world without seemed at times, by contrast, a veritable desert of depravity. In a city such as London the busy doctor is constantly confronted with life's more sordid aspects, with painful examples of the weakness and folly, the selfishness and shabby self-indulgence of human nature. Behind closed doors, in the privacy of my consulting room, I saw men without their masks, and often the sight was not a pretty one. To what sad ends were brought those who "with unbashful forehead, wooed the means of weakness and debility"!

At this particular period, through prejudice, lack of educational and public effort, the incidence of social disorders was appallingly heavy in the city. Statistics compiled by one of the great insurance companies showed that in the year 1925 the death rate from syphilis, locomotor ataxia, and general paralysis of the insane attained an all-time high. It was not my purpose to engage in moral dialectic, or harrow the feelings of my readers with the sorrowful history of these patients who found their way in shame and suffering to my consulting room. Yet there is one tragic case which I venture to record, since it was so different, in its beginning and in its end, from all the others.

On a warm June afternoon, when the practice was in a quiet phase and I sat debating whether I might steal an hour from duty to visit the tennis championships at Wimbledon, the doorbell rang and presently a young man and woman were shown to my consulting room. A pleasant sight they made together, as they entered, sustaining each other with a sidelong glance, half-humorous and intimate. There was about them something of the promise of this early summer day, and instinctively my glance sought out the engagement ring which sparkled on the second finger of the girl's left hand.

One does not readily get to know one's neighbours in a London terrace, yet I recognised her as one of a family named Anderson living a few doors down the street. She was fair and pretty, not over-tall, with blue eyes and a certain simplicity, an artlessness of manner which was attractive. She could not have been more than nineteen.

Her companion was about twenty-three, I judged, slight of figure and sensitive-featured, but alert and active. He introduced himself as Harry Charvet; then, after a short silence, he gave me a rather sheepish look.

"It's ridiculous to trouble you, Doctor . . . , but, well, Lucy insisted that I should come." He smiled boyishly at his fiancée. "She's ordering me about already, you see."

"You are to be married then?" I gazed from one to the other.

"Yes, Doctor. In a month."

"And he's been doing too much lately," Lucy interposed. "He had quite a nasty turn this afternoon."

"Oh, it was nothing, really," Charvet protested. "We were walking in the park when I suddenly felt giddy. . . . The sun perhaps . . . , or too much lunch. I know it's nothing. I've had the same sort of thing before."

"Come along, then. We'll put you through your paces. You're run-down, perhaps. You may want a tonic, or something simple like that. At any rate, we can't let it be the cause of the first family quarrel!"

I asked Miss Anderson if she would go for a few minutes to the waiting room. But she excused herself, saying that she was expected at home. Some friends were arriving for tea—for that matter, she hoped I would not keep Harry too long.

When she had gone I sat on the edge of my desk in a friendly and unprofessional manner.

"Now, young fellow. What kind of turn did you have?"

"Oh, just as I told you," he answered with a half laugh. "I seemed to come over groggy. My head felt dizzy and I had to sit down. I suspect it was the heat."

I nodded.

"We'll just make sure. Suppose you stand out in the middle of the floor. That's right. Hands by your sides, feet together, head up."

I waited while Charvet carried out these instructions; then I added:

"Now, close your eyes."

Standing erect and unsupported in the centre of the floor, he obeyed this injunction. And immediately swayed like a reed in the wind. A drunken man could have balanced better. In fact he threatened to fall flat upon his face, and soon, with a little gasp, he opened his eyes and clutched at the wall for support.

"There!" he exclaimed, as though astounded at having so aptly demonstrated his odd complaint. "That's exactly how it takes me." And rather doubtfully he smiled.

But now I could give him no answering smile. I had used the Romberg test merely as a matter of routine, never expecting anything but a negative result. Yet the test was positive. Slowly I got up from the desk and, taking Charvet's wrist, drew him back to the window. In the strong light I examined his eyes carefully, extremely carefully, covering one, then the other, with my hand and sharply withdrawing it. Then in a manner even more altered I said:

"Sit down a moment and cross your legs. Here, in this chair."

He sat down, and taking a small, rubber-capped percussion hammer, I tapped each knee in its turn, sharply.

There was no answering jerk. The reflex was dead.

"What's all this fuss about, Doctor?"

At first I did not answer. I walked up and down the room for a moment, and then, with a serious air, I said:

"As you've taken the trouble to come in, Harry, I want you to let me have a real good look at you."

He gazed at me in amazement, but there was something in my tone which compelled obedience. He submitted, and slowly peeled off his clothing. Then, with an impassive face, I made a complete examination of the now disturbed young man. It was extraordinary with what scrupulous intensity I made my examination, which must have seemed to Charvet both singular and alarming.

I examined his hands. I examined the reaction and condition of his muscles. For a full fifteen minutes, using the ophthalmoscope this time, I examined his eyes, and finally, asking him to repeat certain difficult words, I made a close investigation of his speech. When at last I had finished, something like a sigh rose and was stifled in my throat.

Silently, I put away my instruments and sat down in my chair by the desk with my eyes fixed upon the prescription pad in front of me. A long time I sat like this. But at length I lifted my eyes and looked straight at young Charvet.

"You are an only son?"

"Why, yes," Harry stammered and he flushed, as he did so easily. "I had two brothers, I believe, born abroad, like myself. But they both died when they were very young."

"Is your mother alive?"

He shook his head.

"Your father?"

Again that vivid colour mounted to his brow.

"I do not know, Doctor." He paused, went on constrainedly, "My parents' marriage was not a happy one. My father had business interests—a ranch—in South America. And for some years we lived with him there. But he was often away. He was of a gay disposition. . . . He liked the life of cities . . . , Paris . . . , Rio. I am not blaming him, Doctor; he was a handsome, a most attractive man, but to speak frankly, even before my mother died, our home was broken up. We came to England, she and I. . . . I have been here ever since."

Another pause. As I gazed fixedly at Charvet I seemed to see another, mature and dissipated face, the face of a man whose wife, and two of his children, had died prematurely, who had turned the joy of this bright June day into something sinister and terrible.

"Really, Doctor, I don't see what all this has to do with me."

"It has a great deal to do with you, I'm afraid."

"Afraid?"

I still sat heavily at my desk, remembering his impending marriage, swept by an even greater wave of pitying compunction. I could not

217

think what to say, or how to say it. For the first time in my career I felt the utter impossibility of telling the truth. Yet Charvet must be told. There was no other way. I set my teeth.

"I'm afraid this trouble is rather more serious than you imagine. It isn't just that you're run-down, or a little out of sorts. Oh, I don't want to worry you with long-sounding names or technicalities. But I do think we ought to have another . . . a specialist's opinion."

"A specialist!" Charvet exclaimed. "You can't be serious. I haven't time to see him. I'm too busy. I must go down to Devon to see about the cottage we're renting for our honeymoon. Hang it all, Doctor, remember I'm being married next month!"

There was a silence in the sunlit room.

"I think it might be as well," I said in a low voice, "if you made up your mind . . . to postpone your wedding. . . ."

"Postpone my wedding! But it's all arranged. Everything! Why do you look at me so strangely? What's wrong with me?"

I kept my eyes steadily upon the young man. It was not easy to say that single word, still less so to explain that the scourge which had fallen upon him, which would ravage his nervous system, was a congenital condition, a legacy, insidious and terrible, in-herited at his birth. But I had to do it.

A long bar of silence throbbed within the room, while the meaning of my words dawned upon him. He remained absolutely still, pale to the lips, then a violent spasm of denial shook him.

"No!" he cried. "I can't believe you. It's inconceivable. I'll go and see someone else."

"That's what I suggest," I agreed gently. "You must let me send you to Dr. Barton. He's the man who really will advise you. . . ."

"I don't want advice," he answered, with heaving breast. "I only want to prove you're wrong. Oh, it's too cruel . . . , too insane."

"So long as you go to him." I took up my pen. "Wait, I'll give you a letter for him now."

Charvet said no more, but he waited, ashen with resentment, un-til I had finished writing; then, without a word, he took the letter from my hand.

218

All that afternoon I felt troubled and oppressed. In the practice of my profession, I had often known the pity and terror of sudden calamity striking across the sweet brightness of life. But this, bursting out of a summer sky, turning happiness to misery and joyful prospects, in a flash, to certain pain, was the most terrible I had ever known.

There were few patients at the evening surgery—all of London seemed to be in the country or at the seaside, enjoying a holiday week end. But toward nine o'clock the doorbell rang. I went to the door myself and opened it.

Harry Charvet stood there. Although his face was pale, he seemed calm, and his voice was quiet and controlled.

"I'm sorry to be so late. One or two things have kept me. But perhaps I might see you for a moment."

He followed me into the sitting room calmly—no anger, dismay, or nervous agitation.

"I want to apologize." He fixed his dark eyes steadily upon me. "I behaved rather badly this morning. You see, it was a shock to me." A pause. "You were right, of course—absolutely right."

"I wish to God I had been wrong."

"The specialist was extremely kind," Charvet went on in that same matter-of-fact tone. "Just as kind as you were, Doctor. He confirmed your opinion. There's no doubt at all. I made him tell me everything."

The impersonal voice broke suddenly, revealing a depth of tortured bitterness.

"So I know what to look forward to. These giddy attacks will get more frequent. Soon I'll begin to stagger all over the place like a drunken man. In a year or two I won't be able to walk at all. Then my eyesight will suffer and my speech may go. Oh, yes, I know all about it. I made him give me the whole story. So there I'll lie, paralysed and incurable . . . , helpless until I die. A pretty picture of a bridegroom, Doctor."

Aware of the utter inadequacy of any comfort I could give, I nevertheless made the effort to console him.

"I've been trying to think things out for you, Charvet. It's hard, I know, but wouldn't it be better if you went away from London for a bit, just cut off to a sanatorium in the country?"

He looked across at me with a twisted face.

"Dr. Barton said something like that, too. He wanted me to go to a nerve home up in the Mendip hills."

"Yes, that's right."

"And wait there, I suppose," went on Harry with a note of dreadful satire in his voice, "until they carry me out on a stretcher. Wait until I lose my reason. There's no treatment, no cure for this thing, and you know it."

"You mustn't talk that way. You've got to face it."

There was a silence. Harry sighed. His calmness returned. He was not looking at me now, but into the distance; he spoke like a man talking to himself.

"Yes," he said, "I've got to face it. No use making a fuss. You've been very patient and kind. I'm afraid I've not appeared too grateful."

"You'll take my advice?" I said quickly.

He nodded slowly. "I'll get out of London. It's best for all concerned."

"Come in here tomorrow and we can make all the arrangements," I insisted. "I'll do everything I can." I paused. "But you . . . you must tell Lucy."

"I shan't tell her just yet." He spoke without any visible trace of emotion. "I have one or two things I must do first. Arrangements to make and unmake. For instance, I must go and settle about the cottage." He smiled at me with a new courage. "You knew we'd arranged to spend a month there, at Teignmouth. Lucy's fond of the sea. And she loves Devon. That's why we planned our honeymoon there. But now I'll have to cancel it. I'll go at the end of the week. And then Lucy must be told."

At this he rose abruptly, held out his hand to me, thanked me once again, and in a moment he had left the house and set off, swaying a little on his feet, down the street.

I moved slowly upstairs. Charvet's behaviour under this crushing

220

blow served only to increase my sympathy for him. The miserable injustice of it all, the impossibility of escape, pressed down upon me. I could not banish from my mind the picture of Harry and Lucy standing together, laughing, brightening the waiting room by their presence.

A week passed and next Saturday came. At four o'clock I entered the house and went to the living room for tea. My wife was there, but she offered no greeting, did not give me her usual smile. An early edition of the evening paper was in her hand.

"Have you seen the news?" These were her first words. "It's dreadful. Poor fellow . . . poor young man."

Silently, she handed me the sheet, marking a front-page paragraph with her finger.

"Tragedy in Devon: Boat Capsises in Rough Sea: Holiday-maker Drowned."

"This morning, off the coast of Teignmouth a tragic fatality occurred. A visitor named Henry Charvet, aged twenty-six, having hired a rowboat from the jetty, set off on a fishing expedition to Pollock Deep some two miles off shore. The sea was choppy but not rough. It appears, however, that, while sculling, Mr. Charvet unfortunately lost an oar and in reaching for it capsised his skiff. When the overturned craft was observed a launch from the boat pier went at once to his assistance but without avail. The body was not recovered. The accident is rendered more painful by the fact, we understand, that Mr. Charvet was about to be married."

A heavy silence in the room. I could not speak. Now I understood Harry's ready acquiescence—the best, the only remedy—a quick and certain way out, indeed.

After the first intolerable shock, Lucy bore up bravely. She had sweet and happy memories to sustain her. No one dreamed of the real facts of the case. There was no scandal, no malicious gossip, only sympathy and regret. But for many days afterward I was haunted by a strange vision, not of poor Harry Charvet, but of an older man, that debonair and handsome man, who had liked, so much, the gaiety of cities.

# Chapter Twenty-five

SUICIDE IS, OF COURSE, an indefensible act. But surely there are extenuating circumstances which merit, at least, the grace of Christian burial and not, as in olden times, that midnight interment at a lonely crossroads without benefit of bell, book, and candle, with a stake through the poor wretch's heart. I shed no tears for the stockbroker who, having lost his fortune in a market gamble, throws himself out of the nearest tenth-story window, or for the embezzler who, rather than face the clients he has defrauded, puts a bullet in his brain. But there are other instances which cannot be so easily dismissed as "the coward's way out."

Many times, through my association with the Camden police office, I was called upon to view the bodies of those unfortunates, the lost souls of this great city, who had died by their own act, and now lay rigid and pitiful, upon the cold marble of the mortuary slab. For those who seek an adventure in realism, a salutary lesson in the vanity of human wishes, nothing more suitable could be recommended than a periodic visit to the Metropolitan Morgue.

An old woman fished out from the Serpentine, a sodden bundle of rags, bloated from long immersion, yet starved, destitute—there was not a penny in her tattered purse—one of life's lost people; I never even knew her name. I remember also that ex-corporal of World War I, badly shell-shocked, in and out of hospitals for fifteen years, martyred perpetually by his nerves—we found him hanged, by his braces, in a Nottinghill doss house. Nor shall I readily forget

Mrs. Stacey—that was not her real name—for whom I had no sympathy whatsoever.

She was a widow of forty, good-looking in a florid way, and very comfortably off, who, with another woman, her lifelong friend, and a man, a naturalized Swiss, Georges Lanier, owned and managed a small, extremely high-class hotel near the park. Georges and Mrs. Stacey were acknowledged lovers. She had met him in Geneva, where he was a waiter in a lakeside café, some years before, had brought him to London and given him an opportunity in this excellent and profitable partnership which, since Lanier's experience in the business was useful, seemed to work out admirably. But one day, unfortunately, she discovered that the three-way partnership existed in more than a commercial sense—in brief, she discovered Georges in bed with her best friend, in circumstances which precluded the explanation that they were merely changing the sheets. She made a frightful scene. Georges, however, was now financially independent. He shrugged the situation off coolly. He was sick of her, he told her, and infinitely preferred her friend. Hysterically, Mrs. Stacey retired to her room with a bottle of fifty veronal tablets. When they called me next morning the bottle was empty. Without her make-up and her artificial teeth, she was a very ugly corpse.

One of the most truly remarkable instances of suicide which I met with in my practice was the case of the Chattertons. Again, Mr. and Mrs. Chatterton kept a boardinghouse—Bayswater teemed with these establishments. The Chatterton house was modest, took only a few guests, but was most admirably run by Ada Chatterton, a great, solid, muscular, plain-featured woman who was a magnificent housekeeper and a miraculous cook. Ada, in fact, did everything, from roasting and carving the joint to carrying up the coals, and did it the more readily since Alf, her husband, a tiny shrimp of a fellow with a sunken chest and a hollow cough, was not strong, capable only of light duties in the office. Ada was devoted to Alf, utterly so, and in her fondly aggressive maternal way she coddled him like a child, washed his woollens, bullied him out of smoking too many cigarettes, and above all, she fed him well, with steaks and chicken, nourishing soups and creamy puddings. No relationship could have

223

been more admirable than that of this big, bossy woman and the meek, delicate little man. . . . They were completely happy and had been so for nearly twenty years.

One day a new boarder came to the Chatterton house, a middle-aged man named Glover who was connected with a sporting arena newly established in nearby Hammersmith. Glover was a huge man, heavy and burly, bigger, almost, than Ada, and he had one of these thick black moustaches, waxed to a point, which one associates with pictures of old-time strong men. And, indeed, Glover had been a weight-lifter in his day, then had turned professional wrestler and travelled the country with a famous circus.

Some weeks later when I heard gossip that Ada and Glover had, as my informant phrased it, "gone off the deep end," I could not believe it. Yet it was so. After years of soft maternal fondness, Ada discovered, at a dangerous age, a different variety of love, and Glover, apparently, was carried away by an equal passion. They were always together, out every evening in Glover's car, committing the wildest of indiscretions, in what was, admittedly, a saturnalia of sexual indulgence.

As usual, the husband was the last to guess the truth. Poor little chap, how I pitied him—how could this delicate little atom hope to survive against these two huge, brutal creatures linked by an over-powering, sordid passion? I waited, with compassion, for the inevitable denouement.

What actually happened defies description. I cannot explain it. I only know what I found, one chilly January morning when summoned, at dawn, to the back yard of the Chatterton house. Ada and Glover had locked themselves in Glover's car inside the lean-to garage. They had written out a mutual suicide pact, put their arms around each other, then started the engine. Within fifteen minutes both were asphyxiated.

Was it remorse? The triumph of weakness over strength, or right over wrong? Who knows? Perhaps Alf does. He sold the business, bought a Bath chair, and went to enjoy the placid existence of a semi-invalid on the promenade at Brighton.

This dissertation upon suicide would not be complete without the mention of one final episode which is, perhaps, the most singular of all.

On a wet November night, toward one o'clock, I was awakened by a loud knocking at the door. It was my friend Blair, sergeant of police, in dripping helmet and cape, mistily outlined on the door-step. A suicide case, he told me abruptly, in the lodgings round the corner—I had better come at once.

Outside it was raw and damp, the traffic stilled, the street deserted. We walked the short distance in silence, even our footsteps muffled by the fog, turned into the narrow entrance of an old building. Then, as we mounted the steps of a creaking staircase, my nostrils were stung by the sick-sweet odour of illuminating gas.

At the open door of a small flat on the upper story an elderly woman, the landlady, received us and, in great agitation, showed us to a bare little attic where, stretched on a narrow bed, lay the body of a young man.

It took only a glance to recognise the unmistakable symptoms of carbon monoxide poisoning. But although the youth was apparently lifeless, there remained the barest chance that he was not quite beyond recall. At least any gleam of hope, faint though it might be, could not be ignored, and with the sergeant's help, I began the work of resuscitation. For an entire hour we laboured without success. A further fifteen minutes and, despite our most strenuous exertions, it appeared useless. Then, as we were about to give up, completely exhausted, there broke from the patient a shallow, convulsive gasp, followed by another, and still another. It was like a resurrection from the grave, a miracle, this stirring of life under our hands. Half an hour of redoubled efforts and we had the youth sitting up, gazing at us dazedly and, alas, slowly realizing the horror of his situation.

He was a round-cheeked lad, with a simple, countrified air, and the story that came brokenly from his swollen lips was painfully simple too. His parents were dead, an uncle in the provinces— anxious, no doubt, to be rid of an unwanted responsibility—had found him a position as clerk in a London solicitor's office. He had been in the city only six months. Utterly friendless, he had fallen victim to the loose society of the streets, had made bad companions, and, like a young fool, eager to taste pleasures far beyond his means, had, under their influence, begun to bet on horses. Soon he had lost all his small savings, had pledged his belongings, owed the bookmaker a disastrous amount. Then, pressed, threatened on all sides, he had, in an effort to recoup, taken a sum of money from the office safe for a final gamble which, he was assured, was certain to win. But this last resort had failed and, terrified of his employer, of the prosecution which must follow, muddled, sick at heart, sunk in despair, he had chosen the easy way out, had shut himself in his room and turned on the gas.

A long bar of silence throbbed in the little attic, chilled by the night air, when he concluded this halting confession. Then, gruffly, the sergeant asked how much he had stolen. Pitifully, almost, the answer came: seven pounds ten shillings. Yes, incredible though it seemed, for this paltry sum, not more than thirty dollars, this poor misguided lad had almost thrown away his life.

Again there came a pause in which, plainly, the same unspoken thought was uppermost in the minds of us three who were the sole witnesses of this near tragedy. And indeed, almost of one accord, we voiced that thought—our desire to give the youth, whose defenceless nature rather than any vicious tendencies had brought him to this extremity, a fresh start and a second chance. The sergeant of police, at considerable risk to his job, resolved to make no report upon the case, so that no court proceedings would result. The landlady, who seemed attached to her lodger, offered a month's free board until he should get upon his feet again. While I, making the last, and perhaps the least, contribution, came forward with seven pounds ten shillings for him to put back in the office safe.

Twenty years later, in the summer of 1949, I was crossing the Atlantic, returning from America to England, and, on the second day out from New York, while making the round of the promenade deck, I suddenly became aware of the scrutiny to which one of the other passengers was subjecting me. There could be no doubt about it. He was watching me, following me with his gaze every time I passed, his eyes filled with a troubled, almost pathetic intensity.

226

He was around forty, I judged—out of the corner of my eye—
rather short in build, with a fair complexion, a good forehead from
which his thin hair had begun to recede, and clear though rather
shortsighted blue eyes. His appearance was certainly not that of a
man who strikes up an acquaintance with strangers, and his dark suit,
sober tie, and rimless spectacles, in fact everything about him, gave
evidence of a serious and reserved disposition.

At this point the bugle sounded for lunch and I went below. The
rest of the day I spent in my cabin. But on the following forenoon,
as I came up for exercise at the same hour, I again observed my
fellow voyager watching me, with that identical earnestness, from
his deck chair.

And now I perceived that a lady was with him, obviously his
wife. She was about his own age, very quiet and restrained, with
brown eyes and slightly faded brown hair, dressed in a grey skirt
and grey woollen cardigan. And she too was looking toward me with
an interest that matched her husband's, her expression holding also
that same hint of diffident hesitation, even of distress, which marked
his gaze.

The situation by this time had begun to intrigue me, and from the
passenger list, supplied by my steward, I discovered that they were
a Mr. and Mrs. John Quilter, of Ealing, near London. Yet when
another day passed without event, I began to feel that my curiosity
must remain unsatisfied—Mr. Quilter, I decided, was too shy to
carry out his obvious desire to approach me. However, women are
the braver sex, and on our final evening at sea it was Mrs. Quilter
who, with a firm pressure on his arm and a whispered word in his
ear, urged her husband toward me as I passed along the deck.

"Excuse me, Doctor. I wonder if I might introduce myself." He
spoke almost breathlessly, offering me the visiting card which he
held ready in his hand and studying my face to see if the name
meant anything to me. Then, as it plainly did not, he went on with
the same awkwardness. "If you could spare a few minutes . . . ,
my wife and I would so like to have a word with you. . . ."

I let him take me over and introduce me to his wife. A moment
later I was occupying the vacant chair beside them. At first the

conversation went haltingly, but when I asked him whether they had been spending a holiday in America he was quick to respond. Yes, he told me, it was their first visit, and after the years of austerity at home, the experience had proved particularly pleasant. Yet it was not entirely a holiday trip. They had been making a tour of the northeastern states, inspecting many of the summer recreational camps provided for young people there. Afterward, they had attended centres in New York and a number of the larger cities to study the methods employed in dealing with youth groups, especially in respect of backward, maladjusted, and delinquent cases.

There was in his voice and manner, indeed in his whole personality, a genuine enthusiasm which was most disarming. Despite the peculiarities which had prefaced our meeting, I found myself liking him instinctively, drawn, as it were, by a bond of natural sympathy. Questioning him further, I learned that he and his wife had been active for the past fifteen years in the field of youth welfare. He was, by profession, a solicitor, but, in addition to his practice at the courts, found time to act as director of a charitable organization devoted to the care of boys and girls, mostly from the depressed areas and city slums, who had been so unfortunate as to fall under the ban of the law.

As he spoke with real feeling, his wife joining in with an occasional restrained word, her grave eyes remaining all the time upon my face, I got a vivid picture of the work which they were doing— how they took these derelict adolescents, many of whom were physically unfit, delinquent and reformatory cases, "first offenders" on probation, or under suspended sentence from the juvenile court, and, placing them in a healthy environment, restored and re-educated them, healed them in mind and body, sent them back into the world, trained in a useful handicraft, no longer potential criminals, castaways of society, but fit to take their place as worthy members of the community.

It was a work of rehabilitation and redemption which stirred the heart, and after a momentary silence, I asked him, with interest, what had directed his life into this particular channel.

The question had a strange effect upon him, for immediately, without giving himself time to pause, he took a sharp breath and exclaimed:

"So you still do not remember me?"

Surprised and puzzled, I shook my head: to the best of my belief I had never seen him in my life before.

"I've wanted to get in touch with you for many years," he went on, under increasing stress, "but I was never able to bring myself to do so." Then, bending near, he spoke a few words, tensely, in my ear. At that, slowly, the veils parted, my thoughts sped back almost a quarter of a century, and with a start, I remembered the sole occasion when I had seen this man before. He was my little clerk, the boy who had tried to gas himself.

The ship moved on through the still darkness of the night. There was no need of speech. With a quiet gesture, almost unobserved, Mrs. Quilter had taken her husband's hand. And as we sat in silence, hearing the sounding of the sea, and the sighing of the breeze, soft as the beat of wings, a singular emotion overcame me. I could not but reflect that, against all the bad investments I had made throughout the years, those foolish speculations for material gain, producing only anxiety, disappointment, and frustration, here at last was one I need not regret, one that had paid no dividends in worldly goods, yet which might stand, nevertheless, on the profit side, in the final reckoning.

# Chapter Twenty-six

"Doctor, I can't . . . I won't have a child."

It was four o'clock in the afternoon, the hour of my "best" consultations, and the woman who spoke so vehemently was tall, distinguished, and handsome, fashionably dressed in a dark grey costume, with an expensive diamond clip in her smart black hat.

I had just examined her, and now, having dried my hands methodically, I put away the towel and turned toward her. "It's a little late to make that decision now. You should have thought of it two months ago. You are exactly nine weeks pregnant. Your baby will be born toward the middle of July."

"I won't have it. . . . You've got to help me, Doctor. You simply must."

How often had I heard these words before. I had heard them from frightened little shopgirls in trouble; from a shamed spinster, aged thirty-five, who told me in a trembling voice, exactly like the heroine of old-time melodrama, that she had been "betrayed"; from a famous film actress defiantly resolved that her career should not be ruined; above all had I heard them from selfish and neurotic wives, afraid of the pangs of childbirth, afraid of losing their figure, their health, their life, afraid—most specious pretext of all—of "losing their husband's love."

This case was somewhat different. I knew my patient, Beatrice Glendenning, socially; knew also her husband, Henry, and her two grown-up sons. They were wealthy people, with a town house in

Knightsbridge and a large estate in Hampshire, where the pheasant shooting was excellent and where, indeed, I had spent several pleasant week ends.

"You understand . . . , it isn't just money, Doctor. . . . I must get out of this business, and to do so I'll give anything." She looked me full in the face.

There was no mistaking her meaning. Indeed, that same offer, indescribable in its implications, had been made to me before, though perhaps never so blatantly. It had been made by a young French modiste, estranged from her husband, who had compromised herself with another man and who, slim, elegant, and bewitching, with affected tears in her beautiful eyes, leaned forward and tried to take my hands in hers.

Doctors are only human, they have the same difficulty in repressing their instincts as other men. Yet, if not for moral reasons, from motives of sheer common sense, I had never lost my head. Once a doctor embarks upon a career as abortionist he is irretrievably lost.

There were, however, many such illicit practitioners in the vicinity, both men and women, plying their perilous undercover trade at exorbitant rates, until one day, inevitably, the death of some wretched girl brought them exposure, ruin, and a long term of imprisonment. Perhaps desperation blinded such patients as came to me, yet it always struck me as amazing how few of them were conscious of the infinite danger involved in illegal abortion. Under the best hospital conditions the operation holds a definite risk. Performed hastily in some backstairs room with a septic instrument by some brutal or unskilled practitioner, the result almost inevitably is severe haemorrhage, followed by infection and acute peritonitis.

There were others too, among these women who believed it was within my power to relieve them of their incubus by such a simple expedient as an ergot pill or a mixture of jalap and senna. Others, too, who confessed to having tried the weirdest expedients, from boiling-hot baths to such eccentric gymnastics as descending the stairs backward, in a crouching position. Poor creatures, some were almost comic in their distress, and there were among them many

231

who needed sympathy and comfort. This they got from me, with much good advice, but nothing more.

Beatrice Glendenning, however, was neither comic nor ignorant, but a strong-minded, intelligent woman of the world who moved with considerable éclat in the best society.

My only possible attitude was not to take her seriously. So I reasoned mildly:

"I daresay it's rather inconvenient . . . , with these two grown-up sons of yours. And it'll spoil your London season. But Henry will be pleased."

"Don't be a fool, Doctor. Henry isn't the father."

Although I had half expected this, it silenced me.

During these country week ends I had met the inevitable family intimate, a close friend of Henry's, who went fishing and shooting with him, a sporting type, one of these "good fellows," whom I had disliked on sight and who obviously was on confidential terms with Henry's wife.

"Well," I said at last, "it's a bad business. But there's nothing I can do about it."

"You won't help me?"

"I can't."

There was a pause. The blood had risen to her cheeks and her eyes flashed fire at me. She drew on her gloves, took up her bag. A rejected woman is an enemy for life.

"Very well, Doctor, there's no more to be said."

"Just one thing before you go. . . . Don't put yourself in the hands of a quack. You may regret it."

She gave no sign of having heard, but swept out of the room without another word.

The interview left me not only with a bad taste in my mouth, but in a thoroughly bad mood. I felt that I had lost an excellent patient, an agreeable hostess, and the half dozen brace of admirable pheasants which I had come to regard as my annual autumnal perquisite. I never expected to see Mrs. Glendenning again. How wrong I was—how little I knew of that invincible woman's character!

About ten days later the telephone rang. It was Henry Glenden-

232

ning himself. Beatrice, he told me, had a frightful cold, an attack of influenza, in fact. Would I be a dear good chap and pop round to Knightsbridge as soon as convenient? Pleased by this *rapprochement*, I arrived within the hour at the Glendenning town house and was shown directly to Beatrice's room.

Attended by a nurse, a heavily built, middle-aged woman with a face like a trap, the patient was in bed. She appeared, at first sight, rather more ill than I had expected—fearfully blanched, with bloodless lips and every indication of a raging fever. Puzzled, I drew back the sheet . . . , and then the truth burst upon me. The thing had been done—botched and bungled—she was thoroughly septic and had been haemorrhaging for at least twelve hours.

"I have everything ready for you, Doctor." The nurse was addressing me in a toneless voice, proffering a container of swabs and gauze.

I drew back in a cold fury. I wanted, there and then, to walk out of the room. But how could I? She was *in extremis*. I must do something for this damned woman, and at once. I was fairly trapped.

I began to work on her. My methods, I fear, were not especially merciful, but she offered no protest, suffered the severest pangs without a word. At last the bleeding was under control. I prepared to go.

All this time, as she lay there, Mrs. Glendenning's eyes had never left my face. And now, with an effort, she spoke:

"It's influenza, Doctor. Henry knows it's influenza. I shall expect you this evening."

Downstairs, in the library, Henry had a glass of sherry ready for me, concerned, naturally, about his wife, whom he adored, yet hospitable, as always. He was in stature quite a small man, shy and rather ineffectual in manner, who had inherited a fortune from his father and spent much of it in making others happy. As I gazed at his open, kindly face, all that I had meant to say died upon my tongue. I could not tell him. I could not.

"Nasty thing, this influenza, Doctor."

I took a quick breath.

"Yes, Henry."

"Quite a severe attack she has, too."

"I'm afraid so."

"You'll see her through, Doctor."

A pause.

"Yes, Henry, I'll see her through."

I called again that evening. I called twice a day for the next ten days. It was a thoroughly unpleasant case, demanding constant surgical attention. I suppose I did my part in maintaining the deception. But the real miracles of strategy were performed by Beatrice and the nurse. For Henry Glendenning, who lived all that time in the same house, who slept every night in the bedroom adjoining the sickroom, *never for a moment suspected the true state of affairs.* The thing sounds incredible, but it is true.

At the end of that month I made my final visit. Mrs. Glendenning was up, reclining on the drawing-room sofa, looking ethereal and soulful in a rose-coloured tea gown with pure white lace at cuff and collar. Flowers were everywhere. Henry, delighted, still adoring, was dancing attendance. Tea was brought, served by a trim maid—the grim-visaged nurse had long since departed.

Toying with a slice of teacake, Beatrice gazed at me with wide and wistful eyes.

"Henry is taking me to Madeira next week, Doctor. He feels I need the change."

"You do indeed, darling."

"Thank you, sweetheart."

Oh God, the duplicity, the perfidy of woman . . . the calm, deep, premeditated, and infernal cunning!

"We'll be alone together for the first week," she concluded, sweetly. "A second honeymoon. Then we expect George to join us. We're both very fond of George."

Her eye sought mine, held it, and did not for an instant falter.

"More tea, Doctor, dear? You must come and shoot with us when we get back."

When I rose to go, Henry saw me to the door, shook my hand warmly.

234

"Thank you for all you've done, Doctor." And he added, "Confoundedly nasty thing, that influenza."

I walked all the way home across Kensington Gardens, gritting my teeth and muttering, "That creature, oh that damned, that most damnable creature!"

But in September I got my half-dozen brace of pheasants. They were nice, tender birds!

# Chapter Twenty-seven

UNQUESTIONABLY, IN a great city, the doctor sees much of the seamy side of marriage. Previously, when I practiced in the northern countryside and in the mining villages of Wales, I found the institution of the family regarded with infinitely more respect. In these remote districts, where its members worked together to extract a livelihood from the land or from the mine, the family was the essential unit of the community, existing and surviving through its own indispensability. In Tannochbrae, particularly, parents and children alike rose early and set about their appointed tasks: tending the stock; milking the cows; plowing and harrowing the fields; baking, cooking, and canning; scrubbing and rinsing through the steamy rigours of the weekly washday. There was a sense of duty in this hard and simple life, and a strong religious feeling too, manifested in the evening gathering for family prayers. Pleasures were infrequent, though none the less enjoyed, and despite its obvious austerities, the family had its own rewards and satisfactions, was closely united, almost indestructible.

But in London the picture was completely changed. Here all the conveniences, pleasures, distractions, and excitements provided by this vast metropolitan concentration of so-called civilization exerted a strong disruptive influence upon the home. That innate cohesion which, in more primitive communities, holds the family group together, was sadly lacking, in consequence of which, in many instances that I met with, the family simply fell apart.

With the metropolitan divorce courts in active operation, many heartbreaking examples of broken marriages came under my observation. When one considered the misery, the bewildered, disillusioned children, the bitter rancours and resentments, the chaotic mess which so often resulted, the situation seemed so calamitous I used often to ask myself, how, under high heaven, sane persons ever permitted it to come about.

Unquestionably, the main cause of the breakdown of so many marriages is that people enter into the wedded state too lightly, too rashly, and with an utterly false conception of its real meaning and purpose. Unfortunately, however, the idea of sex appeal as the primary basis for matrimony, steeped in a sickly romanticism and sugared with the false promise of an eternal honeymoon, has become an integral part of the modern dream. Physical attraction has its place in marriage—in the most successful partnerships I have known, this has lasted for twenty, thirty, even forty years. But there are other, infinitely more important qualities than ruby lips, sparkling eyes, or the much advertised allure of a peach-and-cream complexion. The rocky road of life demands stronger apparel than sheer silk negligee, stouter footwear than a pair of high-heeled shoes. Love at first sight is a dangerous illusion; nothing is truer than that wise old adage: marry in haste, repent at leisure. If only half the young people who, at the first note of the cuckoo, fall swooning into each other's arms could be educated to those realities, how much of that wretched postnuptial "letdown" would be spared them. To every infatuated young man about to marry I would quote Kipling's description of woman: "a rag and a bone and a hank of hair"; to every young bride I would say: "your hero, your great lover, is just another average man."

That immortal character, the Vicar of Wakefield, in his opening remark, comes very close to the point: "I chose my wife," he says, "as she chose her wedding gown, *for qualities that would wear well.*" Not, mark you, because she was another Aphrodite. In my native Scotland, so often the target for humorous criticism, courtship is regarded as a serious affair. A couple will "walk out" together for several years, getting to know each other in steady companionship, discussing the future in detail, saving their money, making practical

237

arrangements for their life together, so that when, after this period of probation, they finally settle down, they do so on a solid foundation of understanding and respect, faced by none of those dangers which so often blight the beginnings of matrimony.

Certainly the early months of any marriage are by far the most crucial. The excitement of the wedding ceremony is over, the exacting raptures of the honeymoon have diminished, and not infrequently the newlyweds come down to earth with a heavy and unexpected jolt. They are not quite used to living together, nor do they yet have the maturity or experience to adapt themselves to a routine which appears, all at once, to bristle with the stubborn facts of life—problems of finance and household management, doubts and difficulties with regard to sex, relatives, religion, even commencing irritations in respect of each other's personal habits. They believed that all they had to do to gain perpetual bliss was to marry. Both built up a glittering edifice of expectations. And now what? Nothing but a pile of greasy dishes by the kitchen sink, an unmade bed, the slam of the apartment door as the young husband snatches a perfunctory kiss and makes a frantic rush to catch a bus to the city. At such a moment life suddenly seems sour, stale, insufferably humdrum. And then it is that the insidious thought may be given birth in the subconscious of each partner: Was I wise to take this fateful step? Wouldn't I have been better off if I had kept my freedom?

In a seedy two-room flat in a back street of Bayswater I came across just such a couple. They had been married only a year, but now, disillusioned by the drabness of their environment, the limitations imposed upon their personal ambitions, and the frequent clashes of their temperaments, they had decided that the time had come to separate. He was an architect, a clever young fellow who, rather than continue his present work with a large firm of contractors planning semidetached suburban dwellings, was resolved to go to Rome to resume his studies—he wanted to build a great, a tremendous cathedral. She, a college graduate with a passion for art, was not a whit behind in her fierce determination to abandon her hated cooking, washing, and ironing, in favour of a fuller and freer life on the Left Bank in Paris. Each separately confided these intentions to me with a bitter intensity rendered more pathetic by the fact that they really loved each other. There is no knowing what folly they might have committed. But fortunately nature took a hand, and as their physician, I was able to inform them that they would shortly have a child. This wholly unsuspected contingency brought them up short, caused them to realise their responsibilities, and, as there was a great deal of good in both of them, made them determine on a fresh start. They now have four children, and while he has not achieved his Italian cathedral, nor she her place of honour in the Louvre, they have safely weathered their early troubles, prospered financially, and made a fine comfortable home for themselves.

Without doubt, children are the greatest saviours of the marriage state—statistics show that by far the largest number of divorces occur between childless couples. The coming of a child into the family brings a sense of achievement, of fulfilment, to the young parents. It binds them more closely, with a new solidarity, creates fresh interests and delights in watching and guiding the baby from infancy onward, gives to them an opportunity, a purpose, to develop an individual who will be a credit to society and themselves. Make no mistake—children are not entirely angelic creatures "trailing clouds of glory from above," ready to cure all parental woes, to straighten out all family conflicts. More often than not the arrival of a baby upsets the household arrangements, by night as well as by day, disturbs the balance between husband and wife, creates new hazards, problems, and anxieties. But the baby is worth all this, a hundred times over. How wise are those couples who redeem the ill fortune of a sterile union by the kindly process of adoption! Husbands who shirk the responsibilities of parenthood, wives who refuse to fulfil the functions of motherhood, are prostituting the marriage state.

At my University, when I graduated, we had an old Highland professor of medicine who used to give his class this valedictory advice: "Go out and get married, lads. Have children. Raise them fine, strong, and healthy. And bring them up to be a credit to you." He was a wise old man, versed in the snares and pitfalls of the world, and he practiced what he preached . . . ; he had a son who became, later, one of Europe's foremost physicians.

Such an attitude of mind demands that marriage and the family be taken seriously. We have to work, and work hard, for the joys and satisfactions that come from family life. We must learn to make adjustments, to meet trials and hardships not easy to bear, develop understanding and self-control, practice the silent virtues of patience and self-sacrifice. How often was I brought face to face with examples of such heroism, acts of courage and devotion, unheralded and unsung, which nevertheless spoke volumes for the strength and richness, the finely knit texture of family ties. I have known a wife who suffered for months, without a murmur, a painful and dangerous malady, refusing to tell her husband lest it upset him during some protracted business negotiations vital to his future. On another occasion, I was called in to an elderly woman, a widowed mother, who had literally starved herself into a breakdown to save some extra money so that her brilliant son might take his degree at Trinity College. And how vividly do I recollect that young man who called to engage me for his wife's confinement . . . their first child. When he nervously opened his wallet in my consulting room two cardboard slips fell out, quite by accident, upon my desk. I picked them up. They were pawn tickets. Confusedly, he explained that lately he had been working only half time and had pledged his watch to pay a deposit on my fee. I told him at once that this was unnecessary, that he could pay me when his circumstances improved. Then, curiously, I asked:

"And the other ticket?"

He became more embarrassed than ever, finally made this halting admission. Tomorrow was his wife's birthday. He couldn't, simply couldn't, let it pass. He had pawned his war medals to buy her a present, a little silver brooch.

The home is built on such instances of thoughtfulness and self-denial. It is no place for the selfish, self-indulgent man or woman. Marriage is no joy ride. But those who do not disown their responsibilities, who face up to the hard facts and overcome them, will reap a rich reward in the warmth and intimacy of family life, the joy of a house which is not merely a place to sleep in, the common interests, sympathies, and pleasures of a united home. If I speak feel-

240

ingly here, it is because of the happiness which my own marriage has brought me, a happiness due to that stroke of fortune which gave me a wife so finely moulded by her early training; so patient, self-sacrificing, and wise; above all, so completely staunch in every vicissitude of our partnership of thirty years that life without her now would be unthinkable.

Many times I have been asked to name the virtue most necessary to secure such perfect unity. Undoubtedly, the answer is: loyalty. The worst offense against the marriage state, the rock upon which the family happiness is most often shipwrecked, is infidelity. In too many instances, alas, the standard of morality has fallen to a new low. Unfaithfulness is a shoddy business, a despicable betrayal of mutual trust, the meanest sin in the book of human wrongdoing.

But there are other disloyalties which, while physically less obvious, are in their own way just as dangerous. In my practice I knew a family—mother, father, adolescent son, and daughter—in which, despite affluent circumstances and a superfluity of the good things of life, there existed a constant undercurrent of disharmony. The wife was unquestionably a virtuous woman. She would have scorned the barest suggestion that she might be even remotely untrue to her husband. Yet all day long her unconscious desire seemed to be to disparage him in the eyes of the children—raising her brows, exchanging an ironic glance with her son or daughter, when he made a simple remark, appearing somehow to criticise his opinions, his dress, even his appearance.

This inherent disloyalty is equally manifested by wives who discuss their husbands behind their backs, husbands who mourn to other women how much they are misunderstood, wives and husbands who fly for sympathy to a friend, relative, or mother, bearing sad tales of this and that injustice, of her extravagance and his cruelty—all the catalogue of human defects which they see in the other party but fail to recognise in themselves.

No partnership can survive under such conditions; a house divided against itself will never stand. Such people should bury their bickering in their own back yard, smile, if they can, at each other's failings, try to laugh off that dreadful grievance which, magnified

241

and distorted, makes John such a monster and Jane a heartless slut. Of all the aids to family equilibrium, none is more blessedly useful than a sense of humour.

How well do I remember one evening in the early months of my marriage, coming home to the shabby lodgings which we occupied in Tregenny, that rough Welsh village where I had started, and was trying to build up, a medical practice. I was depressed, worried about a bad case, dead-tired after a hard day's work in the rain, and ravenously hungry. I could have eaten an entire ox. Instead, my young wife gracefully produced one small boiled egg. By a great effort I controlled myself, broke open the shell. It was rotten. At that, everything gave way. I started up with all the adjectives and abuse at my command. Whereupon my spouse, who had wrestled with her own tribulations that day, gave back as good as she received. The exchange went from bad to worse till suddenly, at the breaking point, we stopped short, viewed each other with congested eyeballs, then, struck by the absurdity of it all, dissolved into a wild fit of laughter and fell into each other's arms. Harmony restored, we took the train ten miles down the valley to the nearest town, ate a satisfying supper of "faggots"—which is the Welsh equivalent of hamburger—then went to the tin-roofed cinema to see Charlie Chaplin in *The Kid*. What might have been a tragic rupture ended instead in a joyful reconciliation, all because two young people had sense enough to see the humour in an overripe egg.

Good-natured tolerance does much to make the wheels of family life turn smoothly, and, especially as one grows older, it works wonders to practice that tactful diplomacy which might be called the art of being nice to one another. If your husband begins to lose his hair, to puff slightly as he goes upstairs, do not comment on these brutal symptoms of the passage of the years. Should your wife show signs of putting on weight, onset of that dreaded middle-aged spread, tell her emphatically that in her plumpness she is more attractive than when first you fell in love with her. When your children are noisy and untidy, come to table without washing their hands, or leave footmarks on the newly polished floor, try to achieve better behaviour without losing your temper or indulging in that exer-

242

cise known as "bawling them out." A little generosity, some slight encouragement, can be more effective than a hundred applications of the rod. Thank goodness, we cannot exact from our offspring the priggish, often browbeaten, submissiveness of the Victorian age. But we can replace it with an affectionate comradeship infinitely better.

Tenderness and good will are potent factors in promoting the unity and stability of the family. Most powerful of all, however, is the need for some manifestation of religious spirit. Doubtless we have come a long way since those days when the Bible was read aloud in every home. It may be also that the picture of the child murmuring his prayers at his mother's knee is now viewed by many with due derision, as a sentimental chromo of the past. But unless some regard is paid to spiritual values in the home, the family therein will inevitably founder. Man does not live by bread alone. A family will never flourish unless it draws its inspiration from above. "The family that prays together, stays together."

From the beginning of time man's basic desire has been to take himself a mate, to have children, to provide them with shelter, fire, and food, to protect them from dangers threatened by the outside world. The coming of Christianity served to hallow and dignify this primal impulse. And thereafter, through the centuries, the family has taken foremost place, not only in the safeguarding of morality, but in the evolution of human culture. Wherever the family flourishes in a state of vigour and unity, there will be found a strong and sound society. In an era of fear and restlessness, when man, ringed by hostile forces, feels isolated in a dark loneliness, it is his main, his ultimate hope . . . his hope for self-preservation, for maintaining human dignity, and the decencies of life.

# Chapter Twenty-eight

Of all the patients who passed through my consulting room—a long procession—none were more lamentable than those brought there by their own excesses. As I sat at my desk, my eyes shaded by my hand, listening in silence, like an *abbé* in his confessional, to some disastrous history of self-indulgence, I could not but reflect on the sweet virtue of moderation. And often, wryly, I called to memory the prophetic words of my puritanical old grandmother whose ancestor had died for the Covenant at Bothwell Bridge and who, when I was a child and detected in some misdemeanour, would call me to her knee and, having first placed her steel-rimmed spectacles in her Bible to mark the place, inform me that I should not receive from her my usual Saturday "fairing," then solemnly adjure me: "You see now . . . *it pays to be good.*"

But, in this last court of appeal, when the patient was stripped for examination on my couch, it was seldom a smiling matter. There were the gluttons, the voracious eaters who, unable to resist the lure of rich meats and succulent sauces, of *pâté* and pastries and truffles, had already dug their own graves with their teeth. The old lechers, with soggy prostates, weakened sphincters, and all the load of misery which the goddess Venus joyously bestows upon her acolytes in reward for a lifetime's service. Then the drug addicts, of every shape and variety—from the pitiful old scrubwoman who used to beg tremblingly for a bottle of laudanum "to ease her colic"—and who usually got it, poor creature—to the smart society girl, glibly sure of herself but with twitching nerves, flashing a false heroin prescription and vainly asking me to oblige her by filling it, "as the chemist's was closed."

Finally, there were the dipsomaniacs.

"You're wanted at once, Doctor."

"What for?"

"It's Murray, Doctor. At Lee's lodginghouse in the Lane."

"I've no patient called Murray. What's the matter with him?"

"Drunk. Dead drunk again."

"Damn it all. That's no business of mine."

"I think it better be." The shady-looking youth with close-cropped head and evasive eyes, who had brought the message to the surgery side door, shrugged his shoulders enigmatically. "Or else he's sure going to croak."

I bit my lip. How I detested these calls to Nottinghill Lane! They always meant trouble. Then, with an ill grace, I said that I would be along as soon as I was free.

Presently, then, I made my way through the nest of slums which made up the district of "the Lane" and hammered on the blistered door of a doss house which bore a soiled card: "Good Beds: Men Only." A young slattern in a shawl, who, despite the notice prohibiting her sex, seemed quite at home, admitted me.

"Murray?" I growled at her.

"All right, all right. Keep your blinking hair on. There's his room —up there."

It was a small cubicle at the rear of the house. Because of the back-to-back construction in that congested area, the room was so dark I had to stand for a moment until my eyes adjusted themselves to the gloom. Then I made out a man lying on the torn straw mattress of a truckle bed, still wearing his clothes and boots. He was unshaven, his coat foul with mud, his collar ripped open at the neck, his eyes staring with a sort of horror into infinity. Around him was the evidence of poverty, wretchedness, misery—a bare table, an old burst trunk, a score of battered books. The squalid confusion of the room, the pitiful extremity of its occupant, forced an exclamation from me.

"My God," I muttered involuntarily. "What a mess!"

245

The sound partly roused the man upon the bed: he began to mutter incoherently to himself. He was in a thoroughly bad way, with dilated pupils, general muscular tremor, and so deeply cyanosed I could tell at once that his heart was in the Stokes-Adams syndrome. But the symptoms of delirium tremens are not particularly inspiring; I shall not dwell upon them. As I gave him a hypodermic of strychnine he raved at me feebly—the painful rhetoric of imagination driven mad by alcohol, a stream of nonsense forced from his sick, tormented mind. But as the spasm passed and he fell back exhausted on the bed, he suddenly quoted:

*"Quos deus vult perdere, prius dementat."*

The sharp contrast from besotted ranting, the manner in which the lines were spoken took me aback. I looked at Murray more closely, trying to pierce beneath the beard and grime. He did not look old, not more than thirty-five. His hair was still thick and dark, his brow remained unlined, his features were not yet blurred or spoiled. Yet there lay upon him an air of ageless experience that was sad as death itself.

I waited until he fell into a troubled sleep, tidied up the room as best I could. I picked up a book: it was the *Aeneid*. Another: *Paolo and Francesca*. I sighed. Then I squashed a last bug under my heel, shook myself free of fleas, listened for a moment to Murray's breathing, then stepped out of the room.

In the hallway I questioned the woman, who was waiting there. I could get nothing out of her. However, I had other sources of information and, as I was determined to learn something of my patient, I made a detour on my way home and called upon my good friend Alexander Blair.

"So you've seen Murray." The police sergeant laid his pen on the charge desk. "Well, there's a story there, all right. But it's a short one. Damned short. Drink." A pause. "Poor devil, to look at him now you wouldn't believe he'd been to Harrow and Oxford—yes, one of the best scholars that ever came out of Balliol College. All sorts of things were prophesied for him—from a professorship at Oxford right up to a seat on the woolsack. And what is he now? We've known him for about five years here, and though we had to run him in once or twice, we've done our best to give him a hand. We got him on the *Clarion* as a reporter. He did a first-class job, charmed them all for three months, then came out on his neck in the space of twenty-four hours. Faugh! It doesn't bear thinking on! Take my advice, Doctor, and leave well alone."

Nevertheless, next morning I went to see Murray again, and on several subsequent mornings. I am no altruist—visits for which I would never see my fee did not as a rule entice me. Yet something drew me to David Murray—perhaps at first his helplessness; then, later, the rare pathetic charm of the man himself.

There was no doubt of Murray's charm. Scholarly, sensitive, persuasive, witty, he was the most delightful company. As I sat listening to him I forgot the squalid room and the poverty which dwelt there— he captivated me completely.

And so it happened, one afternoon, when Murray was almost recovered from the attack and able to stagger shakily to his legs, that I braced myself and said:

"Why don't you keep off the stuff? For good, I mean. I'll do everything I can to help you."

He stared at me sideways, then, with the first touch of bitterness he had displayed, he gave a short laugh.

"The friendship treatment, eh? You drop something in my tea when I'm not looking. Tasteless. Odourless. And I'm cured next morning. God! It's a marvellous suggestion, if only for its novelty."

I coloured.

"I was just thinking. . . ."

"It's no good thinking, Doctor," interposed Murray in a milder voice, "and it's no good doing, either. Don't you think I've tried before? I've had a dozen doctors—in Liverpool, London, in Berlin, too. I've been in sanatoria till I'm sick of them. I'm the uncrowned king of inebriate homes. I've tried everything. But it's no use. The thing's ingrained in me. It is me. I'm rotten with the rotten thing. I am the rotten thing. Rotten, I tell you." His voice rose as he went on. "I'm a drunkard, a habitual, confirmed drunkard. The minute I'm able to leave this house I'll go round to Marney's pub. I've got my corner there. They know me. I entertain the boys. When I'm half tight I tell them bawdy stories from the French. When I'm whole tight I convulse them with Greek epigrams. They think it's Chinese—but what's the odds, they like me there. When I'm drunk, you understand. At any rate, that's where I'll go . . . and sponge on my friends. With luck I'll last six months till I get another go of d.t.'s. When the d.t.'s arrive I'm laid up for a month. My rest cure, you see. It sets me right for the next six months' drinking."

I averted my eyes.

"If that's the way of it, then, I suppose there's nothing more to be done."

He was silent, then a sudden impulse seemed to swing him to an opposite decision. He offered me his hand.

"Since you're so good, Doctor," he declared, "let's have a shot at it, for luck."

His manner, slightly ironic, was not altogether convincing, but I could not draw back now. That same day I sent him one of my older suits, some shirts, socks, and ties, a pair of shoes and a small advance, enough to enable him to spruce himself up. Then I set about trying to find him suitable employment. It was not easy; none of the large department stores where I had hoped to place him would take him as a salesman. But finally I had a great stroke of luck.

One of my wealthier patients, Jacob Harrison, manager of the Camden Insurance Company, had a son who was preparing to take the difficult, competitive examination for entry to the Foreign Office. The boy was weak in classics and wanted someone to give him an intensive cramming for the next three months. When I mentioned that I knew of an excellent tutor, the father jumped at my suggestion. I sent David Murray along; he was interviewed and engaged.

I could not, at the outset, discern in Murray any great enthusiasm for his new position. He liked his pupil well enough and promised to pump into him an adequate amount of Euripides and Virgil, and yet there was a lack of enthusiasm, an evasiveness about him which disappointed me, made me suspect that he was not keeping his side of our pact.

But one afternoon he appeared unexpectedly at my house, burst into the consulting room.

"Doctor," he exclaimed, pale and breathless, "I'm going to do it. For good this time."

"But I thought . . . we'd agreed. . . ."

"I've been deceiving you. I haven't really been cutting it out. But now I actually mean it."

As I gazed at him, he continued, with unmistakable determination.

"Why shouldn't I? I can do it if I want to. I've never wanted to before. But now I do. I do. Will you help me, as you said?"

"Yes," I answered slowly, "I'll help you."

If there had been doubts of Murray before, now there was none—in the weeks which followed, while I stood by him, helping him as a doctor, as a friend, by every means in my power, I saw him drain the cup of suffering to the bitter dregs. In the mornings the light hurt his eyes, he felt intolerably ill, dying for a drink. He knew the agony of maddening, sleepless nights. When the craving had him by the throat he would weep from very impotence. But he held grimly on. It looked indeed, as though he would win through at last.

Oddly enough, it had never entered my head to seek a deeper motive in Murray's struggle for redemption. But one May evening, as I stood at a window of my house, I glimpsed a situation I had not even dreamed of. Across the street, walking together, were Murray, his pupil, and a girl of nineteen whom I recognised at once as young Harrison's sister Ada, lately returned from a convent finishing school in France. There was nothing especially disturbing in the sight of these three, laughing and talking together; it was the look on Murray's face as he gazed at Ada, a look which shook me to the core.

When next I met him I mentioned, casually, the name of Ada Harrison. Immediately his face was lit by animation.

"Isn't she lovely?" he exclaimed. "Lovelier than a rose." And as though to himself, he murmured the line: "Hither all dewy from her convent cell. . . ." He broke off with a smile. "You know, Doctor, it's quite incredible. She really likes me. We walked in the park yesterday, I made her laugh at my nonsense. I could see she was enjoying herself. The first time I met her I hardly dared look at her. But now it's different. I'm beginning to find my feet again."

It was as I had feared. He was in love. She was sweet, innocent, beautiful, and nineteen, the darling of a wealthy father. He was thirty-four, a penniless outcast, his constitution damaged beyond repair. What could one say to him? Nothing . . . nothing that would not break his heart.

Time went on. Young Harrison sat his examination and a few days later I met him in the street, in the highest spirits—he had passed well up on the list.

"We're terribly grateful to you for recommending Mr. Murray." He beamed. "Father wants him to take me for a vacation in France, all expenses paid. Sort of reward, you know."

"I'm very glad for Murray's sake."

"Oh, and by the by, Doctor, we thought, as he's almost a friend of the family now . . . , we thought we'd invite him to the wedding."

"What wedding?"

"Ada's. It's fixed for next month." He mentioned the name of the man she was marrying, a junior partner in his father's firm, and then added, "Your own invitation will be along quite soon."

The invitation duly arrived. And that same evening, after my surgery, I walked slowly to Murray's lodging. I felt he might have need of my comfort and support. He was not in.

"Where can I find him?"

The woman of the house gave me her bold, scornful glance, which held now a glint of triumph.

"You might try Marney's Bar."

Oh, no, surely not that, I thought as I hastened down the street and through the swing doors of the corner tavern. Yet it was so.

There was Murray, back in his old corner, surrounded by his coterie, swinging on his seat, blind drunk. With fumbling declamatory gestures he was quoting Homer to them: "Gods, the old oracle returns." And while they still sat agape, he set them guffawing with a new version of Uncle Toby and the clock. Suddenly, through the smoke, amidst the racket, his gaze caught mine. He broke off, turned clay-white, and into his eyes came the dreadful look of a soul tortured in the forsaken depths of hell.

"Curse it," he groaned, "why am I not dead?"

But laughter drowned the words, his glass was filled up, someone started a song. And there I had to come away and leave him.

# Chapter Twenty-nine

It is a cliché to say that time flies when one is fully occupied, yet clichés have a way of being true. We had now been five years in Bayswater, our two boys were attending kindergarten, our lives moved so regularly and smoothly that my dear wife had the delusion we were permanently settled, that nothing would now arise to ruffle the even course of her life.

Only an inverted modesty, the worst kind of affectation, could make me pretend that we had not succeeded, amazingly, in our assault upon London, which had once intimidated us and seemed so difficult to conquer. The nucleus which I had taken over from Dr. Tanner had grown tenfold, and the practice now extended in scope and character far beyond its original limits. I had come to know many of the leading physicians and surgeons of the day, and called in consultation men like Lord Horder, Sir Arbuthnot Lane, and Sir Morley Fletcher. Recently I had been appointed medical officer to that great department store, Whitely's Limited.

Yet I was not satisfied: for some time past I had been specializing more and more in eye work, attending several ophthalmic clinics and hospitals. Already I had begun to establish myself in that field, and it was my intention to move, presently, to Harley Street.

One morning, however, my ambition was shaken by an unusually severe attack of indigestion, a condition which I had endured periodically since my student days and which, since doctors are constitutionally indifferent to their own complaints, I had merely staved off with increasing doses of bicarbonate of soda. On this occasion, however, I felt that I might profitably seek a more suitable prescription, and that afternoon, as I was passing his consulting room in Wimpole Street, I stopped in to see my good friend, Dr. Izod Bennett, a physician whose knowledge of the maladies of the human organs of digestion had made him nationally famous.

I expected a bottle of bismuth and an invitation to play golf. Instead I received the shock of my life. He did not treat my symptoms lightly, and after several tests, X-ray examinations, and a barium meal, Bennett told me, seriously, that I had a chronic duodenal ulcer, which would certainly perforate if I did not take myself in hand. With feeble jocularity I protested that it was a breach of medical etiquette to endow a fellow doctor with so unpleasant a complaint, but he was not amused and his sentence, in the traditional manner, was immutable—low diet and, without question, as soon as I could arrange it, six months' complete rest in the country. Shaken, I rose from the couch in his consulting room. . . . How could I possibly leave a practice so completely individual as mine for such a period? With my impatient temperament I had never been able to endure an assistant. A locum tenens—how well I knew the breed—would ruin my years of careful work within six weeks. Then, as I began to put on my shirt, a strange, irrational thought—call it madness, if you wish—suddenly transfixed me. I stood for a moment, with distant eyes and, doubtless, a foolish expression upon my face, looking back toward the longings of my youth. Then, like a Chinese mandarin, I nodded, slowly and solemnly, to myself. It was the most important gesture of my life.

For two weeks I said nothing of my interview with Bennett; then, one spring afternoon, I came in, sat down, gazed at the ceiling, and out of the blue, in that dreamy voice which betokens my most irrational decisions, remarked:

"It's high time we cleared out of here."

My wife stared at me.

"What on earth do you mean?"

"Precisely what I say, my dear."

A strained pause. Then sun was streaming into our dining room, pleasantly touching the mauve hyacinths she had planted and the

253

new curtains she had hung only the week before. Outside, the air was warm, the pavements dry, the familiar street filled with agreeable bustle. Bayswater and our home had never looked more attractive. The blood rushed to her head.

"You don't know when you're well off. We're happy here, absolutely settled, with the children and everything. You've always had that bee in your bonnet, never content, wanting to dash off at a minute's notice. You've dragged me around so much since we got married you ought to have bought me a caravan. But I've had enough of it. I won't stand any more." She had to pause for breath. "In any case, you're much too young to think of Harley Street."

"I'm not thinking of Harley Street."

"Then what in heaven's name are you thinking of?"

"Selling the practice."

"You never could sell the practice here." She brought out the argument triumphantly. "It's much too large and personal."

"My dear . . . , please don't get mad. . . . I'm afraid I have sold it."

She turned white. She couldn't believe it. Then she saw that it was true. She was beyond words. She had been reading fairy stories to the children the night before, and now, ridiculously, she thought of Aladdin's wonderful lamp, which had brought its possessor everything he wanted, and which, unappreciated, had been so foolishly, so stupidly flung away.

She whispered palely:

"What are you going to do?"

I was silent with, for once, a shamefaced air.

"As a matter of fact . . . , I'm going . . . to try to write."

"Oh God," she gasped, bursting into tears. "You *have* gone crazy."

At this point I felt I had better establish my sanity. I explained, trying not to alarm her, what Izod Bennett had told me. Then I went on, in a low voice, apologetic yet firm:

"I've always had this queer urge to be a writer . . . ever since I was a youngster. But naturally if I'd told them that back home in Scotland, they'd have thought I was wrong in the head. I had to do

254

something sensible, instead. That's why I went in for medicine. It was safe and practical. Oh, I admit I liked it all right. I like it quite well now, I might even go so far as to say that I'm good at it. But all the time I've felt this other thing at the back of my mind. When I've been attending my patients, seeing people as they really are—yes, even as far back as the Rhondda days, when we came up against life in the raw—I kept thinking what stories I could make out of them. I wanted to describe the characters I was meeting, get something down on paper. Of course, I hadn't the time; you need quiet and detachment for that sort of thing, and we were always tearing so hard to get on. Well, now we have got on. I can take six months, even a year, to give myself a chance to write. At least I'll get the bug out of my system. It's a million to one I'm no good. And if I'm not, I can always come back to the treadmill."

There was a long silence. She could not deny that, through the years, she had suspected in me this desire for self-expression. But she had never taken it seriously. When, after dinner and a hard day's work, I had vaguely mentioned my longing to do a book, she smiled at me kindly over her knitting and led me on to talk about my golf handicap. But this was different. This wild project, this disruption, once again, of our pleasant domesticity, seemed to her sheer lunacy.

And it was all fixed, settled, and arranged. What a man! Had he no thought of the children or of his wife? She boiled with anger and dismay.

"Remember that chap Gaugin," I reminded her diffidently. "The Paris stockbroker who, without warning, suddenly threw up his humdrum life and walked off without warning to paint pictures—and good ones—in Tahiti."

"Tahiti," she moaned, "and after that I suppose it will be Timbuktu. For heaven's sake, be sensible. What did Dr. Bennett say was wrong with you?"

"Oh, just a gastric condition. But I must have a rest."

"Yes . . . , yes . . . ," she murmured unsteadily. "You haven't really been well lately. . . ."

Torn by conflicting emotions, she gazed at me glassily, smiled

255

wanly, then—as upon a previous historic occasion—resolved the crisis by laying her head upon my shoulder and again dissolving into tears.

The place selected for our preposterous adventure was Dalchenna farm, a small steading situated on Loch Fyne, a few miles from Inveraray, in the western Highlands of Scotland. And three weeks later, when all the details of the transfer of the practice had been settled and Dr. Green, the new incumbent, was satisfactorily installed, we set out for this remote spot, the car jammed with our belongings, our two boys wild with excitement.

I will acknowledge that, with suitcases falling on my head at every curve, my mood was scarcely a confident one. Yet as we sped along, that fine June day, my heart lifted—after all, we had not had a real holiday in years. And when at last, after a twelve hours' run, we reached the moors and mountains of our native countryside, I stopped the car and turned to my wife. Her glance was as tender as my own, and suddenly, forgivingly, she threw her arms around my neck. Lambs were frisking in the meadow, a stream, fretted by the sunshine, rippled by the roadside, our children, released from the back seat, were gathering wild daffodils.

"It's wonderful to be back again," she whispered in my ear. "You'll get well here, dear . . . , well and strong. We'll have a lovely time. . . . And we'll forget all about that stupid old book."

# PART FOUR

# Chapter Thirty

The Highland clachan of Inveraray, little more than a cluster of whitewashed cottages huddled about the castle of the Duke of Argyll, lies among a wild grandeur of mountains at the head of the lovely inlet of the sea which was once the haunt of that delectable fish, the Loch Fyne herring. But the herring, for no known reason other than that it is unpredictable in its habits, had some years before abandoned these waters, extinguishing a profitable industry, sending the trawler fleet to Lossiemouth and Frazerburgh, leaving the village in all its native solitude. Dalchenna farm, which I had rented, was some two miles down the lonely loch shore, and despite the remoteness of the scene, we fell in love with it at first sight. The farmhouse was a snug building, with nasturtiums and scarlet fuchsias climbing its grey stone walls; on all sides green meadows surrounded us; beyond were woods of alder carpeted with bluebells and mitred bracken into which, as we approached, a roe deer bounded; while above towered the heather-clad hills, source of a stream, filled with trout, that tumbled down in golden spate toward the loch.

For the two boys, aged four and seven, who really had no recollection of anything but city life, the place was truly a wonderland. Barelegged and in kilts, they roamed the woods in company with my wife, climbed the hills, bathed, boated on the loch, fished in the stream, chased the rabbits, gathered shells and starfishes on the shore, helped Will, the herdsman, to milk the cows, and Annie, the dairymaid, to churn the butter. For the mother and her sons, the day was one long, perpetual delight—they grew brown as berries, ate

259

like hawks, and slept like hunters. But for me, alas—for the poor parent who was the instigator of the scheme—the picture was somewhat different.

Having emphatically declared before my entire household that I *would* write a novel—tacitly implying, of course, that it was the fault of every other member of the household that I had not written twenty novels—I found myself faced with the unpleasant necessity of justifying my rash remarks. All I could do was to retire, with a show of courage and deep purpose, to the attic of the house which had been at once selected as "the room for Daddy to write in." Here I was confronted by a square deal table, by a pile of twopenny exercise books, a dictionary, and a thesaurus. Nor must I forget the pablum prescribed by Dr. Bennett and treasured in some suitable domestic background, for I am proud of that bland stimulus. Too often in the bad old days brandy has been the chief inspiration of novelists.

It was the morning following our arrival. Amazingly, for that latitude, the sun shone. Our little dinghy danced entrancingly at anchor on the loch, waiting to be rowed. My car stood in the garage, waiting to be driven. The trout in the river lay head to tail, waiting to be caught. The hills stood fresh and green, waiting to be climbed. And I—I stood at the window of the little upstairs room. Wincingly, I looked at the sun, the loch, the boat, the car, the river, and the mountains; then sadly turned and sat down before my deal table, my exercise books, and my dictionary. "What a fool you are," I said to myself gloomily, and I used an adjective to magnify my imbecility. How often during the next three months was I to repeat that assertion—each time with stronger adjectives.

But in the meantime I was going to begin. Firmly I opened the first exercise book, firmly I jogged my fountain pen out of its habitual inertia. Firmly I poised that pen and lifted my head for inspiration.

It was a pleasant view through that narrow window: a long green field ran down to a bay of the loch. There was movement. Six cows, couched in the shadow of a hawthorn hedge, ruminated with steady rhythm; an old goat with an arresting beard tinkled his bell in search, I thought, of dandelions; a yellow butterfly hovered indesively above a scarlet spurt of fuchsias; some white hens pottered about, liable to sudden excitements and pursuits.

It had all a seductive, dreamlike interest. I thought I might contemplate the scene for a minute or two before settling down to work. I contemplated. Then somebody knocked at the door and said, "Lunchtime." I started, and searched hopefully for my glorious beginning, only to find that the exercise book still retained its blank virginity.

I rose and went downstairs, and as I descended those white-scrubbed wooden steps I asked myself angrily if I were not a humbug. Was I like the wretched poet d'Argenton in Daudet's *Jack,* with his "Parva domus, magna quies" and his *Daughter of Faust,* which, as the days slipped on, never progressed beyond that stillborn opening sentence: "In a remote valley of the Pyrenees . . . teeming with legends." Was I like that? I carved the mutton glumly. My two young sons, removed by their nurse to a remote distance in order that they might on no account disturb the novelist, had returned in high spirits. The younger, aged four, now lisped breezily:

"Finished your book yet, Daddy?"

The elder, always of a corrective tendency, affirmed with the superior wisdom of his two additional years:

"Don't be silly. Daddy's only half finished."

Whereupon their mother smiled upon them reprovingly:

"No, dears, Daddy can only have written a chapter or two."

I felt not like a humbug, but a criminal. Determinedly I called to mind the aphorism of an old schoolmaster of mine. "Get it down," he used to declare. "If it stays in your head it'll never be anything. Get it down." So after lunch I went straight upstairs and began to get my ideas down.

I could fill a volume with the emotional experiences of those next three months. Although the theme of the novel I wished to write was already outlined in my mind—the tragic record of a man's egotism and bitter pride—I was, beyond these naïve fundamentals, lamentably unprepared. Most novelists who suddenly blaze into print in their thirties have practised their vice secretly for years. But I, until this moment, had written nothing but prescriptions and scientific papers. It took great determination to drive me through my inhibitions, like a circus rider through a paper hoop.

I had no pretensions to technique, no knowledge of style or form. The difficulty of simple statement staggered me. I spent hours looking for an adjective. I corrected and recorrected until the page looked like a spider's web; then I tore it up and started all over again.

Yet once I had begun, the thing haunted me. My characters took shape, spoke to me, excited me. When an idea struck me in the middle of the night I would get up, light a candle—we had, of course, no electricity in this remote spot—and sprawl on the floor until I had translated it to paper. I was possessed by the very novelty of what I did. At first my rate of progress was some eight hundred laboured words a day. By the end of the second month I was readily accomplishing two thousand.

For the next three months, through all that lovely summer, while the others enjoyed themselves, I remained chained to my desk. Despite their pleadings that I should take a day off, I kept myself on the rack relentlessly, all day and part of the night, coming down late for my peptonised meals, answering the children absently, seemingly anxious only to get back to my private treadmill.

Although at the time I maintained a stoic, a sphinxlike silence, I will now confess to the miseries I went through. There were redeeming moments when, carried away by what I had written, living with my characters in the drama they were enacting, I dared to hope that I was doing something fine; but for the most part I felt that all my drudgery was quite useless, that I was wasting my time in sheer futility.

The worst moment came when I was halfway through the book, and the typescript of the first chapters arrived from a secretarial bureau in London. As I read the opening pages, a wave of horror swept over me. I thought, Have I written this awful stuff? No one will ever read it. No one will ever publish it. I simply can't go on!

I had the impulse there and then to throw up the whole project, destroy everything I had written. It was irresistible. I got up with a set face, took the manuscript to the back door, and flung it in the ash heap.

When the news was known, a dire silence fell upon the house. At lunch, the very children were silent. I remember so well—it started to rain, a dank Scots afternoon, and, scared by my scowl, my wife and the two boys left me without a word.

Drawing a sullen satisfaction from my surrender, or, as I preferred to phrase it, my return to sanity, I went for a walk in the drizzling rain. Halfway down the loch shore I came upon old Angus, the farmer, patiently and laboriously ditching a patch of the bogged and peaty heath which made up the bulk of his hard-won little croft. As I drew near, he gazed up at me in some surprise; he knew of my intention and, with that inborn Scottish reverence for "letters," had tacitly approved it. When I told him what I had just done, and why, his weathered face slowly changed, his keen blue eyes, beneath misted sandy brows, scanned me with disappointment and a queer contempt. He was a silent man, and it was long before he spoke. Even then his words were cryptic.

"No doubt you're the one that's right, Doctor, and I'm the one that's wrong. . . ." He seemed to look right through me. "My father ditched this bog all his days and never made a pasture. I've dug it all *my* days and I've never made a pasture. But, pasture or no pasture"—he placed his foot on the spade—"I cannot help but dig. For my father knew and I know that if you only dig enough, a pasture can be made here."

I understood. I watched his dogged figure, working away, determined to see the job through at all costs. In silence I tramped back to the house, drenched, shamed, furious, and picked the soggy bundle from the ash heap. I dried it in the kitchen oven. Then I flung it on the table and set to work again with a kind of frantic desperation. I would not be beaten, I would not give in. Night after night, keeping myself awake by sheer will power, I wrote harder than ever. At last, toward the end of September, I wrote *"Finis."* The relief was unbelievable. I had kept my word. I had created a book. Whether it was good, bad, or indifferent I did not know.

With a sigh of incredible relief, I packed the manuscript in an old cardboard box, tied it with farmyard twine. Then, having found a publisher's address in a two-year-old almanac, I dispatched the untidy parcel and promptly forgot about it. Like a man who has lost a heavy burden, I began to bathe and fish and row with the boys, to roam the hills and the moors with them, to behave once again like a normal human being.

The days succeeded one another, and nothing happened. That nondescript package might well have disappeared forever into the void. By stern parental edict the subject was taboo in the family, and when the younger son inadvertently made innocent reference to "Daddy's book," he received the blackest of looks.

In point of fact, I had no illusions—I was fully aware that aspiring authors acquire rejection slips more readily than cheques, and that first manuscripts usually come back a score of times before being accepted—if indeed they are ever accepted at all. My surprise and delight may therefore be imagined when, one morning in October, I received a wire from the head of the publishing firm which I had selected, informing me that the novel had been accepted for publication, offering an advance of fifty pounds, and asking me to come to London immediately.

As we read the telegram, a stunned awe fell upon the farm living room. Fifty pounds, cash down, seemed a lot of money, and perhaps later there might even be a little more, on account of royalties. Pale and rather shaky, I muttered:

"Maybe, with luck and economy, I can make a living as a writer. Get the timetable and find out when the next train leaves for London."

Looking back upon the events which followed, it seems incredible, even now, how swiftly, how amazingly, from that uncertain moment, the flood tide of success was loosed. This first novel, *Hatter's Castle*, written despairingly on twopenny exercise books, thrown out and rescued from the rubbish heap at the eleventh hour, was published in the spring of 1930. It was acclaimed by critics, chosen by the Book Society, translated into twenty-one languages, serialised, dramatised, and filmed. It went into endless editions, has sold, to date, approximately three million copies, and goes on selling still. It launched me upon a literary career with such an impetus that, once and for all, I hung up my stethoscope and put away that little black bag—my medical days were over.

# Chapter Thirty-one

WHEN WE MOVED south from Dalchenna it became necessary for us to find a house. Authors who arrive at sudden prosperity are often tempted to a way of life far beyond their means. But my native caution rejected all such boldness.

"This may not last," I warned my wife. Instead of purchasing a historic mansion we rented a small apartment in a quiet part of London.

However, with my second novel, our literary good fortune showed no signs of abating, and when my wife declared that the time had come for us to have a place in the country, I agreed. After some months of searching we were lucky enough to find at Sullington in Sussex, set well away from motoring roads and traffic, a Georgian rectory with great charm and character, an old-world walled garden, age-mellowed outbuildings, and a glorious view of the Downs.

The house had been built of hand-quarried stone a century and a half ago by the vicar of Sullington, who had lived there with his wife for close on sixty years—a mere bagatelle in a district where centenarians are common as blackberries in the hedgerows. Rich, hospitable, and a decided "character," the reverend gentleman was matched in amiable eccentricity, as the years advanced, by his lady. The pair was universally beloved. The vicar lived *en prince*—kept his carriage, ran his farm, and rode his own hunters to every meet for miles around. His wine cellar was the envy of the district, the delight of his friends, butler, and herds—for, if rumour did not lie, he doctored his sick cows on bottled college claret! As for his spouse, her charity was boundless. Disdaining the carriage, she mounted her tricycle and pedalled stoutly on her errands of mercy, a basket of eggs or a boiled chicken dangling from the handle bars, her only concession to increasing age and bulk being sixpence paid to the village boys to push her up the steep incline of Sullington hill.

The property was now in the hands of the Ecclesiastical Commissioners and, after much formal negotiation, the sale was completed and we moved into our new home. Here, since the past few months had been somewhat trying, I looked forward to a period of relaxation.

But if I had expected to enjoy a measure of seclusion, isolated by the privacy of my small estate, I was rudely undeceived. The new world in which I found myself was more frantic than the old. There is a penalty exacted by success, and soon I discovered how multitudinous could be the demands upon an author lucky, or unlucky, enough to occupy the public eye. Upon such a one come requests to open welfare centres, garden fetes and charity bazaars; to speak at club breakfasts, literary luncheons, and gala dinners; to deliver ponderous anniversary orations on the birth of Burns and the death of Dickens; to lecture all over the country on Proust, Shakespeare, Shaw, Dostoievsky, and the function of the novel; to broadcast appeals for charitable institutions, infant hospitals, and homes for aged mariners; to accept membership in a score of dining-out societies designed to propagate culture and cirrhosis of the liver; to sign books in department stores, preside at dull authors' committees, inaugurate book fairs, make the commemoration address and give away the prizes at school speech days; in brief, to stand perpetually in the limelight in the public cause.

Now at one time I might have been delighted to do these things. And no doubt for one who had, only a few years before, struggled in obscurity, it was flattering to be sought after by the great and the near-great, to have one's mantelpiece crowded with important gilt-edged invitation cards, to be made life governor of a famous hospital, proposed for membership on important national committees, pressed repeatedly to stand as an election candidate for Parliament, above all, to receive in shops, theatres, restaurants, and the public street that immediate recognition and obsequious attention which is the most subversive, the most vulgar form of popularity.

Yet lately a strange change had taken place in me. When I sat beside the Duchess of B—— at the County Annual Banquet I was profoundly bored and only maintained a pretence of politeness through a sheer effort of my will. At the Guildhall, when I got to my feet, after eight deadly courses—proceeding from turtle soup through the rich textures of turbot, quail, and haunch of venison—and delivered to an audience of pink-jowled, equally surfeited, city fathers, an oration on the need for morality in letters—a speech filled with platitudes, flavoured with humorous anecdotes well calculated to make obese bellies ripple with amusement, and ending in a high-flown peroration on the virtues of patriotism, religion, and motherhood which brought down the house in a rattle of applause, I knew only too well that I was behaving like a mountebank. I saw myself, with a sombre inner eye, as completely insincere, the betrayer of a principle I had never recognised before. It was a singular paradox. For years, driven by that thirsting and insatiable demon, that desire for success, implanted by my early penury, forced on by the less worthy element of my personality, I had sought relentlessly, step by step, the golden apples of the Hesperides, gift of Gaea to Hera, and now that the fruit was within my grasp, all ready to be plucked, I saw it suddenly as dross, a lure both tawdry and worthless.

What was the reason of this extraordinary change of mind and heart? It sprang partly from the fact that, for the first time in my life, no longer in a state of perpetual activity, I had leisure to reflect. And the question which began to haunt me was: Wherein, exactly, lies the value of all this? From my earliest student days everything that I had attempted had "come off." Even this latest, and most difficult, venture into the field of letters had been unbelievably successful. Now my novels sold in large numbers. Even in the remotest districts my name hit back at me from the local bookstore. Apart from royalties, film and serial rights brought me an income greater than I had ever dreamed I would possess. I was rich. Was I happy? I cannot pretend that I was miserable. Nevertheless I experienced,

basically, a feeling of emptiness and dissatisfaction, a growing realization of the futility of my objectives and, indeed, of all material
achievement. And more, I began dimly to discern how much attention I had paid to the wrong things in life, and how little to the
right. To the exclusion of all else, my energies had been concentrated
upon worldly affairs. I had forgotten, or ignored, the kingdom of the
spirit. My gods had been false gods. And now, with a shock of dis-
enchantment, my eyes were opening to the vanity of human comfort,
and the need of those things that are everlasting.

In this discovery I was aided by a chance encounter. At this time
I was frequently in the company of a man from my home town who
had been my contemporary at school and at Glasgow University and
whom, for convenience, I have named Chisholm. Endowed with many
brilliant attributes, suave, handsome, and glib-tongued, Philip Chisholm had forsaken the medical profession for a political career with
such success that he was now a member of Parliament for a northern
borough and a junior minister of the shadow cabinet. In the inter-
vening years I had not once heard from him, but when I became
known, he was quick to acknowledge our friendship—and this, perhaps, is a fair index of his character. When we talked together, after
dinner at the Garrick Club or at tea on the terrace of the House of
Commons, he had the habit of looking back across the years, with
humorous derision, to our student days. He and I, of all the members
of our group, were the only two who had achieved real fame. We
had rocketed upward, leaving the ruck far behind. There was, of
course, no limit to the possibilities which the future might hold
for us. As for the rest, with the world at our feet, we rather pitied
them.

In May of that year Chisholm asked me to go fishing with him.
A wealthy parliamentary colleague, Sir Harold B——, who owned a
beat on the Hampshire Avon, one of the best and most exclusive
salmon rivers in England, had been called to a council session in
Geneva, and in his absence offered Chisholm his lodge for a fortnight.
The opportunity was too good to miss. We set off together.

The river was in excellent condition and the fish were running
269

well. Chisholm, a true *bon viveur* and man of the world, an amusing conversationalist with an excellent repertoire of stories, made an agreeable companion. Our host, even *in absentia*, kept an admirable table.

Two days after our arrival, the lodge housekeeper slipped on the pantry floor and damaged her kneecap. It looked like a displacement of the patella, but when we two renegades from the healing art offered our assistance the good dame would have none of us. No one would suit but her own village doctor, of whose skill and notable achievements she drew an enthusiastic picture that made Chisholm glance at me and smile.

An hour later the practitioner arrived, with all the quick assurance of a busy man. In no time he had silenced the patient with a reassuring word and reduced the dislocation with a sure deft touch. Only then did he turn toward us.

"My God!" exclaimed Chisholm, under his breath. "Carry!"

Here, indeed, was someone from that past to which Chisholm so often, and so scornfully, referred. We had first known him as a boy, small, insignificant, and poor, who hung on to us, so to speak, by the skin of his teeth—barely accepted by our select band of adventurous youths in the town of Levenford.

If he was in any way remarkable, it was through his defects. He was quite comically lame, one leg being so much shorter than the other that he was obliged to wear a boot with a sole six inches thick. To see him run, saving his bad leg, his undersized form tense and limping, the sweat breaking out on his eager face, well—Chisholm, acknowledged wit of our band, hit the nail on the head when he dubbed him Dot-and-Carry. It was shortened subsequently to Carry. "Look out!" someone would shout. "Here comes Carry. Let's get away before he tags onto us." And off we would dart, to the swimming pool or the woods, with Carry dotting along, cheerful and unprotesting, in our wake.

That was his quality, a shy, a smiling cheerfulness—and how we mocked it! To us, Carry was an oddity. His clothes, though carefully patched and mended, were terrible. Socially he was almost beyond the pale. His mother, a gaunt little widow of a drunken loafer, sup-

270

ported herself and her son by scrubbing out sundry shops. Again Chisholm epitomized the jest with his classic epigram: "Carry's mother takes in stairs to wash."

Carry supplemented the family income by rising at five o'clock every morning to deliver milk. This long milk round sometimes made him late for school. Then a small lame boy would be halted, hot and trembling, in the middle of the classroom floor, while the master drew titters with his shafts.

"Well, well. . . . Can it be possible ye're late again?"

"Y-y-yes, sir."

"And where has your lordship been? Taking breakfast with the provost, no doubt?"

"N-n-n-"

At such moments of crisis Carry had a stammer which rose and tortured him. He could not articulate another syllable. And the class, reading permission in the master's grim smile, dissolved in roars of mirth.

If Carry had been clever, all might have been well for him. In Scotland everything is forgiven the brilliant "lad o' pairts." But though Carry did well enough at his books, oral examinations were to him the crack of doom.

There was heartburning in this fact for Carry's mother. She longed for her son to excel, and to excel in one especial field. Poor, humble, despised, she nourished in her fiercely religious soul a fervent ambition. She desired to see her son an ordained minister of the Church of Scotland. Sublime folly! But Carry's mother had sworn to achieve the miracle or die.

Carry much preferred the open countryside to a stuffy prayer meeting. He loved the woods and the wide spaces of the moor. And while he limped beside us on our rambles he would listen eagerly while we spoke of entering the University as medical students. The truth was, Carry had a tremendous longing to be a doctor.

But obedience was inherent in his gentle nature, and when he left school it was to enter college as a student of divinity. Heaven knows how they managed. His mother scrimped and saved, her figure grew more gaunt, but in her deep-set eye there glowed unquenchable

271

fire. Carry himself, though his heart was not in what he did, worked like a hero.

And so it happened, quicker than might have been imagined, that Carry was duly licenced at the age of twenty-four in the cure of souls according to the Kirk of Scotland. Locally there was great interest in the prodigy of the scrubwoman's son turned parson. He was proposed for the parish church assistantship and named to preach a trial sermon.

A full congregation assembled to see "what was in the young meenister." And Carry, who for weeks past had rehearsed his sermon, ascended the pulpit feeling himself word-perfect. He began to speak in an earnest voice, and for a few moments he went well enough. Then all at once he became conscious of those rows and rows of upturned faces, of his mother dressed in her best in a front pew, her eyes fixed rapturously upon him. A paralysing shiver of self-distrust swept over him. He hesitated, lost the thread of his ideas, and began to stammer. Once that frightful impotence of speech had gripped him he was lost. He laboured on pitifully, but while he struggled for the words he saw the restlessness, the significant smiles; heard even a faint titter. And then again he saw his mother's face, and broke down completely. There was a long and awful pause, then falteringly Carry drew the service to a close by announcing the hymn.

Within the hour, when Carry's mother reached home, she was mercifully taken by an apoplectic seizure. She never spoke again.

The funeral over, Carry disappeared from Levenford. No one knew or cared where he went. He was stigmatised, branded contemptuously for life, a failure. When some years later news reached me that he was teaching in a board school in a farming district, I thought of him for a moment, with a kind of shamefaced sorrow, as a despairing soul, a man predestined for disaster. But I soon forgot him.

I was working in Lochlea when Chisholm, now first assistant to the Regius Professor of Anatomy, dropped into my rooms one evening. "You'll never guess"—he grinned—"who's dissecting in my department. None other than our boyhood friend, Dot-and-Carry."

Carry it was. Carry, at nearly twenty-five years of age, starting out to be a doctor! A strange figure he made, with his shabby suit, his limp and stoop, among the gay young bucks who were his fellow students. No one ever spoke to him. He occupied a room in a poor district, husbanded the slender savings from his teacher's pittance. His age, appearance, and traitorous stammer hampered him. But he went plodding indefatigably on, refusing to admit defeat, the old dogged cheerfulness and hopeful courage still in his eyes.

And here, again, was Carry. Yes, Carry it was. But not the shy, shabby, stammering Carry of old. He had the quietly confident air of a man who, within himself, is at last secure. In a flash of recognition he greeted us warmly, and pressed us to come to supper at his home. Meanwhile, he had an urgent case to attend.

It was with an odd expectancy, half excitement and half lingering derision, that we entered the village doctor's house that evening. What a shock to find that Carry had a wife! Yet it was so. She welcomed us, fresh and pretty as her own countryside. Since the doctor (she gave the title with a naïve reverence) was still engaged in his surgery, she took us upstairs to see the children. Two red-cheeked girls and a little boy, already asleep. Surprise made us mute.

Downstairs, Carry joined us with two other guests. Now, at his own table, he was a man poised and serene, holding his place as host with quiet dignity, unafraid to bow his head and murmur a reverent grace. His friends, both men of substance, treated him with deference. Less from what he said than what was said by others we gathered the facts. His practice was wide and scattered through the valley of the Avon. His patients were country folk, silent, hard to know. Yet somehow he had won them.

Carry was a force now, permeating the whole countryside, wise and gentle, blending the best of science and religion, unsparing, undemanding, loving this work he had been born to do, a man who had refused defeat and won through to victory at last. As we sat in his little study after dinner I chanced to observe on his desk a small framed card. It bore this brief quotation: *"Whatever thou takest in hand, remember thy last end and thou shalt never do amiss."* This, without question, was the motive of his life.

273

Late that night as we left the doctor's house and trudged through the darkness, silence fell between Chisholm and myself. Then, as with an effort, he declared:

"It looks as though the little man has found himself at last."

Something patronising in the remark jarred me. Shamed by the thought of our joint vanities, I could not resist a sharp reply.

"Which would you rather be, Chisholm—yourself, or the doctor of Avon?"

"Confound you," he muttered, "don't you know?"

# Chapter Thirty-two

THIS CHANCE MEETING with Carry, inconsequential though it might appear, accelerated a change in me which, no doubt, was already on the way. The dormant half of my nature, so long overlaid and suppressed, began at last to awaken and, persuasively, to assert itself. Was it the spirit, prim and puritanical, of my mother's Covenanting ancestors? Or a whisper, far back on my father's side, from some Celtic mystic rapt in the dim interior of a turf-roofed *tuath* on the hill of Tara? I cannot attribute it to senility, since I was not yet forty and full of health and vigor. Yet whatever the primal cause, the effects were apparent enough.

The word "conversion" is thoroughly obnoxious to me, suggestive of a revivalist meeting where, under stress of mass emotion, the erstwhile sinner leaps forth with a hysterical promise of atonement. Nor am I prig enough to claim for myself any great and dramatic moral regeneration. I was no Saul of Tarsus, no Augustine impelled by a sudden vision to swift and passionate amendment. Nevertheless there was manifest in me about this time a new attitude toward life, and especially toward religion. This in itself was a remarkable reversal since, because of the peculiar circumstances of my upbringing, I had long maintained a show of indifference toward organised belief.

I may be better understood when I explain that my mother, a Montgomerie, branch of one of the oldest and most Protestant Scottish families, had, when only nineteen, fallen deeply in love with a young Irish Catholic, had run away from home, married him, and, in the excess of her affection, voluntarily adopted his faith. As the sole

275

child of this union, I was baptised into the Catholic Church and for seven years knew nothing but the sweet stories of the saints and the untroubled tranquillity of a happy home. Then, quite suddenly, my father died. He had always lived to the full extent of his resources; beyond the memory of his beloved and handsome figure, his open-handedness and inextinguishable charm, there was little he could leave us. For two years my mother struggled to make ends meet; then, inexorably, through sheer necessity, she was forced to return to the paternal roof.

What a homecoming for one who had, in the eyes of a stern father, disgraced her lineage! And for me, unwanted grandchild, intolerable incubus, the little Papist, what a sad change of circumstances and scene! When I was sent to a Protestant school, my religion, soon discovered, brought upon me the jeers of the class, and indeed of the master, a sadistic brute who took delight in openly baiting me upon such matters as the forgiveness of sins and the infallibility of the Pope. For many months thereafter, a pariah harassed and badgered by a predatory mob, I suffered to the full—since I stubbornly refused to deny the creed into which I had been born—the cruel intolerance of a small Scots community. In that era bigotry was rampant throughout the west of Scotland. On such days as commemorated, for example, the birth of John Knox and the anniversary of the Battle of the Boyne, I saw racial and religious hatreds stirred to the dregs, witnessed the bitter antagonisms of the sects, knew only the worst side of Christianity. In this wilderness I wandered alone, a solitary little boy, swept by doubts and fears, desperately striving to prove to myself the truth of this faith which was so derided and despised.

Later, I grew harder, fought off the worst of my tormentors, laughed with the others at my difficulties, became popular through my skill at games. Then came the time when, winning a series of scholarships, I was able to attend the University, and here the latent revolt brewing within me against the hampering hair shirt of my religion came actively to a head. Proud of my critical faculties, I found impossibilities in the Scriptures, objections to the immortality of the individual soul extremely convenient to my new status as a student of biology. My anatomical studies and scientific training

276

confirmed me in this new attitude of indifference. And when I married, although from a perverse sense of honour I maintained the outward form of Catholicism, I had little thought of carrying out its tenets and obligations. The forces of nature were, in fact, stirring strongly within me. If my conscience troubled me, I buried it beneath a mass of worldly interests. While I never openly disowned Christianity—I was too much of a coward to do so—I conveniently forgot about it. I had reached the supreme goal of egoistic existence.

With such a history, at this late stage of self-deception and self-indulgence, it might seem inconceivable that I should have sought peace of mind and soul in returning to my childhood faith, despite those words of encouragement: "Unless you go back and become like little children you shall not enter the kingdom of God." Yet it was not strange to me, for in truth, however much I beat against them, its bars had always enclosed me, and intermittently in my heart, sounding quiet through the tumult of the world, I had heard the echo of that voice which would not be denied. And even while "I fled Him, down the nights and down the days . . . , down the labyrinthine ways of my own mind . . . , in the mist of tears and under running laughter," I still could hear the beat of those pursuing feet, that secret whisper, "Rise, clasp my hand, and come."

It was not an easy step to take, and one bitter to self-love. For years I had gone on in pride and self-complacency. But that growing interior desolation was irresistible in its compulsion. I stumbled forward, my last defences beaten down, yielded to the craving in my soul. And by whatever means it was accomplished, my period of rebellion against Heaven at last was ended.

There is little virtue in this experience, which is simply the inevitable circuit made by many weak and ordinary souls who, despite the crosscurrents of the world, have not been able to escape the inexorable appeal of the Cross. Indeed for some, encased in their armour of scornful contempt, such "repentance" may evoke no more than a pitying smile. In my defence I cannot even offer visible evidence of the imprint of grace resulting from my surrender. Unlike those who at one lightning stroke consider themselves as "saved" and thereafter walk upon their toes, wearing the prim presanctified smile of the elect, I was still filled with my old imperfections—with ill temper, jealousy, and selfishness. The secret sources of my greatest faults would not dry up. Nor, while I tried to make my pillow less luxurious, could I bring myself to renounce completely my pleasure in transitory and ephemeral things. The mystical empire of the saints was far from being mine.

Nevertheless, although I did not completely slough my skin, I was conscious, within myself, of a new ease, a sense of relief. There was fresh joy in my work. The sadness, tension, and gnawing ennui which had assailed me all were gone. I had cried aloud and the sky had heard my cry. When I fell down, bludgeoned by my still dominant passions, I picked myself up again, offered my wrists voluntarily, and with true contrition, to the fetters of an active conscience. I had made the immense discovery of why I was alive.

# Chapter Thirty-three

DURING THIS PHASE of readjustment I withdrew completely from public affairs. There was no hardship, but rather a fresh and novel interest, in this voluntary retreat. For the first time in my life—that bustling, crowded, tense existence wherein, with never a second to spare, I was constantly engaged—I had leisure to undertake some meditative occupation, to fill the gaps in my sketchy education, to explore the fascinating fields of history, architecture, and art, to plod with pleasure through a first folio of Chaucer, to brush up my French and Italian, to read Montaigne in the original text, yes, even to prune a cherry tree reflectively, not breaking my back to finish in an hour, to adjust methodically an old clock that was losing time, to relax completely with my children in a game of tennis or croquet—these were privileges and satisfactions I had not previously enjoyed.

Above all, this new freedom now afforded us the opportunity to travel. It was a thrilling adventure to take a car across the Channel from Dover to Calais, and to set off along the arrow-straight French roads, between the tall sentinel poplars and those flowering haw-thorn hedges beloved by Proust, through cobbled villages ablaze with roses, past red-tiled farmhouses and graceful churches, brassy *estaminets* and crumbling old châteaux, green canals with barges on them, woods, meadows, and orchards already pink with apple blossom. . . . Ah, how wonderful to escape to such delights!

Paris in the spring was a silver city. What enchantment in the fresh morning streets, to view the hurrying crowds and blue-cloaked policemen; the early housewives with arms crooked on laden baskets;

a Zouave in scarlet trousers; two concierges gossiping across their brooms; an old street cleaner sending a swirl of water along the gutter; pushcarts of vegetables clattering from the Halles; and all this cut by sharp, sudden cries, the chatter of many tongues, a slow chime of bells—against the background of soft grey buildings, the graceful white bridges, the lovely river sparkling in the sun.

Ascension Day in Chartres. There, in the great cathedral, jewel of French architecture, the sun streaming through the rose window, staining the plinths and peristyles with all the colours of the rainbow, the Cardinal, magnificent in scarlet, led the Easter procession behind swinging censers to the high altar and, supported by celestial choristers, intoned the Mass. Afterwards, at La Veille Maison across the square, we lunched appropriately—*escargots à la Burgoyne,* and *quenelles de brochet,* with a carafe of *vin rosé* to aid digestion. Then southward, to the château country, through Blois and Tours, idling along the lazy Loire, to spend the night in Angers, home of France's most fragrant liqueur. And, indeed, at dinner in the Hotel d'Anjou a special *soufflé au Cointreau* appeared, light as foam, soft as a cloud, as spring air, as a maiden's first kiss, enough to tempt a dying anchorite to eat.

Next day, another easy southward drive, through Chauteauroux and Clermont-Ferrand, into the beautiful Auvergne. Everywhere the wild spring flowers were blooming, field after field, carpeted with lily of the valley and golden-eyed narcissus, while from the plain, feathery with cedars, primitive as a Botticelli landscape, little pinnacles of rock arose, Vezelay, Sentier, and Puy-de-Dôme, each crowned by its mediaeval keep, like enchanted castles in a fairy tale.

Carcassonne came next, with its old walled city, then Arles, Hyères, San Tropez, where for days on end one may savour, like an effervescent wine, the sunshine of the Midi sparkling upon the Mediterranean sea.

Nor did this end our opportunity to wander and take possession of new quarters of the world. I had cut myself adrift from lion-hunting hostesses. Now there was no long list of patients to compel us to return, no telephone bringing calls every hour of the day, no night bell to make me its unwilling slave. Instead there was Spain, with its languid dignity and sunshine; the green mountains of Teneriffe, Madeira, Estoril, embowered in gorgeous mimosa and camellia trees; Bruges, placid and peaceful, with pigeons fluttering in the square; Budapest, murmurous with gipsy music, strung upon the Danube like a pearl upon a silver thread.

There was nothing of indolence in these journeyings. Each, indeed, was a source of literary nourishment. The writer must needs refresh himself with frequent change of scene, and in his trade he is privileged above all others in that he may work when and where he pleases. In my case, since I did not use a typewriter, my sole essential luggage was a fountain pen.

I made many notes upon these pilgrimages which formed the basis of future books. And often, too, there was some striking incident, some unusual contact with the mysterious and unforeseeable which would move me to that sadness, or delight, in the oddness of life, which is a basic element of the novelist's attitude.

I remember, for instance, one lovely June afternoon in Italy. As we drove through the foothills of the Alps, two small boys stopped us on the outskirts of Verona. They were selling wild strawberries, bright scarlet berries that looked delicious against the dark green leaves lining the wicker baskets.

"Don't buy," warned Luigi, our cautious driver. "You will get fruit much better in Verona. Besides, these boys . . ." He shrugged his shoulders to convey his disapproval of their shabby appearance.

One boy had a worn jersey and cutoff trousers; the other, a shortened workman's tunic gathered in loose folds about his skinny frame. My wife spoke to the boys, attracted by their brown skins, tangled hair, and dark earnest eyes, discovered that they were brothers. Nicola, the elder, was thirteen; Jacopo, who barely came up to the door handle of the car, was nearly twelve. We bought their biggest basket, then set off toward town.

Verona is a lovely city, rich in history, with quiet mediaeval streets and splendid buildings of an exquisitely pale honey colour. Romeo and Juliet are reputed to have lived and died there, yet, undeterred by that ancient tragedy, and the pinch of economic necessity, the Veronese maintain their gaiety and pride.

Next morning, coming out of our hotel, we drew up short. There, bent over shoeshine boxes beside the fountain in the public square, doing a brisk business, were our two young friends of the previous afternoon.

We watched for a few moments. Ordinarily, I should have passed on, but now I had to reckon with a new taskmaster—the insatiable curiosity of the writer. As trade slackened, I beckoned them over. They greeted us with friendly faces.

"I thought you picked fruit for a living," I said.

"We do many things, sir," Nicola answered seriously. He glanced at us hopefully. "Often we show visitors through the town . . . to Juliet's tomb . . . and other places of interest."

"All right," I smiled, "you take us along."

As we made the rounds, my interest was again provoked by their remarkable demeanour. They were childish enough, and in many ways quite artless. Jacopo, although his lips were paler than they should have been, was lively as a squirrel. Nicola's smile was ready and engaging. Yet in both these boyish faces there was a seriousness which one respected, an air of purpose far beyond their years.

In the week which followed we saw them frequently, for they proved extremely useful to us. If we wanted a pack of Virginia cigarettes, or a special brand of tooth paste, or seats for the opera, or the name of a restaurant that could provide good ravioli, Nicola and Jacopo could be relied upon to satisfy our needs, with their usual cheerful competence.

What struck one most was their unremitting willingness to work. During these summer days, under the hot sun, and in the long evenings when the air blew chill from the mountains, they shined shoes, sold fruit, hawked newspapers, conducted tourists round the town, ran errands, exploited every avenue which the troubled economy of the town left open to them.

One night, we came upon them in the windy and deserted square, resting on the stone pavement beneath the pale arc lights. Nicola sat upright, his face drawn by fatigue. A bundle of unsold newspapers lay at his feet, while Jacopo, his head pillowed upon his brother's shoulder, was asleep. It was nearly midnight.

"Why are you out so late, Nicola?"

He had started sharply as I spoke, but now he gave me his independent glance.

"Waiting for the last bus from Padua. We shall sell all our papers when it comes in."

"Must you keep at it so hard? You both look rather tired."

"We are not complaining, sir."

His tone, while perfectly polite, discouraged further inquiry. But next morning, when I went over to the fountain to have my shoes shined, I said:

"Nicola, the way you and Jacopo work, you must earn quite a bit. You spend nothing on clothes. You eat little enough—when I see you having a meal it's usually black bread and figs. Tell me, if the question is not impertinent, what do you do with your money?"

He coloured deeply under his sunburn, then grew pale. His gaze fell to the ground.

"You must be saving to go to college," I suggested.

He looked at me sideways, spoke with an effort.

"We should greatly like to have an education, sir. But at present, we have other plans."

"What plans?"

He smiled uncomfortably, with that remote air which never failed to baffle me.

"Just plans, sir," he answered in a low voice.

"Well," I said, "we're leaving on Monday. Is there anything I can do for you before we go?"

Nicola shook his head, but suddenly Jacopo's nostrils quivered like a puppy's and he piped up eagerly.

"Sir," he burst out, "every Sunday we make a visit to the country, to Poleta, thirty kilometres from here. Usually we hire bicycles. But tomorrow, since you are so kind, you might send us in your car."

I had already told Luigi he might have the Sunday off. However, now I was more curious than ever, and I answered:

283

"I'll drive you out myself."

There was a pause. Nicola was glaring at his young brother in vexation.

"We could not think of troubling you, sir."

"It won't be any trouble."

He bit his lip, then, in a rather put-out tone, he said:

"Very well."

The following afternoon we drove to the tiny picturesque village set high upon the hillside amidst sheltering chestnut groves, with a few pines on the upper slopes and a deep blue lake beneath. I imagined that our destination would be some humble dwelling. But, directed by Jacopo's shrill treble, we drew up at a large red-roofed villa, surrounded by a high stone wall. I could scarcely believe my eyes, and before I could recover breath, my two passengers had leaped nimbly from the car.

"We shall not be long, sir. Perhaps only an hour. Maybe you'd like to go to the *albergo* in the village for a drink?"

They disappeared beyond the corner of the wall.

When a few minutes had elapsed I followed. I found a grilled side entrance and, determinedly, rang the bell.

A pleasant-looking woman with a ruddy complexion and steel-rimmed spectacles appeared. I blinked as I saw that she was dressed in the white uniform of a trained nurse.

"I just brought two small boys here."

"Ah, yes." Her face lit up, she opened the door to admit me. "Nicola and Jacopo. I will take you up."

She led me through a cool tiled vestibule into the hospital—for hospital the villa had become. We traversed a waxed and polished corridor between well-equipped wards. We went upstairs to a southern balcony which opened to a vista of the gardens and the lake. On the threshold of a little cubicle the nurse paused, put her finger to her lips, and with a smile bade me look through the glass partition.

The two boys were seated at the bedside of a girl of about twenty who, propped up on pillows, wearing a pretty lace jacket, was listening to their chatter, her eyes soft and tender. Despite the faint flush high upon her cheekbones and the queer inertness of her posture,

284

one could discern at a glance her resemblance to her brothers. A vase of wild flowers stood on her table, beside a dish of fruit and several books.

"Won't you go in?" the nurse murmured. "Lucia will be pleased to see you."

I shook my head and turned away. I felt I could not intrude upon this happy family party. But at the foot of the staircase I drew up and begged her to tell me all she knew about these boys.

She was eager to do so. They were, she explained, quite alone in the world, except for this sister, Lucia. Their father, a widower, a well-known singer at La Scala, had been killed in a midnight car smash on the Grand Corniche. Quite improvident, dissipating his salary before he received it, he had left no other legacy than a mass of accumulated debts, writs, and notes of hand. His three children, their home sold, were thrown upon the streets. They had always known a comfortable and cultured life—Lucia had herself been training as a singer—and they had suffered horribly from near starvation and exposure to the cold Veronese winter.

For months they had barely kept themselves alive in a sort of shelter they built of billboards with their own hands in a waste lot near the river. They were proud, they sought help from no one, and because they loved each other, they were determined to survive. The two boys, especially, despite their extreme youth and insignificant size, refused to let poverty break their spirit. They faced it with dignity and courage.

The nurse broke off, then with even deeper feeling she went on:

"I cannot tell you how fine they were, these two. And then, when they were finding their feet again, their sister fell sick . . . seriously. She was suffering from tuberculosis of the spine."

She paused, took a quick breath.

"Did they give up? I do not have to answer that question. They brought her here, persuaded us to take her into the hospital. In the twelve months she has been our patient she has made good progress. There is every hope that one day she will walk . . . and sing . . . again.

"Of course, everything is so difficult now, food so scarce and dear, we could not keep going unless we charged a fee. But every week, Lucia's brothers have made their payment." She added, simply: "I don't know what they do, I do not ask. Work is scarce in Verona. But whatever it is, I know they do it well."

"Yes," I agreed, "they couldn't do it better."

I waited outside until the boys rejoined me, then drove them back to the city. They sat beside me, not speaking, in a mood of contentment. For my part, I did not say a word—I knew they would prefer to feel that they had safely kept their secret—yet I was resolved that aid should reach them. Next morning, before we left for Venice, I sent an envelope to the hospital at Poleta to be delivered to them when next they went there. On it I wrote, simply this: "For two gentlemen of Verona."

# Chapter Thirty-four

NEVER BEFORE HAD the beauty of the world been so apparent. Never had life appeared so charged with potentialities for happiness. Yet through it all, like a strange dissonance in a lovely symphony, there existed everywhere in Europe harsh undertones of hatred and of fear. In the quiet valleys of Bavaria we heard the tramp of soldiers and the roar of artillery practice. We saw caisson after caisson, thundering from the factories of Silesia, loaded with the weapons of war. Munich was an insane blaze of bunting, a mad parade ground for strutting uniforms. In Vienna, gayest and gentlest of all cities, the opera continued, the bells of St. Stephen's still rang merrily, the festival of the new wine was bravely held, yet beneath, one sensed a feeling of dread, of fatalism amounting to despair. It was coming . . . coming . . . , an avalanche of horror and destruction . . . , a total war which would engulf and destroy millions of innocent people who wished no part of it, yet were powerless to prevent it. Why, oh why, in the name of suffering humanity, must this be?

In the winter of 1938 we rented a chalet for the season in the village of Arosa, seven thousand feet up, on the high slopes of the Tschuggen. Majestic white peaks, made rosy by the sunrise, the cheerful jingle of the horse-drawn sleighs, *ski-wasser* and hot coffee with double cream in the bright little cafés of the village, the sweet smell of cows in the wooden straw-packed sheds, the ring of curling stones on ice, the spotless cleanliness, the wholesome goodness of Swiss food, the creak of new snow beneath one's feet, at night that exquisite tiredness after a long day's ski run to St. Moritz, the polished glitter of the stars, lights extinguished, one by one, in the village houses, leaving only eternal stillness and the liquid moonlight. For our boys, for whom this holiday was an unexpected adventure, there was a joyous novelty in skiing and skating, in hurtling downhill on the toboggan run at breakneck speed, winding up with ruddy cheeks, head over heels in the soft snowbed at the bottom.

But to me, despite the stimulation of these surroundings, the world situation, rapidly deteriorating, was a constant source of sad foreboding. My outlook had changed in these last years. No longer living from hour to hour, I had, for better or worse, acquired the habit of reflecting each day upon certain aspects of existence less material than those which had previously engrossed me. Thus no doubt my state of mind was propitious to what occurred. For it was here, in Arosa, one Sunday, when I went to church—an ordinary excursion, undertaken with no unusual piety—that I met with the strangest spiritual experience of my life.

I had seen many churches: the great cathedrals of Chartres and Rheims, the Chapel of the Black Virgin at Montserrat, St. Peter's in Rome, Giotto's exquisite campanile and baptistry in Florence. . . . This was different—a small, bare, pine-wood chapel, sweet-smelling with the tang of resin, perched amidst the snow-encrusted pinnacles of the Alps. Here, in these azure altitudes, cleansed by the still pure air, stricken by the blinding beauty of snow and sky, one felt oneself upon the very threshold of high heaven.

The congregation was mainly peasant, the clear-eyed, sturdy, industrious people of this German-speaking canton of Switzerland. The men wore stiff dark suits, their necks bronzed above unusual collars. There was little finery among the women, at the most a lace headdress or a treasured embroidered shawl. A scarlet kerchief, sported by a little boy, made a splash of colour that set the place alight. The service was one to which I was habituated and which, accordingly, evoked no new sensation. But perhaps there was more simplicity, a greater directness in these devotions. At any rate, there was for me a queer immanence, an odd expectancy vibrating in the air. And then it was time for the sermon.

As the congregation sat down with a rustle and the clergyman came up to the plain wooden pulpit, my companion cast at me a swift glance of commiseration and regret. I had come with a middle-aged Englishman, of undemonstrative habit, who had been a patient of mine in London and who was now taking the tuberculosis cure at a *Heilanstalt* in the village. He spoke German fluently, while I knew not one word of that bewildering tongue. Under the deprecating twinkle in his eye I felt consigned, through my own illiteracy, to an hour of gibberish and boredom.

And yet, as the preacher took his stand and faced his audience I felt again that queer compelling thrill. There was much in the quiet surpliced figure to rivet my attention. He was dark, short and thick-set, still in his virile thirties, with a sallow skin, a noble head and a full, magnetic eye. His manner was both vibrant and composed, charged with a fearless humility. His voice as he gave out his text was restrained yet deeply resonant, filling the tiny church and echoing from the roof. He stood very still, having uttered his premise, and then, in that wholly foreign speech, he started upon his sermon.

Now I am no revivalist. I have listened to many a windbagful of sermons in my day. Of late, especially, I had come to dread the timid bleatings, the milk-and-water flapdoodle of play-safe parsons. But this man was different: different as tempered steel from sounding brass. And as his discourse took shape, despite my utter ignorance of its content, I fell unconsciously under some strange and mystic spell. I caught one word: *Christus.* And one other, which was *Führer.* And then, as by a breath, the scene dissolved, church and congregation vanished. I saw suddenly, and with a stabbing clarity, the countries of the earth and the pestilence that lay upon them. I saw the great dictator states, controlled by one hand, one voice, deifying the doctrine of blood and iron. I saw the great democracies, sleek with good living, jealous of their vast possessions, fearful lest some vandal's hand should rob them of their gains.

I saw in every land the billion tons of armaments piled high. I saw the ever-multiplying shells and guns, the stores of poison gas and bombs, the skies darkened by death-compelling planes. I saw children taught from their cradles to bluster and to hate, to strut in military parade when they could scarcely walk, to nurse a rifle as though it were a cherished toy. I saw half the world's wealth buried as useless yellow metal in a concrete tomb. I saw wheat burned by the million bushels in one corner of the globe, while in another thousands of human creatures went hungry for lack of bread. I saw everywhere the blind surges of mankind, the frightened rushes hither and thither searching for security, the restless plunges into momentary pleasure, the fevered striving for material gain. And over all, amidst the sound of jazz and the chink of coins, I saw the omnipresent ghastly dread, the approaching spectre of self-created doom.

It was a vision which chilled the heart, which moved one to icy terror: this lovely fruitful earth, overflowing with plenty, riven from end to end by hate, aggression, and brutal cruelty, which, if unchecked, must surely crumble civilization to the dust. And less than a quarter of a century before, nine million of the world's finest men had yielded up their lives under the promise of an everlasting peace.

Such agonizing recollection could not but evoke the instant bitter query: Why, in the name of reason and sweet mercy, had this iniquitous bedlam come to pass? The question was not new, yet it struck at me with fresh relentless force. And across my mind flashed the endless explanations advanced by human ingenuity. The talk of economic stress, of boom and slump, of unemployment and the rest. Of the rise and fall of nations, the need for colonies, the survival of the fittest, the whole bag of tricks. How fatuous, how futile they all seemed now!

For it was clear, acutely clear. There was only one reason, one basic explanation: *man had forgotten God*. Millions now living were blind and deaf—dead indeed—to the knowledge of their Creator. For countless human souls that Name was nothing but a myth. For others, an inherited tradition to which lip service must be paid. For others, a convenient oath. For others, a bland hypocrisy.

Yes, that was the blind and naked truth. False gods as evil as the golden calf of old now stood upon the altars of the Christian people. Paganism bestrode the modern earth. To all but a few the very mention of the Christ evoked a smile of mockery and contempt.

Yet here, in this mad search for leadership, was the one Leader who could save the world. Here, forgotten amidst the wild quest for

290

ideologies, was the one creed that promised salvation. Not a hard creed to comprehend. Nor yet to follow. A creed of beauty and simplicity. To live decently in the sight of Heaven and one's fellow men. To love one's neighbour, to be uncovetous of his goods. To be tolerant, charitable, humble. To recollect always that life, as we know it, is but a fragment of eternity.

Oh, that an army of new crusaders might arise to spread afresh in every land this long-neglected counsel, to unfurl once again the faded banner of the forgotten King! Oh, that more ministers of religion might abandon their platitudes, cease to be prudent and become sincere, forsake their empty churches and sally forth like soldiers to justify themselves in valiant conflict beneath the darkening sky! Then indeed might the world come back to sanity, and poor, bemused, and tortured humanity back to God.

Quite suddenly I felt a shock, and the swift flow of my thought was interrupted. With a wrench that was almost physical I came back to earth, and saw that the preacher had at that moment reached the end of his peroration.

We came out of the church into the unblemished brightness of the winter day. And as we made our way down to the village I related to my companion the full account of my striking meditation.

He heard me with ever-growing amazement. As I concluded he faced me in stark bewilderment.

"But don't you realise!" He almost gasped for breath. *"That, almost word for word, was the pastor's sermon."*

# Chapter Thirty-five

WITH EVERY DAY the danger was growing, the handwriting on the wall becoming clearer, and finally, as a few wise men had foreseen, the dogs of war once again were loosed upon the world.

Another war! To those of us who had been involved in that first world conflict and whose sons were now called upon to fight in this, it seemed only yesterday since the thunder of the guns had been stilled, since the little black-coated politicians in whose hands we trustfully place our destinies had promised us, in florid phrases, lasting terrestrial harmony.

What under heaven was wrong with the human race? People, as individuals, as I had met them everywhere, were, in the main, amiable, goodhearted, peace-loving. Why, then, this mass, recurrent impulse to fall upon their neighbours, this blind hysterical urge toward slaughter and self-destruction? What folly . . . , what purposeless, unending lunacy!

But the mortal struggle had begun, and disasters came thick and fast upon us. The surrender of Belgium, followed swiftly by the evacuation of Dunkirk, and the occupation of Holland—these were great misfortunes. But when France fell and the streets of Paris echoed with the tramp of the invaders, it seemed as though freedom could not survive, as though violence and tyranny had prevailed.

Then came the bombings, the guided missiles, all that human ingenuity and malice could devise, a ruthless and indiscriminate holocaust from the air. Women, children, and old people alike were killed, wounded, and maimed, mangled in a bloody mist of pain.

Homes, hospitals, churches, great works of art were shattered and brought to ruin by these vultures of the sky. Everything which the genius of man had created to adorn and inspire the world seemed doomed to destruction. And hunger followed, a gaunt spectre, stalking among the rubble, in what seemed the twilight of the universe.

It was small wonder that the faint of heart despaired. And when, at last, the smoke of battle cleared, how little there seemed left of the world we once had known!

When the opportunity was given me, some months after the armistice, to make an extended tour of Europe, I set out upon this mission with a heavy heart, convinced in advance that however earnestly I sought I should find no gleam of light in the settled gloom that hung upon these devastated lands. Yet I was wrong. The human spirit, although it may be bruised and crushed, is indestructible. The evidence that I discovered was slight, perhaps, based on chance personal contacts, intangible and widely scattered. Nevertheless, it carried more weight with me than a host of cold statistics.

I went first to Vienna, that exquisite city which in the past I had known so well and loved so much. Since morning, when the transport plane had landed me at the airfield, my mood had grown progressively more melancholy. There was no accommodation at the Bristol, and the room they had finally found for me in a drab house in the Kartnerstrasse was sparsely furnished and unheated. For lunch there was only vegetable soup and a slice of black *Kartoffel* bread.

In the afternoon, as I set out in the cutting wind on my tour of inspection, past the shattered Cathedral of St. Stephen and the ruins of the Opera House, my heart sank further. The little palace of the Empress Eugénie where I had lunched so gaily with Count Von Zsolnay and Franz Werfel, the Hall of the Clothmakers where I had lectured to the Kulturbund . . . where, alas, were they now? Was this the lovely, festive city where I had known such joyful days and exhilarating nights, where I had heard Lehmann sing in *La Bohème* and driven afterward in an open carriage through the gaily crowded thoroughfares to celebrate the *Heurige,* the festival of the new wine? I had come prepared for material destruction, for shat-

293

tered houses, heaps of rubble, bombed buildings, yes, even for the melancholy spectacle of the blown-up Danube bridges. I had foreseen affliction, but not this empty, silent desolation which, like a chill miasma, pervaded these grey and dingy shuttered streets.

As it crept into my bones a blind anger grew within me, a sullen resentment against Providence that such things should come to pass. To make matters worse, as the frigid February twilight fell, it began to rain, a heavy, freezing sleet that threatened to penetrate the army mackintosh which I wore over my woollen coat.

I was now somewhere in the eastern suburbs, and to escape I took shelter in a neighbouring building—a small church which had escaped destruction. The place was empty and almost dark, the shadows relieved only by the faint red flicker of the sanctuary light. Impatiently, I sat down to wait until the worst of the downpour should pass.

Suddenly, I heard footsteps, and turning, I saw an old man enter the church. He wore no coat, and his tall figure, gaunt and stiffly erect, clad in a thin, much-mended suit, was painfully shabby. As he advanced toward the side altar I observed with surprise that he was carrying in his arms a child, a little girl of about six, dressed also in the garments of poverty. When he reached the railing of the altar he put her down gently. I perceived then, from the helpless movements of her limbs, that she was paralysed. Still supporting her with great patience, he encouraged her to kneel, arranging her hands so that she could cling to the altar rail. When he had succeeded, he smiled at her, as though congratulating her on her achievement, then he knelt, spare and erect, beside her.

For a few minutes they remained thus, then the old man rose. I heard the thin echo of a small coin falling into the box, then saw him take a candle, light it, and give it to the child. She held it in one transparent hand for a long moment while the glow cast a little halo about her, making visible the pleased expression on her pale, pinched features. Then she placed the candle upright on the small iron stand before the shadowed altar, admiring her little gift, dedicating it with the rapt upturned tilt of her head.

Presently the old man got up again and, lifting the child, began to carry her in his arms out of the church. All the time that I had watched them I had felt myself intruding on their privacy, guilty of a sort of sacrilege. Yet now, though that feeling remained, an irresistible impulse made me rise and follow them to the church porch.

Here, drawn to one side, was a small homemade conveyance—a rickety wooden box with lopsided sticks for shafts, mounted on two old perambulator wheels which had long ago lost their tires. Into this equipage the old man was bestowing the child, spreading an old potato sack across her limbs. Now that I stood close to them I could plainly confirm what I had already suspected. Every line of the old man's drawn face, the cropped grey moustache, the fine nose, the proud eyes under deep brows, showed him a true patrician, one of those noble Viennese to whom, through no fault of their own, the war had brought total ruin. The child, whose peaked features resembled his own, was almost certainly his granddaughter. As with his veined, fine hands he finished tucking the sack around her, he glanced at me. A rush of questions was on my tongue, but something, the spiritual quality of that face, restrained my curiosity. I could only say, with awkwardness:

"It is very cold."

He answered me politely:

"Less cold than it has been this winter."

There was a pause. My gaze returned to the child whose blue eyes were fixed upon us.

"The war?" I said, still looking at her.

"Yes, the war," he answered. "The same bomb killed her mother and father."

Another, and a longer pause.

"You come here often?" I regretted this crudity immediately it escaped me. But he took no offense.

"Yes, every day, to pray." He smiled faintly. "And also to show the good God we are not too angry with Him."

I could find no reply. And as I stood in silence he straightened himself, buttoned his jacket, picked up the shafts of the little buggy and with that same faint smile, that polite inclination of his head, moved off with the child into the gathering darkness.

295

No sooner were they gone than I had again an insufferable desire to pursue them. I wanted to help, to offer them money, to strip off my warm coat, to do something impetuous and spectacular. But I remained rooted to the spot. I knew that this was no case for common charity, that anything which I could give would be refused. Instead, it was they who had given something to me. They, who had lost everything, refused to despair; they could still believe. A feeling of confusion rose in me. Now there was no anger in my heart, no concern for my own petty deprivations, but only pity and a pervading sense of shame.

The rain had gone off. But I did not go out. I hesitated. Then I turned and went back toward the little faithful beacon which still burned at the side altar in the no longer empty church. One candle in a ruined city. But while it shone there seemed hope for the world.

# Chapter Thirty-six

From Austria I went to Italy. Every morning, during my brief stay in the battered little Italian village of Castelmare, near Livorno, I would see old Maria Bendetti. Small, slight, and shrunken, barefooted, clad in rusty black, a black scarf bound about her head, her frail shoulders bowed beneath the big wicker basket on her back, she typified the prevailing tragedy. Her thin brown face, so set and careworn, seemed moulded by calamity into lines of irreparable sadness.

She sold fish, those odd and unappetizing Mediterranean fishes which, eked out by a scant ration of macaroni or spaghetti, formed the meagre diet of this broken seaside community. I had known the village in its days of carefree, joyous peace. Now there was no music and laughter in the little square, where bomb-gutted buildings sprawled drunkenly among the dusty rubble, a scene of utter heartbreak, over which the scent of flowering oleanders lay poignantly, as upon a tomb. The place was dead, and because I had loved it so well, its final desolation saddened me anew.

Most of the young men and women had moved away. But the children and older people remained, moving, it seemed to me, like ghosts, wresting a hand-to-mouth existence from the sea with their patched-up boats and mended nets.

And among these was Maria. Occasionally she was accompanied by her niece, a thin barelegged waif of ten, who trotted beside her and cried in a shrill insistent voice, *"Pesci . . . pesci freschi!"* as though determined to establish beyond all doubt that their fish were of the freshest quality.

One morning, as they passed through the ruined square, I spoke to them. Yes, they had been through the bombardment; the war had been a bad affair, they agreed. They now lived, with the utmost frugality, in a dark little cave of a room in the Via Eustachia, a narrow street in what remained of the poorest quarter of the town.

In a culmination of that mood which burned within me, which was, of course, the reflex of my own pessimism and discontent, I asked abruptly:

"Why don't you leave the village? Here there is no future . . . all destroyed . . . completely finished."

There was a pause. The old woman slowly shook her head.

"This is our home. We do not think it is finished."

As the two moved away it appeared that they exchanged a secret glance.

That glance provoked my curiosity. During the next few days I found myself observing their movements with a queer, unwilling interest. In the early part of the day they had their fixed and visible routine, but in the afternoon, astonishingly, they were nowhere to be found. Several times after my picnic lunch I walked to the Via Eustachia only to discover that the little room was empty. Could it be that the two were less simple than I had supposed, that their absence every afternoon concealed some underhand affair, smuggling perhaps, or some devious working of the black market?

Prompted by this thought, I went earlier one day to the Via Eustachia, at an hour when I usually took a siesta on the beach, and stationed myself in a doorway near the old woman's room. I had not long to wait. A few minutes after one o'clock Maria and her niece emerged. Each carried upon her back an empty wicker basket, and hand in hand, with an air of purpose, they set off briskly along the shattered street. Stealthily, almost, I followed them.

Through the piles of rubble went the old woman and the child. At the outskirts of the village they took a sun-baked path which led down to the dry bed of the river. Here, as I took up a vantage point on the high bank, I saw to my surprise that other figures were working with pick and spade in the flinty channel. Maria and the girl unslung their baskets and set to work. At first, I fancied they were digging some kind of bait, then I made out that the child was filling her small basket with white sand while Maria, stooping and making her selection with great care, was gathering a load of square white stones. When the panniers were full, the two shouldered their loads and slowly ascended the steep and narrow path.

They passed close to me, yet if they were conscious of my presence, they gave no sign. When they had gone a few paces ahead I followed.

The way led to the summit of the ruined town, a plateau dominating the landscape, which, in my wanderings, I had not reached before, the one site in all the wasted terrain that had escaped destruction. There, amidst a grove of acacia trees, a larger group of the village people were at work. Quietly, talking in low tones, with a restraint which gave to their actions a strange solemnity, they were mixing mortar, carving and facing the fine white stones, forming the walls of a large new structure.

For an instant I was puzzled; then, all at once, from the shape already risen, I realised what they were building. I caught my breath sharply. These people, who had barely a roof above their heads, upon whom lay the blight of overwhelming destruction, these women, children, and old men whom I had seen merely as beaten and extinguished shadows, had chosen, as their first united act, to construct, solely by their own effort, a new and splendid church. Not a makeshift chapel, but a finer, larger place of worship than ever they had had before.

Maria and the child emptied out their loads. They stood for a moment to recover their breath, then turned to make a fresh descent. As the old woman passed me, with beads of perspiration still upon her brow, she gave me, unexpectedly, from her dark, wise eyes a quick, faint smile, a smile impenetrable in its sweetness, which held, beneath its deep serenity, a touch of friendly malice, as though to say: "Are we finished, then, after all?" All her life was written in

299

that look—the past, the present, and the future. Courage was there, and high endurance, with trust, patient and unshakable—the will to live from day to day, to accept, and above all, to hope.

Confused and humbled, I stood motionless as the old woman and the little girl passed out of sight together. And suddenly my chest heaved, a stab went through me, a stab of anguished self-compunction at my own proneness to despair. What matter the rubble and the ruins? If the very young and the very old could show such faith, there was hope for the world after all.

I stood there a long time, and as I went down at last, consoled and lifted up, the first star was rising, pale yet luminous, in the eternal sky, and in the soft mist that crept up from the waters the ravaged village disappeared. There rose instead a shining city of the spirit.

# Chapter Thirty-seven

AND THEN I WAS in France. That same month of June, as I drove through the orchards of Normandy, within view of Mont-Saint-Michel, a turn of the road brought me suddenly to an old French château. The sight of this stately dwelling, set in a verdant park behind an avenue of lime trees, caused me to draw up. And as an old countryman was passing, I inquired:

"Who lives there?"

He stopped and smiled—a spontaneous smile which lit up his weathered face, wrinkled and ruddy as a ripe cider apple.

"Why, none other than Monsieur le Maire."

Surprised by this answer, I exclaimed:

"But surely . . . that must be the home of an important person . . . some nobleman. . . ."

The old man nodded his head in amiable indulgence.

"Oh, yes. Monsieur le Maire is certainly a marquis. . . . He has one of the best names in France. But he is also mayor of our village. And that, monsieur . . . , that is how we know him."

Something in the peasant's tone and manner—he would not be drawn further, but ambled off along the dusty lane—whetted my curiosity, gave me the feeling that I had stumbled on a story. And as I had time on my hands, instead of pushing on toward Saint-Malo as I had intended, I turned off at the adjoining village and put up at the tavern there—the Pomme d'Or. I felt a strong desire to meet Monsieur le Maire.

This, the landlord of the inn assured me, would not be difficult—

the mayor was accessible to everyone—and following his voluble directions I crossed the pretty village square and entered the little red-roofed town hall. Here, in a tiny, bare whitewashed room, seated at a scrubbed deal table, under the flag of France, I found the man I sought.

He was of middle age, slight and spare, clean-shaven, with well-marked features, rather hollow cheeks, and a penetrating yet strangely tranquil gaze. He was dressed very plainly, in corduroy breeches, stout stockings and boots, and an old-fashioned Norfolk jacket with narrow lapels and a belt at the back. And he wore, round his waist, the tricolour sash that was the badge of his office. Although he held himself erect as he rose to greet me, I thought that he did not look particularly robust, and he seemed tired, as from a hard day's work. Nevertheless, he smiled cordially and offered me his hand, declaring that he had just been marrying a young couple from an outlying farm, an exercise of his civil functions which—he added—always delighted him. When I gave him my card his eye showed a friendly interest and after some moments of animated questioning he startled me—for I had not expected such hospitality —by inviting me to dinner.

The cool of evening was falling when we left the town hall and walked down the single street. Passing a group of young men returning from the fields, some women washing clothes by the bridge, a band of children playing outside the school, one could not but remark the extraordinary blending of familiarity and respect with which these people of the village greeted my companion. There was nothing of deference in their manner, still less of servility, but rather a kind of camaraderie, a sense of affection, understanding, and good-fellowship.

Then we came to the wrought-iron gates of the château, passed into the avenue, and immediately I was struck by signs of straitened circumstances which had not been apparent to me from a distance. There were deep ruts in the driveway, weeds sprouting between the cobblestones of the courtyard, great cracks in the ornamental urns which flanked the balustrade of the terrace. When we entered the mansion itself—despite the ageless beauty of the exterior—this impression was borne out by the silence of the lofty rooms, the absence of servants, the complete negation of all that grandeur and display which might normally have been found in such a setting. At the end of the vaulted hall a small table covered with a checked cloth was set with cutlery and china, and here, after another place had been laid, an aged white-haired man, quiet and slow-moving, served the dinner.

Now, indeed, the austerity of this establishment was fully confirmed by the frugality of our repast. A thin soup was set before us, followed by a dish of cooked vegetables eaten with dark bread, then came, finally, a cup of unsweetened black coffee. Despite the control which I imposed upon myself, some hint of perplexity must have been visible in my expression. For suddenly, to my embarrassment, my host broke into a low chuckle of amusement.

"If I had known you were coming we should have tried to do better." Immediately he was serious again. "You see, sir, we are glad here even of the simplest fare. For there have been times in our little community when we did not eat at all."

When we had finished our coffee he conducted me outside to a seat upon the terrace, silently offered me a cigarette. Darkness had fallen and, except for the faint hooting of owls in the tall pine woods behind, the stillness was absolute. The moon was not risen, but before us, in the hollow of the valley, the lights of the hamlet made a cluster of low stars. The sight seemed to fascinate the man beside me—his gaze remained steadfastly upon it.

"Do you believe that a place . . . like that village you now see . . . can have a soul?" The question came unexpectedly, and before I could answer it my companion went on, "Perhaps that sounds absurd to you. Yet it is a belief I cling to with all my heart."

There was a pause, then, drawing deeply on his cigarette, suppressing the slight cough which seemed always to trouble him, he began to speak, in a low tone, gazing straight ahead.

He was, he told me, one of a family of three, but both his brothers had been killed in World War I. He himself had spent four years in the trenches in that conflict, had been gassed with chlorine, wounded by shrapnel in the chest. He made this admission lightly,

303

without self-consciousness, remarking with a faint smile that it was not the Boche gas but the Caporal tobacco, which he smoked incessantly, that really had affected his lungs.

In the troubled interim of peace which followed, both his parents had died. Then came World War II. When the Germans broke through, they occupied the château, made it a general staff headquarters, and, suspecting that he was heading a resistance movement, threw him into prison. In this fashion he had spent another four years of his life.

He smiled again, in a reminiscent fashion, and lit another cigarette.

"Someday I would like to tell you of that time in prison. The trials of an active nature with nothing to do. In desperation I bribed my jailor with my cuff links to bring me string. And with this string I made fish nets . . . scores of fish nets. And while I made these nets, I thought. . . . Ah, yes, monsieur, I thought deeply. Heaven knows I am no philosopher, yet it was the result of these reflections in my cell which changed completely my outlook upon life."

He paused in that same gently reflective manner.

"When we were freed by the forces of liberation, for which, believe me, sir, we owe the United States our eternal gratitude, I came back here. This place, the home of my family for centuries, was in a state of indescribable dilapidation and neglect, while I, of course, was ruined." His lips curved with deprecating humour. "In prison I had not been clever enough to beat the depreciation of the franc by black-market speculation. What inflation had begun, taxation finished off. As I surveyed the wreck of my estate I was tempted to throw up the sponge and go away to escape, anywhere, to the furthest ends of the earth. And then, through the mist of my own misfortunes, I became aware of the condition of the village —and of the people there—which was worse, far worse than mine.

"In the severe fighting of the liberation many of the houses had been reduced to rubble. Food was scarce, inflation and black marketing were rife, currency had no value, and for many a poor peasant the slowly accumulated savings of a lifetime, hidden in a stocking in the chimney corner, had suddenly become valueless. Everything

304

we had believed in seemed gone. People were not only without homes, bread, or money, they were without heart, without faith. Yes, they had lost their belief in God, in France, in themselves. And in this desperate plight the new enemy crept in. Yes, monsieur, here in this remote countryside, far from the great cities, in the heart of our beautiful France, we were threatened by Communism. A mechanic at the garage, named Martin, was the leader. He had suffered severely—his business was gone, the piece of land he had bought and cultivated had become so densely overgrown by briars in the war years he had neither the means nor the will to reclaim it. In brief, he was in the mood to preach revolution, he did preach it, and soon he had a large number of the people under his influence."

My host paused here, stared broodingly into the night, before resuming.

"I must confess to you that my family had always kept themselves aloof from the village, had never taken but the remotest interest in it, except as a recruiting ground for their servants, gardeners, footmen. But suddenly, I, the sole survivor of my line, felt a strange responsibility. Perhaps you remember the parable of the lost talent. That, monsieur, in my moment of supreme despondency, was how I felt—that I must go out and seek, without rest, until I found it . . . the talent of the lost happiness and well-being of a ruined village.

"It so happened that the office of mayor was vacant. No one wanted it. It was an anachronism, according to Martin, part of the derelict system that had deceived and exploited the people. Without ostentation I put myself forward . . . and was appointed. And then, instead of looking to the villagers to serve me, I began to serve them."

Again that reflective pause, that quiet smile directed toward me.

"I shall not bore you by detailing my indifferent efforts. There were some fields at the end of this property—these I divided up among such as were eager to till them. For others I established a fishery in the bay—my nets proved not altogether useless, you see—and arranged for a distribution of the catch in Rennes. I used every effort to provide opportunities for work. But the essential thing was to place myself at the disposal of everyone, to be always on hand, to give advice, to settle disputes, to offer all possible assistance.

"Oh, it was not easy. Naturally the people did not trust me, suspected me of an ulterior motive, sneered at me behind my back. But gradually, almost in spite of themselves, some began to come my way. There remained, however, Martin and his following. Every time I passed the derelict garage they would shout abuse, spit on the pavement. Ah, how they hated me."

He turned toward me quickly.

"Make no mistake, monsieur, I did not commit the folly of hating them back. I understood how they felt, indeed I sympathised with them; they were Frenchmen, just as much as I. In those years in prison I had realised how false were the old standards of patriotism. In the old days in the trenches we used to say that a man cannot fight on an empty stomach. How much truer to say that he will not fight *for* an empty stomach. He must *have* something—here in the country, he must have a home, a patch of land, chickens and a cow; above all, a decent, rewarding way of life, to make him a loyal and contented citizen."

His voice suddenly grew intensely serious.

"All over the world, monsieur, that fact is becoming more and more evident. We cannot preach democracy and at the same time tolerate conditions which deny a living wage and equal opportunity to vast sections of our population. Happy people are never Communists. Revolution springs only from discontent and misery. If through our own stupidity we drive the masses in desperation, to that extremity, we have only ourselves to blame."

For a long moment he was silent; then, with a return to his former tranquillity, he went on:

"I need not tell you that we, in France, have felt the good will of America. One day, in the spring of 1948, there arrived in our village the first exciting evidence of *le bon plan Marshal*. It was a tractor, a splendid agricultural machine, complete with plough, harrow, cultivator; in short, with all equipment. I assure you, as it stood there in the square, brand new, its bright vermilion paint gleaming in the sun, it was the centre of attention. Everyone flocked to see it.

"Well, sir, toward evening, when the crowd had gone and the commotion subsided, I saw a solitary figure viewing the machine, at first from a distance, then coming nearer, inspecting the engine, testing the controls, even caressing the heavy tire treads with his hands. To my surprise, I saw that it was Martin. Approaching unobserved, I spoke to him.

" 'Good evening, Martin. It is a nice machine.'

"He started in confusion, angry at being caught there, admiring this product of the hated capitalists. But honesty compelled him to be truthful. He glared at me doggedly.

" 'Yes,' he muttered, 'it is a fine job. Any fool could tell you that.'

"I gazed back at him, and as I did so a sudden idea, call it if you wish an inspiration, came to me. You will recollect that this man was a mechanic who knew and loved machinery. Remember also his derelict farm with only a broken wooden plough to work it. Almost involuntarily, the words came from me.

" 'I am glad you approve of it, Martin. It is yours.'

"At first he did not understand. Perhaps he imagined I had gone mad. Then he thought I was making game of him, and his face turned dusky with anger. But he knew that the machine was under my jurisdiction, and something in my look, which was serious and calm, though I assure you, sir, I was not calm inside, must have told him I was in earnest. He went deadly pale. The struggle within him was painful to observe. He tried to speak but his lips began to tremble; although he set his jaw hard, the muscles of his face were out of his control. I could see the moisture forming in his eyes. Without a word, without even a sign, I turned and walked away."

My companion leaned forward and placed his hand upon my arm, his expression half quizzical, half grave.

"After that, no more trouble. One act of generosity can do more to dispel malice and envy than a hundred burnings at the stake. Of course we all use the tractor in the village. But it is Martin's. He is proud of it. With it he has not only reclaimed his farm. He has reclaimed himself."

When he concluded there was a long silence, a silence filled with meaning, in which, through the veils of vapour that now lay upon the dew-drenched fields, the lights of the tiny hamlet seemed somehow to burn brighter. Slowly I turned and grasped his hand.

"Yes," I said in a low voice, "your village has a soul. I believe that you have saved it."

Next morning it was early as I drove away from the Pomme d'Or. But already, though the place was only half awake, Monsieur le Maire was at his post. He waved as he threw up the window of his little bureau. And in that simple action, it was for me as though a window had been thrown open to the splendour and mystery of service and self-sacrifice. Even now I have the vision of that slight spare figure, that humble aristocrat with his pale, hollow-cheeked face, his cough, his Caporal cigarette, his comic little sash, viewing the world with unfailing sympathy, helping his neighbours, bringing together the highest and the lowest, striving simply, earnestly, unfalteringly, to keep alight the flame of freedom in the country that he loves.

And I thought that if only all of us would work like that, steadfastly and selflessly, forgetting personal expediency, in the cause of the brotherhood of men, then the troubles of this stricken world would end.

# Chapter Thirty-eight

WHEN AUTUMN CAME I was still in Normandy. Now the fields were golden with ripe grain, the orchards heavy with red-cheeked cider apples. Here, in the open country, only a few scars of battle met the eye—some scraps of rusted metal in the ditches, the shattered segment of a tank, half hidden by a hedgerow. It was good to view this healing of the ravaged earth, yet one could not escape a vague sense of regret that so slight a testimony should here endure to the invasion—that great, exalted effort which had freed this fruitful French countryside.

But when we reached the Lion Rouge in the little village near Avranches which was our destination for the night, I came upon a shred of evidence which drew me up . . . and made me smile. Written on the ground-glass panel of my bedroom door, I noticed these cryptic words: "Johnnie Brown, GI, stays here."

The scrawl was in pencil and could easily have been erased. The fact that it remained interested me, and after supper I ventured into the kitchen and mentioned the matter to Madame Delnotte, who owned this simple inn.

As though debating whether or not I were worthy of her confidence, Madame studied me, her sallow features illumined by a gleam from the copper pans which lined the wall. She glanced toward her daughter, Claire, who sat mending some linen at the table. Then, slowly, with an air of quiet reminiscence, she answered me.

Yes, Johnnie had been one of that great American army engaged in the fighting which raged around this focal point between Mortain and Avranches. Impossible now to realise the severity of that conflict —Madame's face grew faintly rigid as she leaned forward in her chair—it was not an ordinary battle but had gone on for weeks, in endless uncertainty and suspense. Mortain, for example, had changed hands no less than seven times. Under such circumstances it was necessary that the exhausted troops should from time to time be billeted out of the line for a few days, to rest and recover. Thus Johnnie had come to the Lion Rouge.

He was a silent, yet smiling, boy with dark hair and eyes, tall for his age—he had just left high school when war broke out, and his home was in Georgia. Despite his reserve and the slow reticence of his soft Southern speech, Johnnie was a general favourite who took good-naturedly any amount of chaff, and Madame knew from his comrades that he was brave in action. Yet there was one special quality which distinguished him above all others: he was a born naturalist.

On his rest periods at the inn he would set out for the woods and meadows, following the leafy trails and winding brooks with an alert and eager gaze, pausing to watch the darting of a kingfisher, lying flat to study the movements of an otter or a water vole, parting the long grasses to view the timid scurryings of a nest of field mice. Only a few short kilometres away the livid hell of battle raged, the roar of heavy artillery filled the air until the very sky seemed blasted, yet Johnnie pursued his beloved hobby unperturbed. And as he returned in the evening bearing some trophy, a rare fern, a strange butterfly, or a tiny lizard from the Salpaire sand pits, his face would beam with achievement.

Then Johnnie had a stroke of luck—he was detailed for supply-route duty at Avranches, with headquarters fixed at the Lion Rouge. Now he was able to make more frequent expeditions. At first he went alone, but presently, as though drawn by the young soldier's absorbed, heroic fervour, Claire went with him. She was his companion when, one day, in a clump of rushes, they found a thrush with one leg broken and a wing half shattered by shrapnel.

Johnnie brought the thrush home, and how gently, how skilfully

310

he attended to its wounds! While Claire and her mother stood by, he splinted the fractured leg, bound back the dragging pinion, and coaxingly pursing his lips to a soothing whistle, induced the quivering bird to peck at a warm mash of bread and milk. When he had laid it in a box of soft hay by the kitchen stove he looked up with his quiet smile.

"Don't you worry," he declared. "It'll soon be okay."

Feeling their eyes upon him, he coloured and tried to excuse himself.

"There's nothing nicer in spring than the song of the thrush."

This selfless interest in the little creatures of field and furrow touched the women to the heart. All around men were killing each other, the air was charged with death and destruction, yet the only thought of this simple, fearless boy was that of succouring a wounded bird.

"Johnnie," Madame said suddenly, "you have a great talent. . . . One day it will make you famous."

Johnnie's flush deepened. Carried away by this unexpected praise, he spoke up. He had always wanted to be a naturalist, even before, as a kid, he had immersed himself in Audubon's wonderful books. Now he wanted to write nature books himself, to collect fine specimens, to send back to the museums trophies which he had discovered abroad. Why, the conditions were so good in these remote Norman woods, he would like to come back when the fighting was over and begin his work.

When the boy finished speaking there was a silence. Then in a low voice, looking shyly into his eyes, Claire said:

"Yes, Johnnie, you ought to come back."

"You bet," said Johnnie, returning her gaze with his steady smile. "I will."

Well, resumed Madame Delnotte after a brief pause, these were happy days. The enemy at last was being pushed back, people dared to think with confidence of the future. Johnnie's thrush recovered and there came a great day when, with his wing completely healed, he hopped and fluttered, then finally took to the air, darting and swooping about the back yard of the inn in a wild delirium of joy.

311

He flew to the woods, of course—Johnnie said it was to find his mate—but he came back from time to time, usually in the evening, to perch on Johnnie's wrist and peck at a piece of apple. After he had eaten, as though to show that he had not forgotten, his little throat would swell and he would break into a series of liquid trills.

"He's paying for his supper." Johnnie grinned.

When autumn came, and the first frost sent the leaves tumbling down, the bird made a farewell visit, then flew away to the south. A little later Johnnie and the rest of his squad were ordered back to the line.

"We were sorry, of course," remarked Madame Delnotte, "yet not overwhelmed. Now it seemed only a matter of crossing the Rhine: the end of the war was in sight."

Again Madame broke off and although I waited expectantly, she did not resume. Then, as the moments passed, and grew oppressive, I seemed to sense the reason for her silence. Covertly, I glanced at Claire, then quickly looked away. Of course! Victory had taken Johnnie back to America, where those promises, made so easily under stress of war emotion, could be as easily forgotten.

"So Johnnie"—I spoke at last—"Johnnie didn't come back."

They both looked at me, as if surprised.

"Oh, but yes!" said Madame, and she smiled oddly at my discomfiture. "In fact, he is quite near here. We go to visit him often. For that matter, we go tomorrow."

"May I come with you?" I asked. I felt now that I would give a great deal to meet Johnnie Brown.

Next morning, after coffee and fresh-baked bread, we all got into the car. It was a sweet morning, the dew fresh upon the grass, the wood smoke spiralling from the cottage chimneys, a morning when it was good to be alive. Under Madame's direction, I drove toward the village of Saint James. Somehow I wondered if I had not heard the name before. We entered the quiet little town, turned left, ascended a pretty hill, and there, at the summit, yes, there, full understanding broke upon me.

In silence, I followed Madame and Claire through the iron gates of the beautiful enclosure, passing between the long rows of plain

312

white crosses, until at last we stood before the grave of Johnnie Brown.

"He was killed by a land mine . . . near Mulhausen . . . only two weeks before the end of the war."

Madame Delnotte's expression, usually so contained, had broken —her lips were trembling. She gazed round the great American Military Cemetery stretching across the hill crest, ordered and peaceful under the morning sun. Her voice fell almost to a whisper.

"You see . . . , Johnnie stays with us . . . forever." Her eyes were wet with tears, "We will never forget them . . . , never . . . , Johnnie and those other dear, brave boys . . . , for what they did for us . . . , for France . . . , and for the world."

A bell sounded softly from the nearby village and at last we turned away. Slowly we drove back along the Highway of Liberation where, marking every kilometre, there stands a stone blazoned with the flaming torch of freedom. A bar of silence lay upon us, binding us in sympathy. Then—was it my fancy?—suddenly and clearly, in a distant hedgerow, or perhaps it was only in my heart . . . I heard the singing of a thrush.

# Chapter Thirty-nine

How OFTEN IN THESE afflicted countries had I seen the eyes of men turn in longing toward America! To those who had suffered much and lost much, who now, despite their striving, found themselves caught in a mesh of economic difficulties, smothered by levies and penal taxation, hampered by edicts and restrictions, embargoes and controls, it stood out as the last great bastion of individual liberty, a country solid and secure, where one might still find opportunity and incentive, a decent way of life, and above all the chance to advance by effort and ability, without the crushing intervention of that curse, that creeping paralysis of the modern age—regimentation by the state. Especially to those parents who wished for their children a fair and favourable future did it seem attractive beyond all other lands.

Was it strange, then, that before the clamps were finally screwed down, making the free movement of the individual impossible or, at best, dependent upon bureaucratic whim, our own gaze should swing toward this far yet hospitable horizon.

Previously we had made several visits to America and been stirred not only by the warmth of our welcome, but by the breadth, vigour, and immense potentialities of this vast new country. I felt, indeed, a curious affinity toward these United States, since, but for an unhappy circumstance, I might well have been born within their borders. At the end of the century my father's brothers and sisters had emigrated to California, and my parents were on the point of joining them when my father was stricken with a serious lung condi-

314

tion, an illness which debarred him from making the voyage and which soon afterward ended his life.

It may be imagined, then, with what interest and sentiment—a nostalgia derived, perhaps, from prenatal influences—I explored this vast segment of the New World. In company with my wife I had fished in Maine, sat at a drugstore counter in the Middle West, eaten a steak in Kansas City, viewed the Grand Canyon, Crawford Notch, and Grant's Tomb, wandered through missions of the Santa Barbara, the old gardens of Charleston and Savannah, the Vieux Carré of New Orleans. Often, on comparing notes, I found I knew more of America than many good Americans. With cousins on the West Coast, nephews and nieces in Chicago, I was very much at home. My transpontine public was a responsive one. In Hollywood my books had been transferred, not unprofitably, to the screen. Most of my business affairs were centred in New York. I had even become a Yankee baseball fan and would stun these kindly cicerones who took me to the Stadium and began, patiently, to explain that the basic idea was to strike the ball with the club, by calmly rattling off, to the last decimal point, Joe de Maggio's batting average for the past five years. But beyond all this, in a troubled and tortured world, I saw America as the bulwark of democracy, the great, perhaps the only, hope for the future of the world.

It was June when we invaded the New World via the port of Boston. This was no mere foray; we were an entire family and had come to stay. For several months we occupied a house in York Harbor, and experienced for the first time the glory of a New England summer. Never had we known such blue skies, such continuous and brilliant sunshine. Then, in the gold and scarlet fall, we purchased a property in Connecticut and settled down for good.

As I have described it, this seems a smooth and simple undertaking, but in reality it took time to effect the transposition of roots long planted in European soil and to adjust both idiom and ideas to transatlantic standards. Arnold Bennett was once impelled to state that Americans would always be alien to the British—but since this remark followed an unsuccessful lecture tour in the United States, it may be accepted with due reserve. Nevertheless, differences between the two peoples do exist, more than are implied in the pronunciation of such words as "schedule" and "tomato."

Yet our early perplexities soon were dispelled, submerged by the fundamental decencies of this new land, by the basic sincerity and honesty of its people. The individual American is a sure and massive person, with a loyalty to his neighbour and his country unsurpassed elsewhere. There is, moreover, in most Americans a certain breadth of outlook, a genial tolerance of others—emphasised by the lack of fences around their houses—a liberal attitude of "live and let live," and above all, a most characteristic largeheartedness, a supreme generosity of heart and spirit, which far outweighs their minor defects.

Many examples of this magnanimity have come within my personal experience, but none, I think, more poignantly typifies it than an incident that occurred in a town quite near my new home in Connecticut. This book has been burdened by many stories, the only tenable excuse for which is the fact that they are true. Yet perhaps one more indulgence may be permitted me, this final episode is so pertinent to what is in my mind.

It concerns a man, Henry Adams, an accountant for a New York publishing house, whom I had known—being involved in the same trade—for some six years. Henry, about forty-five, turning slightly bald, with rimless glasses magnifying his rather shortsighted eyes, lived with his wife, two daughters of fifteen and thirteen, and his little son, aged six, in a commuting town which I shall call Elmville.

His home, purchased by installments, was of no great size, but he took pride in it—especially the half-acre back-yard garden where he worked in old clothes on Saturday afternoons and Sundays. Aided by his small son, Sam—pressed into service with rake and wheelbarrow at the strictly nonunion rate of a quarter an hour—Henry came near to winning a prize at the Elmville Garden Show. On those fall afternoons, soon after our arrival in the district, when I used to drive over to visit Henry, I would observe these incorrigible confederates, the spare little man and the sturdy little boy, bent together over the herbaceous border, or standing work-proud in the twilight, burning a heap of dry leaves. Sammy, you see, was

316

devoted to his father, and Henry . . . well, without running to superlatives, Henry was rather fond of Sammy.

Apart from horticulture, Henry had no outstanding tastes. He liked a good movie and an occasional ball game. On wet evenings when the children were in bed he settled down to a cigar and a detective story by the open fire and it was hard to move him—though when his wife wanted to get him to a church social she usually succeeded.

Mrs. Adams was an energetic, still pretty woman with a warm smile and soft hair with a wave in it. Her fondness for uplift societies was readily forgiven when you ate her blueberry pie or noticed the smartness of the school dresses which her quick fingers had machined for her two growing daughters, Betty and Louise.

I have spoken of uplift movements, to which Elmville is reasonably addicted. When the war spread its devastating horror across Europe, the town joined in the movement to do something for the children of the stricken lands. Naturally Mrs. Adams was in the forefront of it; she suggested to Henry that they take a refugee child into their home for the duration. Henry, who valued his privacy, did not much care about the idea at first, but he came to see the humanity of it and agreed readily enough in the end.

After the formalities had been completed, word came that a Silesian boy had been allocated to the Adamses. I went with Henry to New York to pick up the youngster. Paul was the boy's name; his family name was so full of entanglements like 'piotro' and 'stanal' it was difficult to get it right at the initial attempt.

I shall never forget the first sight of that nine-year-old product of terror and starvation. Sitting on a high stool, he seemed little larger than a shrimp, pale as a sheet, with pipestem legs and arms, a bony, close-cropped skull, and big dark eyes, frightened yet unfathomable. He could not speak English, and when you spoke to him he had a way of averting his head and letting those slanting eyes slip over the top of your hat. This, then, was my introduction to strange little Paul Piotrostanalsi.

Henry drove him out to Elmville, where a royal welcome awaited him. Louise, Betty, and Sammy met us at the door, and Mrs. Adams

317

came hurrying from the kitchen. A cheerful fire blazed in the living room, the table was lit with candles, the house full of warmth and the smell of roast turkey. As we sat down to supper everyone was eager to make the strange child feel at home.

Paul thawed somewhat as the meal went on. Eating with great speed, he kept watching Sammy across the table with strange intensity. He took no notice of the two girls, who were "mothering" him with all their might; he simply fixed his attention on Sammy. Finally he broke into a shrill, incredible little cackle, reached over and took Sammy's hand in his. It was a funny, touching gesture, which made us all laugh and seemed to be the high light of the evening.

By all the conventions, my story should end upon this pleasing note of promise. But truth does not work to any formula. As the weeks slipped past, a painful disillusionment began slowly to supplant that first tender impression of the Adams's young guest. Nothing you could put your finger on, perhaps. Yet there it was . . . whether due to privation or the war horrors he had witnessed, Paul was not quite—well, not quite normal. He was a queer, detached little creature, with confused ideas of obedience, perfectly untroubled by the slightest moral sense. Small change left about the house disappeared into his pockets. As he acquired the language, which he did with surprising quickness, he proved himself an astounding manipulator of the truth. At school he would entertain audiences with fantastic accounts of his exploits, relating, pale and tense, how he had subjugated lions and killed bad men with his own hands. Other, less amusing, falsehoods came back to the family in unpleasant ways.

When reasoned with for some misdemeanor, Paul would turn quite blank, staring away into space with evasive eyes. It was impossible to be severe with him, for the mere mention of correction caused him to wake up at night in fits of crying which left him, and the entire household, exhausted. In all but one respect he was devoid of gratitude. Passive in this attitude toward Betty and Louise, he blandly tolerated Henry and avoided Mrs. Adams, who was sometimes sharp with him. Toward Sammy he displayed the most abject devotion; in fact, he followed him around in a fashion that was really embarrassing. He had loved the smaller boy at first sight and could scarcely bear to be away from him.

This was the situation when America entered the war. Henry had harder work and longer hours, his salary didn't go so far, a sense of strain seemed to fall upon the Adams home. However, they got through the winter without mishap and with the coming of spring everyone began to feel brighter.

Then, one hot day in June, Paul came down with a sore throat. He was put to bed and no one thought much about it. But next morning he was worse and Mrs. Adams called in the family doctor. When he came down, after an absurdly long time upstairs, his serious words changed the complexion of the case. The boy, disregarding all injunctions, had gone swimming in a nearby creek, a place strictly forbidden to all children. Now he had a septic infection, probably streptococcal, was dangerously ill, and would certainly be worse.

For a week there was misery in the Adams home. Everyone moved on tiptoe while Paul, isolated in his attic bedroom, tossed and muttered in a raging delirium. The doctor held out little hope—it was a virulent germ, the patient's resistance was nil. Yet, by the strange inconsistency of fate, he survived. At the end of a desperate ten days he was out of danger, feebly begging to see his beloved Sammy. This was impossible, because of the danger of contagion, but notes and fruit were sent up by the children, the house came to life again, and everyone was happy and relieved.

On Saturday, two mornings later, when Henry Adams went in to call Sammy for breakfast, he almost dropped from the shock of what he saw. In bed with the sleeping Sammy, his arm thrown around his little friend's neck, breathing close to him, was Paul. He had crept in without disturbing the other boy, content to be beside him, humble as ever in his affection. He sent his sliding gaze past Henry Adams and smiled. As for Sammy, he sickened the same week—never seemed to have a chance, though everything was done for him—and died of the infection four days later. . . .

I was away at the time. The letter I sent Henry, though full of heartfelt sympathy, must have sounded trite and empty to the

319

anguished father. I knew how deep had been this silent man's affection for his son; Sammy had been the mainspring of his life. This was the thought which spurred me to bitter indignation as I wrote bidding him free himself of this insufferable brat for whom he had done everything, who had made him this tragic recompense. There were institutions for such children, suitable orphanages where everything would be done for the unhappy Paul. "For heaven's sake," I said, "get rid of him."

The fall had gone and winter was in the air when I returned from California and went out to visit Henry Adams. As I came round the bend of the suburban road and approached the stricken house, I drew up with a queer pang, between amazement and disbelief. There, working in his garden, covering his herbaceous border, now bleak and flowerless, against the coming frost, was Henry, thinner, rather pinched with the cold, in the same old clothes. And helping him with rake and wheelbarrow . . . a small boy. For an instant my heart turned over within me, I thought that I had seen a ghost—then I saw that it was Paul.

I went slowly toward them.

"Well," I said, after an exchange of greetings, "you still have him?"

"Yes." Henry paused, avoiding my gaze. "He's improved quite a bit lately. . . . He's quieter and brighter . . . some gland tablets they're giving him."

There was a long silence while we both watched the boy carrying fresh salt hay from the wheelbarrow. As he drew near he flushed under my hostile stare: the most human sign I had yet discovered in him. But it was not enough to turn the edge of my indignation. Overcome by a sense of bitter injustice, I exclaimed:

"All I can say . . . , he's lucky, this Paul Piotro . . . whatever his wretched name is!"

"You'll have no more trouble with the name." Henry put his arm round the boy's shoulder, turned, and gave me a quiet, half-ashamed smile. "He's Paul Adams now. You see, we've adopted him."

# *Chapter Forty*

As WE GROW OLDER, the city of the spirit has more and more importance for us. Unless a man be a blind and heedless fool, when he reaches the years of maturity he will pause occasionally, amidst the racket of the world, to ask himself: "Why am I here? And where am I going?"

In youth time moves too fast, distractions are too numerous, and the end of the road seems too far away to permit of such self-analysis. At least, so it was with me. Medical students as a rule are not remarkable for their reverence, and I was no different from others of the breed. In the anatomy rooms, dissecting formalin-impregnated remains, the human body seemed to me no more than a complex machine. None of the autopsies showed anything I could identify with an immortal soul. When I thought of God it was with a superior smile, indicative of biological scorn for such an outworn myth.

But when, as a qualified doctor, I went out into the world, to the mining valleys in South Wales and, in the practice of my profession, saw life at first hand, observed the courage and good humour of my fellow creatures struggling under great hardships, for the first time I began to penetrate into the realm of the spirit. As I assisted at the miracle of birth, sat with the dying in the still hours of night, heard the faint inexorable beating of the dark wings of death, my outlook became less self-assured. Through the slow pangs of experience, new values were made apparent to me. I realised that the compass of existence held more than my textbooks had revealed, more than I had ever dreamed of. In short, I lost my superiority, and this, though

I was not then aware of it, is the first step toward finding God.

I have told you of Olwen Davies, the middle-aged district nurse who for more than twenty years, with fortitude and patience, calmness and cheerfulness, served the people of Tregenny. This unconscious selflessness, which above all seemed the keynote of her character, was so poorly rewarded, it worried me. Although she was much beloved by the people, her salary was most inadequate. And late one night after a particularly strenuous case I ventured to protest to her as we drank a cup of tea together.

"Nurse," I said, "why don't you make them pay you more? It's ridiculous that you should work for so little."

She raised her eyebrows slightly. But she smiled.

"I have enough to get along."

"No, really," I persisted, "you ought to have an extra pound a week at least. God knows you're worth it."

There was a pause. Her smile remained but her gaze held a gravity, an intensity which startled me.

"Doctor," she said, "if God knows I'm worth it, that's all that matters to me."

The words were little enough, but the meaning in her eyes was plain to see. Never for a moment had she implied that she was a religious woman, yet now I realised that her whole existence, in its service and self-sacrifice, was a dedication, a perpetual testimony to her belief in a Supreme Being. And in a flash of understanding I sensed the rich significance of her life and the comparative emptiness of my own.

I am no professor of theology. I have never felt myself called upon to stand up in a public place to lead a prayer meeting. Nor am I concerned here with any one particular sect or creed to the exclusion of all others. I speak simply of belief in God, a subject which many shy away from as though it were in questionable taste, but which is today surely more deserving of attention than at any other period in human history.

Never before, indeed, has the matter been so urgent or so vital. One half of the world, bound by an atheistic ideology, has engaged itself in a relentless aggression against religion, a ruthless and tireless

322

campaign to stamp into the mud forever the concept of a Creator. While we, the other half, despite the spiritual hunger gnawing persistently at our hearts, are in the main so apathetic in our attitude toward God, so dead to the true meaning of existence, as to be heedless of the dreadful dangers to the life of the spirit which now threaten us. For many, indeed, the trend of modern thought, stressing the advances of science and the obsolescence of tradition, has brought the reality of God seriously into question. Others, distrusting a universe which seems clouded with doubt, conflict, and fear, seek only to escape from the future in a variety of distractions.

It is the pressing consciousness of such a crisis in human affairs which leads me to define some of the processes of mind and spirit that have shaped my faith.

At the outset it should be stated that the only motivating power in supernatural faith must be God Himself. God cannot be proved like a mathematical equation, nor can His existence be demonstrated like a problem in a book of Euclid. Obviously an infinite Being cannot be rationalized in finite terms—our human capacity is utterly incapable of wholly understanding Him. Nevertheless there are certain simple arguments which help us to discover Him.

If we consider the physical universe, in its mystery and wonder, its order and intricacy, its awe-inspiring immensity, we cannot escape the notion of a primary Creator. Who on a still summer night dare gaze upward at the constellations, glittering in infinity, without the overpowering conviction that such a cosmos came to being through something more than blind indeterminate chance? And our own world, whirling through space in measured rhythm, unfolding its regular progression of the seasons, surely is more than a meaningless ball of matter, thrown off by merest accident from the sun?

Reject if you will as pure imagery the Biblical presentation of God, shaping the world with His own hands in six days. Smile—should you feel disposed—at Michelangelo's bearded patriarchal figure in the Sistine chapel—prototype of that God the Creator whom men of humble faith accepted in the past—sending the spark of life from His finger into Adam. Accept evolution with its fossils and elementary species, its scientific doctrine of natural causes. And still you are confronted with the same mystery, primary and profound. *Ex nihilo nihil,* as the Latin tag of our school days has it: nothing can come of nothing.

Some years ago in London, where I had in my spare time organised a working boys' club, I invited a distinguished zoologist to deliver an evening lecture to our members. His was a brilliant address, although to my concern rather different from what I had expected. Acting no doubt on the idea that youth should be told "the truth," my friend chose as his subject "The Beginning of Our World." In a frankly atheistic approach he described how, aeons and aeons ago, the pounding prehistoric seas upon the earth's primaeval crust had generated by physicochemical reaction a pulsating scum from which there had emerged—though he did not say how—the first primitive form of animation, the protoplasmic cell. It was strong meat for lads who had been brought up on a simpler diet. When he concluded there was polite applause. In the somewhat awkward pause that followed, a mild and very average youngster rose nervously to his feet.

"Excuse me, sir." He spoke with a slight stammer. "You've explained how these b-big waves beat upon the shore; b-b-but how did all that water get there in the first place?"

The naïve question, so contrary to the scientific trend of the address, took everyone by surprise. There was a silence. The lecturer looked annoyed, hesitated, slowly turned red. Then, before he could answer, the whole club burst into a howl of laughter. The elaborate structure of logic offered by this test-tube realist had been crumpled by one word of challenge from a simple-minded boy.

The truth is, in all the investigations of science into the nature and purpose of these tremendous awe-inspiring processes, these processes stretching backward into the incalculable abysses of time, of which we can have no more than a fleeting glimpse, there is no valid basis for denying the existence of God. Rather is one driven to conclude that in primordial creation, in the motivation of the universe and the operation of the natural laws, there is, has been, and always will be a Supreme Intelligence.

The stumbling block to this belief, for many earnest and well-intentioned people, lies in the evil and pain so widely prevalent in the life of the world. How can this Divine Being be credible, they ask, in the face of a tormented world—a world afflicted by storm and flood, by famine, pestilence, earthquake, and lightning stroke, by dreadful and agonizing diseases, by death in its cruelest forms? Surely, they cry, your God was a most imperfect Architect to produce so ungodly a result.

There is an answer to this difficulty, and nowhere has it been expressed more simply, or in more beautiful words, than in that great cry from the heart which is found in the Book of Job. Here, indeed, was one who understood the true meaning and purpose of the brief span of man's earthly years. But we, alas, in this materialistic age, obsessed by the pursuit of pleasure, driven by an insatiable craving for distraction, forget that mere enjoyment is not the be-all and end-all of existence. If we accept God and our own immortality, we understand that our lives are not meant to be a joy ride but a time—all too short—of preparation; a moment, in terms of eternity, of testing and endurance, when we stand poised, so to speak, upon the threshold of the hereafter. We are indeed destined to suffer, and the more we try to insulate ourselves against suffering the more we shall suffer. One of the wisest yet humblest men who ever lived, Thomas à Kempis, wrote this: "So long as suffering appears grievous to thee and thou seekest to fly from it, so long will it be ill with thee and the tribulation from which thou fliest will everywhere follow thee."

By our acceptance of discomfort and pain, of disappointment and misfortune, by drinking to the dregs the bitter cup of sorrow, we survive the supreme test of submission to the will of God. We acknowledge the vanity of our desires, of the earthly treasures we so feverishly seek and cherish. Strengthened in spirit, we submit. Thus it was with Job when he cried aloud in that sublime, that tremendous act of faith: "Let come on me what will. . . . Though He slay me, yet will I trust in Him." Then went on joyfully, rapt with a new vision: "I have heard of Thee by the hearing of the ear, but now mine eye seeth Thee."

It is this "seeing eye," this inner infusion of light which alone can show us God, for in the last analysis, reason as we may, burrowing inward with our feeble antlike processes of thought, we cannot even

325

scratch the surface of the Infinite. The revelation of God comes only from the heart.

During a recent visit to Italy I drove out from Florence one glorious afternoon to a famous monastery in the hills near Fiesole. There I was privileged to visit the beautiful fifteenth-century church, to examine the exquisite illuminated manuscripts, to view the magnificent works of art, all "raised to the honour and glory of the Lord." But it was later, when I wandered into the little monastery garden, that I discovered the greatest treasure of them all. There I fell into conversation with an old man, a gentle soul, bent with toil and rheumatism yet still bright of eye, who for more than thirty years had tilled that patch of earth, making work his constant prayer, and who, answering the question which I put to him, pointed to the orchard which was his special care and smiled.

"I see my cherry trees in bud, and then in flower, and then in fruit. And then I believe in God."

If we could have one-hundredth part of such faith, such trust, if we could only give ourselves up with such completeness, then should we find ourselves upon the path toward God. The first step is surrender: "I am nothing, I know nothing." Yet the farther our steps continue along that pathway, the greater our confidence becomes, the more our knowledge increases, until at last it reaches a sure conviction. And when one beholds, even though it be faintly, the first glimmer of that ultimate vision, there comes upon one a terrible awareness of the blind futility, the worthlessness of life without it.

While still a practising physician, I attended a man, a public figure in a northern town, who had all his life prided himself upon his atheism. He had quarrelled with his only daughter and disowned her because she married a schoolmaster who was devoutly religious. Toward the end of his life, however, when stricken by an incurable malady, a strange change came over this old sceptic. Now that death's shadow lay painfully upon him he was taken less by a change of heart than by an almost passionate desire to justify himself in the eyes of his son-in-law. Time and time again he would wander round to his daughter's home to engage the younger man in argument. If

326

he wavered he did not show it, for always he concluded with the remark:

"Don't delude yourself. I'm not repentant. I still don't believe in God."

To which one day his daughter, by a stroke of genius, replied:

"But, Father, He believes in you."

This simple remark swept away the last of the old man's resistance. And it is indeed a thought which might serve for all of us. Whatever we may think, whatever we may do, we are still God's children. He is waiting for us. And it takes only one word of faith to acknowledge Him.

Abraham Lincoln went upon his knees each night and turned his thoughts toward heaven. Are we now too worldly-wise to follow this great example? Through the centuries, countless human beings have shaped their lives, with true nobility and shining example, upon God. He has brought courage to the weak, strength to the weary, hope to those lost in the shadows of despair. He is everywhere, above and around, on the ocean and in the sky. He is in each one of us, if we will only seek Him.

# *Chapter Forty-one*

---

It is SPRING AGAIN, a day of sunshine, tempered by a soft west wind. As I enter my study and sit at my desk, the sweetness of the morning makes me disinclined to work. Gazing through the window at the green, gently swaying trees I fall insensibly into a reverie . . . looking backward, in a mood of introspection, of self-analysis.

When a man surveys his past from middle age he must surely ask himself what those bygone years have taught him. If I have learned anything in the swift unrolling of the web of time—and it seems only yesterday since I hastened through Kelvingrove to my medical classes, an eager, fresh-complexioned lad of twenty, bent on conquering the universe—it is the virtue of tolerance, of moderation in thought and deed, of forbearance toward one's fellow men. These were qualities sadly lacking in my furious youth.

I have come also to acknowledge the great illusion which lies in the pursuit of a purely material goal. What slight satisfaction lies in temporal honour and worldly grandeur! What sad futility in that frantic desire for gain which possesses the money-changers of the world, snatching for little scraps of printed paper, feeding an appetite never satisfied! All the material possessions for which I strove so strenuously mean less to me now than a glance of love from those who are dear to me.

Above all am I convinced of the need, irrevocable and inescapable, of every human heart, for God. No matter how we try to escape, to lose ourselves in restless seeking, we cannot separate ourselves from our divine source. There is no substitute for God. Though we may

328

not fully recognise it, we exist in the divine essence. The image of God is found in all mankind.

Yet there are some who, in blindness toward their eternal future, bury this sense of identity with God, who contend that human life springs without meaning from the beasts, that the end of all is nothingness, that they themselves are no more than shuttlecocks of circumstance, victims of sleeveless chance. Such could never be my view. Beneath its visible hills and valleys, I see a pattern in my life, shaping me toward an eventual end, an end which was stamped upon my childish features, perhaps was written even before the hour when I was born.

I was never anything but powerless to escape the creed with which I was endowed at birth. And now, after many vicissitudes, nothing on earth would induce me to abandon it. I have handed myself over, body and soul. It is this surrender, total, unquestioning, in complete and absolute humility, which is the true essential of belief. The disciple Thomas, who, before believing, insisted upon touching the wounds of the resurrected Lord, is the prototype of all those who temper their faith with reason, who strain at the gnat of individual dogma oblivious to the inner meaning of the divine rebuke, "Blessed are they who have not seen and have believed."

Every attempt to adapt Christianity to suit modern temporising, the efforts to rationalise Christ as a prophet, a great man, to explain His miracles in terms of popular science—Lazarus was not dead but in a state of coma, the blind man made to see was merely a hysteric suffering from transient amaurosis—all these are no more than sorry devices to evade what is most demanded of us. When the lepers came and begged to be healed, the answer was, "according to thy faith, so it be done unto thee." Even at the Crucifixion it was the Saviour's purpose to leave us in such balanced uncertainty that belief in His divinity still required an effort of faith. When we clamour for positive proof we become like those Roman soldiers who, mocking yet half afraid, raising on the spear to those thirsting lips the sponge dipped in gall, besought the ultimate miracle which would have made faith unnecessary. "If Thou art the Son of God, come down from Thy cross."

There, then, lies the final choice—all or nothing. When we take, each one of us, that momentous, that mysterious walk to Emmaus, we do so with a Stranger. Yet in those unknown features we must trace the radiant countenance of the risen Lord. It is this voluntary act of recognition which makes faith sublime.

Despite the intensity of my conviction, I am no proselytiser. I have slight desire to go about urging my neighbours to attend my church and threatening them with eternal damnation if they fail to do so. If my early sufferings taught me anything, it was to detest the jealous feuds and malignant hatreds which I witnessed between members of rival denominations. Creed is such an accident of birth, of race and antecedents, even of latitude and longitude, that it cannot, surely, be the exclusive determinant of our salvation. I, at least, have confidence that any man of good will, whether he be Catholic or Calvinist, has full and undiminished opportunity of winning his eternal reward.

That dream which we all cherish, the brotherhood of man, can become reality only if cooperation supplants competition between the creeds. Then indeed would humanity be saved. Yet such a change in the heart of the world can begin only in the heart of the individual, can succeed only if every man who calls himself a Christian would cease to give smug and self-righteous lip service to his own sect and get down to the bedrock of human need. Could we but put in practice the Sermon on the Mount, all the problems of our poor tortured universe would be solved, all the difficulties, apparently insuperable, which confront mankind would melt like mist before the rising sun. Of one thing I am convinced: nothing, no philosophy, no power on earth will restore our shocked and shattered world except the teaching of Him who bore to Golgotha the burden of all mankind.

When the world seems a place of bewilderment and fatigue, that is the gleam of light on the dark horizon, the remedy which offers release from misery and strife. Have we the grace to see that light, to apply the remedy to our souls? The challenge is there, the need is desperate. Despite the cruelty which men inflict upon each other, despite the indifference and confusion, the threats of war and open hostility, the destroyings and dispersings which afflict the nations, I have an inextinguishable hope in the moral regeneration of the peoples of the earth.

All human suffering is an act of repentance. A single contrite tear, one cry out of the depths is enough. The publican, kneeling far back in the shadows of the temple, had but to bow his head in sorrow: "Oh Lord, be merciful to me, a sinner." That is the supreme prayer . . . the prayer for me . . . surely the prayer for all of us.